CAMBRIDGE STUDIES IN AMERICA?

The San Francisco Ren

Cambridge Studies in American Literature and Culture

Editor
Albert Gelpi, Stanford University

Advisory board
Nina Baym, *University of Illinois, Champaign-Urbana*
Sacvan Bercovitch, *Harvard University*
Richard Bridgman, *University of California, Berkeley*
David Levin, *University of Virginia*
Joel Porte, *Cornell University*
Eric Sundquist, *University of California, Berkeley*
Mike Weaver, *Oxford University*

THE SAN FRANCISCO RENAISSANCE

Poetics and Community at Mid-century

MICHAEL DAVIDSON

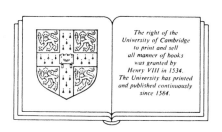

The right of the
University of Cambridge
to print and sell
all manner of books
was granted by
Henry VIII in 1534.
The University has printed
and published continuously
since 1584.

CAMBRIDGE UNIVERSITY PRESS

Cambridge
New York   Port Chester   Melbourne   Sydney

Published by the Press Syndicate of the University of Cambridge
The Pitt Building, Trumpington Street, Cambridge CB2 1RP
40 West 20th Street, New York, NY 10011, USA
10 Stamford Road, Oakleigh, Melbourne 3166, Australia

First published 1989
First paperback edition 1991

Library of Congress Cataloging-in-Publication Data

Davidson, Michael, 1944–
The San Francisco Renaissance : poetics and community at mid-century /
Michael Davidson
p.   cm. – (Cambridge studies in American literature and culture)
ISBN 0-521-25880-4 hardback
1. American literature – California – San Francisco – History and criticism.   2.
American literature – 20th century – History and criticism.   3. San Francisco
(Calif.) – Intellectual life – 20th century.   I. Title.   II. Series.
PS285.S3D38   1989
811′.5409′97461 – dc20   89-1025
                                                                 CIP

British Library Cataloging in Publication Data

Davidson, Michael
The San Francisco Renaissance : poetics and community at mid-century. –
(Cambridge studies in American literature and culture)
1. Poetry in English. California writers, 1945–.
Critical studies
I. Title
811′.54′09979461

ISBN 0-521-25880-4 hardback
ISBN 0-521-42304-X paperback

Transferred to digital printing 1999

For Roy Harvey Pearce

Contents

Preface

This book owes a great deal to all of those well-intentioned English teachers who never said a word about the literary movement going on in San Francisco during the late 1950s and early 1960s. Their silence meant that as a student, growing up across the bay in Oakland, I had to learn about these events on my own through a kind of "vernacular pedagogy." Such an education is created piecemeal out of popular mythology and hearsay and gains much of its impetus by the suppression of its subject matter. The vernacular pedagogy that led to the writing of this book began on a schoolbus sometime in 1959 when an older "bohemian" student loaned me a copy of Lawrence Ferlinghetti's translations of the French surrealist poet Jacques Prévert. It was a book in Ferlinghetti's Pocket Poet series published by City Lights Books. Not only had I never read poems like that (we were still trying to figure out why the horse *did* stop in the woods on a snowy evening), I had never seen books made like that. Its small format and stapled binding bespoke a portability intended for immediate access, a book one was meant to read while on the bus or standing in line. And there was something about the clandestine way that my friend handed the book to me that signaled secrecy and solidarity at the same time.

Like many other teenagers of my generation, I followed the book to its lair, taking the yellow Key Line train across the Bay Bridge to the First Street Station and then walking through the Financial District to Chinatown and then to North Beach, where "it" was happening. I'm not sure I knew then what "it" was, but one thing was certain: It wasn't what was happening in my middle-class neighborhood in Oakland. North Beach was a perpetual theater where all sorts of unpredictable things were going on. People dressed "differently" and spoke the exotic argot of the hipster. In those days, underaged youths could get into clubs (at least those that served food) and hear jazz at The Cellar or The Place, folk music at the Coffee Gallery, or chamber music at the Opus One or the Old Spaghetti Factory, not to mention poetry readings at a number of galleries and bars. My friends and I could sit around Beat shrines like Cafe Trieste or City Lights Books or Dante's (Mike's) Billiard Parlor and forget the fact that we were kids with crewcuts from the suburbs. We may have been living out a fantasy of liberated adulthood, but nobody bothered to tell us so.

I mention these nonliterary contexts because they played an especially important role in what has come to be called the San Francisco Renaissance, a movement in which lifestyle was as important to its dissemination as any specifically literary values. Although in the pages that follow I qualify certain myths of the movement, it is important to stress the value of these stories in creating a sense of community during a period of consensus and conformism. Reception theory and reader response analysis have introduced concepts like a "community of readers," but such critical methods say little about actual historical readers who not only read literature but are made by it. For my generation, exposure to the literary renaissance of the late 1950s and early 1960s involved an awareness of new social forms and practices for which our formal education had little prepared us.

These nonliterary factors in the San Francisco Renaissance worried early critics, who saw in Beat bohemia the destruction of an important barrier between mass culture and high art. Poetry could be heard on street corners and in jazz clubs, and read in the pages of quickly printed, mimeographed magazines. Figures like Kerouac, Ginsberg, and Corso appeared on television talk shows, and their remarks on the state of culture could be read in *Esquire* and *Playboy*. The Beat movement in particular identified with alienated heroes of Hollywood film like Marlon Brando and James Dean, and much of its antiestablishment humor derived from the Marx Brothers and standup comedians like Mort Sahl. Such unashamed assimilation of mass culture brought new audiences to poetry that were not necessarily part of the academic establishment. The movement also reintroduced a new coefficient of contemporaneity (or its more debased version, "relevance") into a literary hermeneutics that had become increasingly technical and formal.

This shift in reception turned the definition of culture away from its Enlightenment associations with "civilizing" and rationalizing activity to an earlier, anthropological meaning that stressed processes of enrichment within the entire community. Raymond Williams reminds us that the term "culture" originally referred to the raising of crops and animals, the cultivation of land. The modern use of the term, beginning in the seventeenth century, applied the idea of cultivation to products of the mind – the cultivation of "Spirit" – and by the mid-nineteenth century the term referred to the process of becoming civilized.[1] We could see the San Francisco Renaissance as reinforcing the earlier, agrarian definition by the ways that it foregrounded primitivist notions of community (the oral tradition, the role of the tribe, the divinity of nature) through which collective activity takes precedence over individual volition. For the writers with whom we shall be concerned, a new poetics implied not only formal innovation but also discovery of alternative social forms. As Robert Duncan asserts, "Surely, everywhere, from whatever poem, choreographies extend into actual space."[2]

Despite the rhetoric of tribalism or mutual aid adopted by many of the writers during this period, the actual development of community was not always so egalitarian. Poets often had recourse to rather exclusive and exclusionist rituals that belied their democratic social ideals. The bohemian bar life of the 1950s was a competitive arena in which many of the power struggles of the dominant culture were acted out in microcosm. Poetry became not only a vehicle of personal expression but a complicated intertextual and dialogical field in which rivalries and sexual preferences could be encoded and defended. The work of this period reveals a tension between certain extravagant claims of transcendence and lived reality, but that tension was also a measure of postwar America's inability to provide a social validation equal to its extraordinary economic success. World War II had catapulted the country into a new stage of capitalist development that moved away from single markets and industries toward global ventures and multinational corporations. If the country was at least economically prosperous, its social dialectic was far less stable, manifesting itself in the "joiner" mentality of middle America as well as in the red-baiting rhetoric of the McCarthy committee. Popular sociological accounts of the period, like those of David Riesman and Daniel Bell, attempted to describe some of the anxieties of the burgeoning middle class – tensions brought on by bureaucratization, mobility, decentralization – but one can see the same sense of disaffiliation within literary bohemia.

In defining the tensions between claim and reality, I have occasionally relied on anecdotal and apocryphal histories of the period, not simply to trade in gossip but to show how a certain literary subject was inventing itself through representations of freedom, emancipation, and participation. A good example is the series of alter egos Jack Kerouac created in his novels to embody the independence and involvement he could never obtain for himself. The same could be said of Kenneth Rexroth's vision of the engaged proletarian artist, Robert Duncan's projection of a heavenly city of art, or Jack Spicer's idealized bar world. Within the "enabling fictions" of community surrounding the San Francisco Renaissance can be glimpsed the utopian hopes for some kind of *Gemeinschaft* that was rapidly being replaced by suburban anonymity and the new corporate state. Such fictions do not diminish the integrity of the movement but suggest the difficulties that postwar writers had in separating themselves from the society they criticized.

The existence of such enabling fictions of community has not been much discussed in recent criticism of American poetry, which, in one version, has attempted to define the canon by reference to the oedipal struggle of "strong" poets with equally strong precursors. The desire there is to identify transcultural principles that embody a distinctly cultural (American) identity, thus leaving aside issues of gender, race, sexual preference, and class in the bargain. Even when issues of culture and history *do* enter the debate, the primary goal is to identify consensus rather than creative dissent. Robert von Hallberg, for example, has argued that the best recent poetry is accommodationist rather than oppositional, that it is concerned with the center, not the margins, of American life. Poets as diverse as John Ashbery, Ed Dorn, Mona Van Duyn, and James Merrill write an Arnoldian "culture poetry" that takes as its primary focus "the feelings, experiences, and difficulties that are considered the irreducible center of public life."[3] Though I respect von Hallberg's desire to study a diversified group of poets "not all read by the same audience, and not all of whom care deeply about each other's work,"[4] I also feel that the mainstream culture that these poets address is an enabling fiction in itself, one created by the critic to explain ideological chasms glimpsed by the poet.

The motivating feature of much recent criticism is a desire to subsume difference and conflict within the great paradox of American literature itself, one announced by Emerson and adumbrated by Whitman: that of a democratic ensemble that empowers the idiosyncratic individual. Within that capacious idea, however, are tensions that even Whitman could not solve, tensions that can be felt in the middle portions of "Song of Myself" and later in *Drum Taps*. What a literary democracy does not tolerate is sectarianism and insularity – poetic movements fighting over turf or poetry wars conducted in little magazines. I will make the unfashionable case that such insularity is often necessary for the creation and survival *of* culture poetry. A poet like Ezra Pound was able to concern himself with what he took to be the central issues of his day only by constantly revising history in his own terms. Through poems, correspondence, essays, and broadsides Pound battled perceived "central" authority (Roosevelt, Jewish bankers, British jurisprudence), and the center he most desired – a fascist millennium – seems to us now the most hideous parody of all such unifying structures. The point is that Pound – like many of the poets I discuss in this book – gained much of his impetus to write by regarding himself as embattled, a "lone ant" on the anthill of decaying European culture. He relied on a complex network of magazine editors, politicians, and other poets as sounding boards for ideas that he regarded as salvational but that his recipients (including Mussolini) regarded as errant nonsense. To neutralize the element of sectarianism and cultural myopia in Pound's work would be to de-historicize radically this most historical of poets.

It may be objected that because of my focus on a regional literary movement I am unable to speak about larger developments in American poetry during the same period. Although I occasionally refer to writers outside San Francisco, my attention remains on figures who lived and participated in the "excitements" (as Robert Duncan called them) of the period from 1955 to 1965. Obviously my remarks about the revival of romanticism could as easily be said about John Ashbery or A. R. Ammons or Elizabeth Bishop as they could be about Robert Duncan or Allen Ginsberg. There are probably more significant aesthetic parallels between Robert Duncan and Charles Olson than there are between the former and, say, Jack Kerouac or Lew Welch. The fact is that such larger continuities *do* exist, and they have been the subject of several important recent books. But in deterritorializing writers for the sake of shared aesthetic continuities, one loses some of the vitality produced by region and community.

It may also be objected that because I am limiting myself to a relatively small area, I must deal with "minor" poets whose impact on the national scene has been minimal or whose work seems less rigorous, complicated, or intellectual than that of others working in the same idiom. In order to answer this objection, it is necessary to examine the means by which a writer attains "major" status – those seemingly universal standards by which one author is anthologized and another ignored. One could usefully employ the example of recent feminist scholarship, which has emphasized the degree to which evaluative terms for literature are determined by gender. These terms marginalize literary works by women, either because the genres in which they write are considered minor (sentimental romance, diary, epistle) or because the idiom is personal, expressive, or confessional. In analogous ways, certain writers of the San Francisco Renaissance have not achieved recognition, either because they have refused forms of literary self-promotion (Jack Spicer, Philip Whalen, Joanne Kyger) or because the interpretive standards of the day will not admit their openly romantic idiom.

Exclusion from the major literary venues not only is a matter of literary taste but includes those questions of lifestyle mentioned earlier. John Crowe Ransom's reasons for rejecting poems by Robert Duncan that he had initially accepted for the *Kenyon Review* were based on his having read the poet's "Homosexual in Society" essay and deciding that the poems were tainted by Duncan's sexual "advertisement." No doubt Ransom felt that he was exercising disinterested critical judgment when he first accepted Duncan's poems as much as disinterested social judgment in subsequently refusing them. Canon formation occurs in the imperceptible fissure between these two forms of disinterest.[5]

A word on the term "Renaissance": The term implies renewal as well as return, and both senses apply to the San Francisco poetry movement. The return was not to an indigenous literary flowering of an earlier era but to the romantic movement itself, which had been thwarted, so the poets felt, by the sedimentation of its ideals during the period of late modernism. Robert Duncan was the most vocal proponent of this view, but it can be felt in Kenneth Rexroth's hope for a literary revival on the order of the one that occurred in Paris in the 1920s and William Everson's celebration of the bardic tradition. At the same time, many who referred to the period as the San Francisco Renaissance recognized the absurdity of an event based on something that had already happened. For the American western poet, deprived of any culture at all, the use of a highfalutin' term like "Renaissance" for a scruffy, proletarian movement had just the right kind of humor attached to it. Hence the "San Francisco Renaissance" refers to a self-conscious attempt to have an inaugural literary movement at the same time as it signals the impossibility of having first things first.

Acknowledgments

The cover photograph for this book shows the Golden Gate Bridge under construction in the late 1930s. Although this moment precedes the San Francisco Renaissance by some years, it nevertheless embodies the spirit of western growth and change that this book chronicles. More important, the incomplete nature of this great western icon provides an image of a literary community already in formation by the time of the bridge's completion. The writing of literary history is also a communal project – an "increment of association" as Pound called it – that re-creates the past as a living presence. I therefore want to acknowledge the community of friends and scholars who have made my task easier.

The inspiration to consider the San Francisco Renaissance as a gathering of literary sects and circles came from Robert Duncan. In many conversations, he and Jess described the psychic geography of San Francisco not only as a historical literary movement but as a visionary topos in the romantic imagination. Their anecdotes and reminiscences (some of them unprintable) provided a vivid sense of a period in which they were central actors. I have been similarly assisted by discussions with Ron Loewinsohn, Paul Dresman, Tom Parkinson, Judy Grahn, Lyn Hejinian, David Bromige, David Meltzer, Robert Creeley, Michael McClure, Susan Griffin, Jerry Rothenberg, Ron Silliman, Bruce Boone, Robert Gluck, Donald Allen, Philip Whalen, and Robin Blaser. Lew Ellingham graciously made available his amazing (and as yet unpublished) manuscript on the Spicer circle, *Poet, Be Like God*. Michael Palmer provided a consistent (if heretical) commentary on all matters poetic and otherwise. His correspondence and conversation are so implicated in my writing that I am not quite sure where "I" begins.

The major impetus to write a book on the San Francisco Renaissance was provided by Marjorie Perloff, who has extended support and constructive comments during the past five years. Special thanks go as well to Jim Breslin and Bob Bertholf for their sensitive readings of the manuscript. The editorial staff at Cambridge University Press (particularly Andrew Brown, Mary Nevader, and Robert Racine) has been responsive and efficient at every stage of production. Albert Gelpi has been a perfect editor, reading the manuscript carefully and thoughtfully and providing much-needed encouragement along the way. His sympathy for the project and his own important work on contemporary poetry have been a great help.

I received incredible scholarly assistance from Lynda Claassen and her excellent staff at the Mandeville Department of Special Collections at the University of California, San Diego. I also received help from the directors and curatorial staffs of several manuscript depositories: the Butler Library, Columbia University; the Bancroft Library, University of California, Berkeley; and the Poetry/Rare Books Collection, State University of New York at Buffalo. I am particularly grateful to the late George Butterick of the University of Connecticut, Storrs, who answered many of my questions about individual authors and whose example as a textual scholar has always been an inspiration. His loss is felt by all of us working in the field he helped to create.

The wonderful cover photograph was made available by Bob David of the Golden Gate Bridge, Highway and Transportation District. I want to express my gratitude to copyright holders for letting me quote from published materials and to poets and estate executors for permitting me to quote from unpublished manuscript and audiotape materials.

Parts of chapters have appeared in journals and magazines, among them *Acts, Ironwood,* and *boundary 2,* for which thanks to editors David Levi Strauss, Michael Cuddihy, and William Spanos. Thanks also to Dawn Kolokithas, who organized the Jack Spicer/White Rabbit Conference, and Michael Lynch, who chaired a special MLA panel on Robert Duncan where sections of the book were presented.

Lori Chamberlain has read more of this manuscript than she wants and has given me more help than she can possibly know. Her presence, patience, and affection are the empowering conditions beyond the text.

Finally, I want to extend my gratitude to Roy Harvey Pearce, to whom this book is dedicated. His pioneering work on American poetry and his willingness to include the "New American Poetry" in a continuity extending back to Edward Taylor and Anne Bradstreet gave permission for many of us to follow his lead. His sensitivity to poetry as a cultural and historical document, "Part of the res itself and not about it," has been central to my thought in writing this book. His personal support as a mentor and colleague is immeasurable.

Introduction

Enabling Fictions

INAUGURAL MOMENTS

The limitless and stretching mountains of the damned
Surround Arcadia; they are the hells that rise above the ground
Of this poetic paradise;

(Jack Spicer)

The writing of literary history invariably takes mythic forms. A new school, movement, or aesthetic credo often emerges from a series of enabling fictions that structure the reading of a given text. Inaugural moments like the premiere of Stravinsky's *Sacre du Printemps,* the Armory Show, the arrival of Tristan Tzara in Zurich, and the meeting of Picasso and Braque have become, for better or worse, the luminous centers around which modernism has been formulated. Such moments galvanize public attention and give to the desultory evolution of literary history the illusion of purpose and direction. But these enabling fictions of origin often obscure creative dissension and opposition that are a part of any literary movement.

The history of what has come to be called the San Francisco Renaissance is no exception. What began as a series of loosely organized readings, publications, and meetings has been read as a unified narrative of the literary and artistic life of the San Francisco Bay Area during the late 1950s and early 1960s. This book is a history of that narrative rather than a narrative of that history, the latter having been written already, often through the filter of those myths of origin just mentioned.[1] My interest is not to debunk that history but to see in the disparity between what has been claimed and what has been produced some of the tensions in contemporary poetry in general.

In this, I am adapting an idea of Jerome McGann, who has discussed

1

the tendency of critics to write the history of nineteenth-century poetry out of a particular "ideology of Romanticism," one produced "by an uncritical absorption in Romanticism's own self-representations."[2] These representations include an emphasis on the creative imagination, enthusiasm, and transcendence to the exclusion of more problematic areas of skepticism, irony, and existential despair. The romantic ideology, as promulgated by Rene Wellek, M. H. Abrams, and others, valorizes aesthetic and psychological issues without considering the political and historical backdrop against which these theories were formulated. What McGann says of romanticism is also true of the way that contemporary poetry, itself an outgrowth of romanticism, has created its own reading based on certain myths of participation, immediacy, and spontaneity. These myths, like those projected by the first-generation romantics, lead the poet to conceive of life in allegorical terms, each moment intersecting with the divine, so that the creation of poetry is directly linked to the creative powers of nature itself. Such an attitude was particularly pervasive during the San Francisco Renaissance, when matters of aesthetics were inextricably confused, in the public perception as well as in the minds of its participants, with matters of lifestyle. The history of the period, then, far from being an objective report, often seems like another chapter from one of Jack Kerouac's novels. And since Kerouac was often the source of this history, any claims to authenticity have to take into account his own complicity in the events.

If one were to write a comprehensive history of the San Francisco Renaissance, it would have to include the myth of the place itself: its colorful bohemian past, its political and social iconoclasm, its impressive physical setting. It would have to make some reference to earlier artistic movements like those in Big Sur during the 1930s and in Berkeley during the late 1940s. It would have to include the opening of Lawrence Ferlinghetti's City Lights Bookstore in 1953 and the subsequent publication of City Lights Books. It would have to make reference to the 1957 issue of the *Evergreen Review,* the "San Francisco issue," which featured many writers of the period along with Harry Redl's stark, somber photographs. It would have to include the publication of Allen Ginsberg's *Howl,* its seizure on the New York docks, and its obscenity trial. It would have to mention the publication of Jack Kerouac's *On the Road* by Viking Press and the various journalistic accounts of the movement spawned by that book. It would have to include accounts of the North Beach scene, its bars and coffeehouses, its poetry and jazz sessions at The Cellar, its occasional conflicts with the local police. Obligatory reference to drugs, sex, and wild parties would probably enter into certain parts of the narrative.

Of all such events, one in particular has come to epitomize the spirit of the age. According to most commentators, the San Francisco Renaissance "began" on October 13, 1955, at the Six Gallery, a small cooperative artspace run by painters associated with the San Francisco Art Institute and located in the Marina District.[3] On this occasion, five poets read, each introduced by San Francisco's senior poet, Kenneth Rexroth. Jack Kerouac was in the audience, cheering things along and keeping everyone well lubricated with liquid refreshments. The poets who read – Allen Ginsberg, Michael McClure, Gary Snyder, Philip Whalen, Philip Lamantia – gained their first public exposure that evening. The Six Gallery reading figures in most accounts of the period but nowhere more enthusiastically than in Jack Kerouac's *The Dharma Bums:*

> Anyway I followed the whole gang of howling poets to the reading at Gallery Six that night, which was, among other important things, the night of the birth of the San Francisco Poetry Renaissance. Everyone was there. It was a mad night. And I was the one who got things jumping by going around collecting dimes and quarters from the rather stiff audience standing around in the gallery and coming back with three huge gallon jugs of California Burgundy and getting them all piffed so that by eleven o'clock when Alvah Goldbook [Ginsberg] was reading his, wailing his poem "Wail" drunk with arms outspread everybody was yelling "Go! Go! Go!" (like a jam session) and old Rheinhold Cacoethes [Rexroth] the father of the Frisco poetry scene was wiping his tears in gladness.[4]

Despite Kerouac's ecstatic picture of it, the San Francisco Renaissance was by no means unified, nor did it necessarily revolve around the figures who read at the Six Gallery. Two of them – Snyder and Whalen – were absent from the scene during many of the crucial years. Rexroth was, for the most part, a reluctant participant – and ultimately an antagonist. Two major poets of the period – Robert Duncan and Jack Spicer, both of whom were intimately associated with the formation of the Six Gallery – were not part of the reading, nor did they identify the Beat movement as "their" renaissance. Sectarian rivalries among persons, manifestoes, and subgroups within the city fragmented the scene, and when journalists attempted to define some kind of common ground, they had to fall back on vague references to exotic religions and anti-establishment attitudes. Even Kerouac's projection of himself as a one-man cheering section conflicts with his tendency elsewhere in his novels to stay in the background – an uneasy and slightly insecure voyeur among his more active central characters.

Kerouac's desire to see all of the poets who read that evening as part of a single movement is belied, as well, by the variety and diversity of the poems that were read. The "big event" of the evening, as we know, was Ginsberg's reading of "Howl," a poem written in his "Hebraic,

Melvillian voice," which chronicles the destructive effects of political and psychological control on the poet's generation. The poem's long lines, its clusters of substantives, its openly confessional style are usually taken as the dominant mode of poets in this period. But Ginsberg was not the only poet on the program. Gary Snyder read "The Berry Feast," a poem based on Amerindian coyote tales. He also read translations from the T'ang dynasty poet Han-shan. Both reflect the influence of Pound's ideogrammatic method and Rexroth's own spare line, a style quite distinct from that of Ginsberg. Snyder's longtime friend and former college roommate, Philip Whalen, read "Plus ça Change . . . ," which also reflects the influence of Rexroth but contains a degree of whimsy and personal directness that distinguishes him from the more literal Snyder and links him to certain eighteenth-century satirists like Pope and Swift. McClure read "Point Lobos: Animism," inspired by Artaud's "visionary gnosticism."[5] Like Snyder's poems, "Point Lobos: Animism" deals with atavistic and ethnological perspectives, but where Snyder's rhetoric is clipped and spare, McClure's is openly declarative and discursive. And whereas Whalen mocks his own seriousness ("What are you doing? / I am coldly calculating / I didn't ask for a characterization"), McClure speaks from an unironic, unitary perspective:

> (I knelt in the shade
> By a cold salt pool
> And felt the entrance of hate
> On many legs,
> The soul like a clambering
> Water vascular system.[6]

Philip Lamantia chose not to read his own poems but those of a recently deceased friend and fellow surrealist, John Hoffman. In some sense, the Six Gallery reading brought together all of the poetic styles that one associates with the period: a vatic, confessional mode; imagist precisionism; satire and self-projection; surrealism; personalist meditation. The point to make here is that, even in its self-described inaugural moment, the San Francisco Renaissance was diverse, relying for its unanimity on a spirit of camaraderie and fellow-feeling more than on shared aesthetic beliefs. It was this spirit that Kerouac caught and passed on to later chroniclers.

Critical attention to the San Francisco scene has not gone very far beneath the surface created by anecdotal histories such as the one described above. Most accounts conflate all literary activity of the area under the general heading "Beat generation," as, for example, do Harold Bloom and David Bromwich in the *Princeton Encyclopedia of Poetry and Poetics.* Under the entry "American Poetic Schools" in that volume, the authors ignore poets like Jack Spicer, Philip Whalen, Gary Snyder, Kenneth Rexroth, and Robin Blaser, seeing the entire San Francisco Renaissance as involving a watered-down version of Whitman in which "the myth has become a mystique in their hands, which merely to invoke is apparently to justify."[7] This "apparently" is meant to account for the Whitman encountered in Ginsberg's whimsical "A Supermarket in California," Duncan's historical speculation, "Poem Beginning with a Line by Pindar," and Jack Spicer's moving translation of Lorca's "Oda a Walt Whitman," three vastly different Whitmans and three vastly different poems.

Daniel Hoffman devotes several pages of his *Harvard Guide to Contemporary American Writing* to the events in San Francisco, and though he gives a more detailed account of separate individuals, he too draws the map around the more public Beat scene: "In California, traditional home of refugees from the burdens of tradition, they became the bards of the cult of complete personal freedom, of the nascent drug culture, of beatific visions and Oriental religions, of communal living."[8] As we shall see, such subordination of actual literary practice to lifestyle is a standard pattern among literary historians. The critic tests the poet's claims of "personal freedom" or "beatific visions" against the hard reality of history, finds them wanting in depth and complexity, and dismisses them accordingly.

More recently, Stephen Schwartz has excoriated the Bay Area literary environment for being long on self-aggrandizement and short on intellectual rigor. He too assumes that the Beats were – and remain – the city's only claim to literary fame, a claim he feels is dubious: "The Beats deserve nothing other than burial, with a minimum of public grief."[9] He deplores what he calls the "leftist miasma" that "covers the entire literary terrain," and at least in this respect Schwartz is unique in finding *any* politics to speak of among the Beat writers. What politics he does find is characterized as neo-Stalinist, a fact that would have surprised anarchopacifists like Kenneth Rexroth and Robert Duncan.[10]

Schwartz's remarks, like those of Bloom, Hoffman, and others, conflate the wide diversity of writing in the San Francisco Bay Area into a single, monolithic Beat ethos, one based less on any particular literary values than on self-presentation. By seizing on the more extravagant claims and actions of Kerouac, Corso, and Ginsberg, critics may avoid reading the work, focusing their attention instead on bad manners. As subsequent chapters will indicate, this critical attitude has much to do with a more pervasive distrust of "popular" movements, even while critics celebrate America's "democratic" potentiality.[11] And although populism was important to the period, it was by no means the only component. What *was* central was the idea that poetry should reach an audience – that it should enchant, invoke, and inspire rather than cause reflection. "We must become singers, become entertainers," Jack Spicer said as early as 1949. "We must stop sitting on the pot of culture. There is more of Orpheus in Sophie Tucker than in R. P. Blackmur; we have more to learn from George M. Cohan than from John Crowe Ransom."[12] It was this kind of attitude – stated here by someone whose work could hardly be called "populist" in the usual sense – that incurred certain critical dismissal, and it was this kind of attitude that enabled the movement to believe in itself.

To some extent this book is about that dismissal, even as it is a reading of individual authors. It explores the ways in which the San Francisco Renaissance was the creation of plural narratives of its origin and gestation, narratives in whose distortions and refractions we may see the postwar period more clearly. We may read these narratives, as have the critics just mentioned, as failed representations of certain millennial hopes for individual freedom and communal unity. But we may also read such critical dismissals as enabling fictions themselves. We may, for example, see in the attacks of the Old Left against the Beats a certain powerlessness and insecurity felt by many intellectuals during the late Stalinist period. We may see in the grumbling over "populism" a continuity, even to the present day, of certain New Critical principles involving the authority of the text. As I have said, many of these critical remarks derive from a willing acceptance of terms laid down by the authors themselves, and so a true reading of the San Francisco Renaissance involves another look at those enabling fictions of place, politics, and poetics. The burden of this introduction is to provide such a look.

In this book I have chosen to focus on poets in a single geographical area and period – that of the San Francisco Bay Area from the late 1940s to Jack Spicer's death in 1965 – in order to study the conflicting strands of an emerging "postmodernism" in a specific locale. The poets who were active in San Francisco during the 1950s and 1960s represent a specific – perhaps extreme – version of the romantic spirit of contemporary poetry in general. Because the literary movement was so closely linked to cultural change within the society at large, it offers us a particularly interesting example of literary bohemia as an aesthetic as well as social formation. The evolution of a new poetics was closely linked to changing attitudes toward religion, psychology, and politics that often served as the ultimate verification of aesthetic acts. To this end, the San Francisco Renaissance represents the closest link to that earlier American Renaissance of the 1850s.

As I have already said, the character of the San Francisco poetry scene is the product of myths propagated as much by the participants as by the popular media, and these myths are inextricably bound to the historical and social circumstances of the postwar period. Although my account is not a sociological study, it draws on a historical record that includes a profound shift in the nature of American self-perception. The forces that generated Allen Ginsberg's "Howl" or Robert Duncan's "Passages" or Jack Kerouac's *On the Road* are embedded in the social traumas of reconstruction and disaffiliation following World War II. If literary bohemia was to be a "poetic paradise," as Jack Spicer said it should be, it would have to coexist with the considerably harsher realities of the Cold War and the McCarthy hearings.

THE WESTERN GATE: POETRY AND PLACE

... & they every one in their bright loins
Have a beautiful golden gate which opens into the vegetative world
(William Blake)

And the gate it is God's, to Cathay, Japan, –
And who shall shut it in the face of man?
(Joaquin Miller)

In the spiritual topography of Blake's epic *Jerusalem,* the West represents the zone of sensation and voice. It is the "gate of the tongue" that has been closed by the restrictive forces of Lockean associationism; it is sexuality, awaiting the reunification of Albion with his emanation, Jerusalem. It would be tempting to read Blake's compass in terms of the San Francisco Renaissance with its revival of the oral tradition, its utopian dream of a city of art, its celebration of sexuality and sensation, its belief in social and political liberation. "[The] west is outwards every way,"[13] Blake says in a phrase that San Francisco poets might easily have adapted to their own "spirit of place" in 1955.

The most generative myth of the period was the myth of San Francisco and the West, both as geological fact and as metaphysical principle. In poems, novels, and paintings of the period the city is invariably a central character, whether as a backdrop in the dark, brooding canvases of David Parks or Elmer Bischoff, in Jack Kerouac's city sketches like "October in the Railroad Earth," or in William Everson's sacramental nature poems. For Robert Duncan, the city is seen through a golden mist, "... the westward edge of dreams, / the golden promise of our days."[14] And for Kenneth Rexroth, the city is a teeming international metropolis of laborers and artists, linked arm in arm against the background of the Sierras. Each version of "the western gate" reflects a private narrative for which the city offers a capacious variety of moods, tones, and colors.

The romantic "spirit of place" among San Francisco writers was based on the city's undeniable physical beauty – its position at the edge of the continent, its hills, its quickly shifting weather patterns, and its wild seacoast. These features captured the imagination of many early literary figures. Writing in *The San Francisco Wave* in 1897, Frank Norris remarked:

> Perhaps no great city of the world is so isolated as we are. Did you ever think of that? There is no great city to the north of us, to the south none nearer than Mexico, to the west is the waste of the Pacific, to the east the waste of the deserts. Here we are set down as a pin point in a vast circle of solitude. Isolation produces individuality, originality. The place has grown up independently. Other cities grow by accretion from without. San Francisco must grow by expansion from within; and so we have time and opportunity to develop certain unhampered types and characters and habits unbiased by outside influence, types that are admirably adapted to fictitious treatment.[15]

Three years after this was written, Norris was to explore the darker effects of this isolation in *McTeague,* a novel in which San Francisco serves as the stage for a drama of human acquisitiveness and greed. Norris was not the first or the last to feel that San Francisco was an island[16] and that its distance from other centers of power exerted a profound psychological effect on its inhabitants. From the Barbary Coast days through the bohemian period of George Sterling and Gertrude Atherton to the North Beach of the 1950s, San Francisco inspired certain "unhampered types" to think of themselves as unhampered – and to provoke others elsewhere to think of the same as provincial. The city is a good place to be alone, so the myth goes, and there are plenty of others with whom to be alone together.

This congenial culture had been such a refuge for trappers, traders, explorers, and refugees from the earliest days of its settlement. Its first literary visitor was Richard Henry Dana, who, like many another after him, encountered the rugged beauty of San Francisco while fleeing from his own genteel East Coast life. *Two Years Before the Mast* (1840) is as much an account of personal self-discovery as it is of the tough rigors of the sea and unexplored coast. But as Kevin Starr observes, Dana was unable to escape the bonds of caste and propriety, maintaining a detachment and even condescension in the face of the "profanity and promiscuity of life" among sailors and savages.[17] When Dana returned to California in 1859 his discomfiture with the place was increased by the acceleration of development and exploitation that had occurred during the intervening twenty years. Dana's California, as David Wyatt observes, "is the place that refuses *déjà vu.* If 'California' is a dim tradition in 1859, what will it prove a generation hence? Any return to such a place is a return to a memory, not a place."[18] As Wyatt goes on to say, with

Dana and other early commentators the story of California was often a fall *out* of Paradise rather than a discovery of an untouched wilderness.

With the Gold Rush of the mid-century and, later, the Civil War, this feeling of belatedness was increased as California recognized and exploited its extraordinary material resources. The period inaugurated San Francisco's first literary boom as well, bringing writers like Mark Twain, Ambrose Bierce, John Rollin Ridge, Bret Harte, and even Oscar Wilde to the area, all of whom stayed long enough to satirize the city's provinciality on the one hand and exalt its physical surroundings on the other. Harte became the editor of the area's first major literary magazine, the *Overland Monthly,* which he edited with Charles Warren Stoddard and California's "poet laureate," Ina Coolbrith. Most first-generation writers left the area (with the exception of Coolbrith) for more exotic cultural centers on the East Coast or in Europe, but it was among such writers during the late 1860s that what might be called a "California literature" began, created out of journalistic satire, sentimental romance, imported aestheticism, and western adventure.[19]

This combination was vividly embodied in the work of Joaquin Miller, whose poetry attempted a kind of epic scope and Whitmanian democratic spirit that might have become a model for a truly indigenous poetry if it had not been for his leaden meters and forced rhymes:

> Lo! here sit we mid the sun-down seas
>   And the white sierras. The swift, sweet breeze
> Is about us here; and a sky so fair
>   Is bending above in its azaline hue,
>   That you gaze and you gaze in delight, and you
> See God and the portals of heaven there.[20]

Despite his love for "the sun-down seas / And the white sierras," Miller yearned for acceptance in the considerably more refined surroundings of European parlors. He brought his western garb and outlandish behavior to the literary shrines of England, visiting Rossetti, Tennyson, Arnold, and others, making up for his lack of culture by fulfilling the European's picture of the frontier rough. As Louis Untermeyer says, Miller "brought to the calm air of literary London a breath of the great winds of the plain. The more he exaggerated his crashing effects, the louder he roared, the better the English public liked it."[21]

In Miller, as well as in the younger writers who gathered at his rustic home in the Oakland Hills – Ina Coolbrith, George Sterling, Edwin Markham, Jack London – we see both the possibilities and limitations of a regional impulse that has always marked California writing. This impulse was fulfilled in later poets like Robinson Jeffers, Gary Snyder, and

William Everson, who drew, if not on the work of these early writers, at least on their example in inaugurating a western regional literature.

William Everson has been the most devout chronicler of this heritage, seeing in the limitations of a writer like Miller the unconscious emergence of a western archetype:

> Thus Miller's low place in American poetry (and for that matter in Californian poetry) cannot permit us to ignore the fact of his emergence. From the point of view of our present perspectives Miller can be credited with scarcely a single achieved poem. But more than with either Dana or Harte or Twain (who after all only sojourned here) he identified with the West and appropriated the archetype into his being, adhering to it as the determining way of his life.[22]

Everson's Jungian perspective tends to ignore the historical specificity of the individual writer in favor of an ahistorical principle informing all writers who confront the West. That principle involves the western writer's supposed proximity to violence. Extreme geography, so Everson's logic goes, leads to extreme psychic states, and the writer who seizes the "western archetype" will be one who lives at the edges of things, geographically as well as psychologically. Although Everson tends to spiritualize place, he is quite right to see Miller's tendency toward self-projection as part of a larger problematic of style in the western writer. The western ethos, he says, is built on participation rather than discrimination and depends on a certain authenticity of lifestyle as the ground for artistic expression. Such authenticity does not mean that the man projected by the poem and the man who wrote it are necessarily the same, but that some attempt at verisimilitude must be maintained. Hence Miller's exaggerated sense of himself as the western bard – his frontier clothing and lifestyle – seems to be a creation of his poems as much as qualities of his personality, a characteristic that we can see in Everson himself. Miller's participatory stance demanded that he *be* the person he claimed he was, much as Whitman sought to provide in the photographs attached to editions of *Leaves of Grass* an image of himself as "one of the roughs."

To some extent the failure of California's early regional writers resulted from the impossibility of fusing a rather genteel literary language, inherited from certain romantic models, with the powerful landscape that was its subject. This attempt led not to an original literature but to more derivative, sentimentalized forms. Miller, Coolbrith, and Markham are interesting in individual poems, but they never quite transcend their similarities to a Whitman, a Browning, or a Shelley. Like the exaggerated, brilliant western landscapes of such painters as Bierstadt and

Remington, California was for the early writer both a place and a state of mind.

At a conference on the San Francisco Renaissance in 1982, Gary Snyder, Robert Duncan, and William Everson discussed this very problem and made reference to the important role of California's early bohemia in creating their own sense of place. To Duncan, California represents a long history of alternative religions, from Indian shamanism to the Blavatskian Point Loma Theosophical Society to his own upbringing in Bakersfield in a middle-class theosophical household. To Gary Snyder, California represents a long tradition of political radicalism, including early environmental activism, IWW labor organizing, and anarchopacifism. For Everson, as I have already pointed out, California embodies an archetype of sensuality and violence, one that defines the creative potential of its inhabitants. For each poet, "place" means different things, but for all three the fact of living in the West means living at the margins, whether this implies a radical political tradition, nontraditional religious practices, or extreme psychological states. The myth of place remains the myth of an alternative society, the attempt to forge out of a somewhat terrifying landscape various alternative forms of participation: "Actually the whole thing is just too big," Everson remarks: "I mean you can put Rhode Island in Inyo County. But it's a great place to be a writer because somehow you can generate more steam, more tension from the marginal position which we are than you can from the center."[23]

Kenneth Rexroth defines this marginality in terms of the city's cosmopolitanism. San Francisco has escaped the Puritan ethos by virtue of having been settled by "rascally and anarchistic types" or by ethnic groups whose cultural heritage was well established before being transplanted to the West Coast.[24] Rexroth's avoidance of the Spanish settlement of California notwithstanding, he fabricates a place out of what he sees as the city's European character. At the same time as he envisions San Francisco's cultural proximity to cities like Milan and Paris, he finds that it is also next door to Kyoto, Peking, and Hong Kong. For Rexroth San Francisco's Asian heritage is more than "incense burners" and chopsticks; it involves cultural, religious, and social structures that inform the city's total personality.[25]

The fascinating thing about Rexroth's numerous creations of San Francisco (not unlike his fabrication of himself, as we shall see) is his emphasis on the city's otherness. Its main advantage is *not* to be New York, a city he associates with all forms of artistic and political revisionism. San Francisco does not simply boast an underground culture like other cities: "It [the underground] is dominant, almost all there is."[26] San Francisco writers do not simply argue politics in coffeehouses and then go back to their academic offices; they are actual proletarians who work in factories, walk picket lines, and identify with a worldwide labor movement. Rexroth's optimistic vision of San Francisco as a politically and culturally sophisticated city and of its writers as engaged proles is like the WPA mural projects on which he worked as a young man – idealized projections based partly on actual history but mostly on his own utopian goals for an alternative society.

When Rexroth invokes the city in his poems, it is invariably as a backdrop for or contrast to a larger ethical point. In the opening lines of "Noretorp-Noretysh," for example, he views the "Rainy, smoky Fall" in Golden Gate Park,

> . . . the peacocks
> Scream, wandering through falling leaves.
> In clotting night, in smoking dark,
> The Kronstadt sailors are marching
> Through the streets of Budapest.[27]

As I develop in Chapter 1, Rexroth often uses place as a prop for historical reflection. He sets the stage in the present (hiking on a lonely trail, camping under the stars, climbing a mountain) and then allows the natural landscape to stand in mocking contrast to the political and social failings of humans. The "smoky Fall" encountered in Golden Gate Park is inverted through invocation of the "smoking dark" of the Kronstadt rebellion. The permanence of nature gives way before the impermanence of history, the enduring value being the poet's ability to bring space and time together in an act of critical reflection.

Rexroth's obvious heir in developing a "poetics of place" is Gary Snyder, though unlike his mentor, Snyder allows the landscape a greater degree of autonomy. Snyder also equates place with history, but whereas Rexroth sees the relationship in allegorical terms – landscape as *paysage moralisé* – Snyder sees the relationship in analogical terms – landscape as ecological model. Snyder's poems on place invariably carry an environmental imperative: Know your place and act by that knowledge. His poems are often catalogues of things seen or done, lists of trees and plants, precise descriptions of landforms and cloud formations. The function of these catalogues is to suggest relationships between poem, individual, and nature that are fundamental to survival itself:

> To do just one of the jobs of poetry, not the only job of poetry – that job is to bring to life the names of the plants and the animals, of the places, to capture the stories of the places, to give song to the places, to vivify the landscape. And our historical role here: to prepare the landscape for future habitation.[28]

This pedagogical dimension of poetry does not end in some Arnoldian cultural theory but in daily practice. It is not enough to use natural ecological harmony as a model of how to live (though this is implicit in all of Snyder's writing); such knowledge is acquired only through daily work and study, activities Snyder equates with sitting zazen and koan study. Thus, to "know your place" means constantly to re-vision it from a new perspective. Snyder gives a graphic illustration of what this means when he describes taking his young sons out to learn the local geography around his home in the Sierra foothills:

> When they were four or five we would go over to Bald Mountain on foot and we could look back and see our place. When they were seven and eight, we went up to Grouse Ridge on foot and we could look down from Grouse Ridge to see Bald Mountain from which you can see our place. A few years later we went on up to the High Sierra and got up on 8,000 foot English Mountain from which you can see Grouse Ridge. And then we went on over to Castle Peak which is the highest peak in that range which is 10,000 feet high and climbed that and you can see English Mountain from there. Then we went on north and we climbed Sierra Buttes and Mount Lassen – Mount Lassen is the farthest we've been out now. So from Mount Lassen, you can see Castle Peak, you can see English Peak, you can see Grouse Ridge, you can see Bald Mountain and you can see our place. That is the way the world should be learned. It's an intense geography that is never far removed from your body.[29]

Snyder's last observation could serve for many poets of the period – Lew Welch, James Koller, Michael McClure, Joanne Kyger, William Everson – for whom the landscape and physiology constantly mirror each other. For these poets, like their romantic forebears, place is both the source and the ground of numinous presence. To name the landscape is to participate directly in its ecological orders, summoning up things past by attending to the present. To walk in the landscape is to establish connections between animate and inanimate realms, the resulting poem being the necessary articulation of those interdependencies. When Lew Welch "circumambulates" Mount Tamalpais or when Gary Snyder takes a "walk" to Benson Lake in the High Sierras, their poems written in response are not intended to be descriptions of the events but reenactments, testifying through the poetics of open form to the vitality of an open universe.[30]

It is instructive to contrast Rexroth's, Everson's, and Snyder's essentially pantheist and rural treatment of place with that of confirmed urbanists like Jack Kerouac, Lawrence Ferlinghetti, and Jack Spicer, for whom the city of San Francisco provides an endlessly diverting parade of sights and sounds. From differing perspectives these poets celebrate the

city for the intense social interaction it provides. As Jack Spicer says, the
city is something created "in our bartalk or in our fuss and fury about
each other,"[31] and in this sense his remark resembles the words of another urbanist on the opposite coast, Frank O'Hara, whose love for New
York takes on a similar tone:

> I have never clogged myself with the praises of pastoral life, nor with
> nostalgia for an innocent past of perverted acts in pastures. No. One
> need never leave the confines of New York to get all the greenery one
> wishes – I can't even enjoy a blade of grass unless I know there's a
> subway handy, or a record store or some other sign that people do not
> totally regret life.[32]

In his sardonic way, O'Hara equates landscape poetry with loss; he prefers the immediacy of people to nostalgia for Eden. The spirit of
O'Hara's remarks might seem to suit writers like Jack Kerouac, Lawrence Ferlinghetti, and Jack Spicer, whose poems often depict the variety
of life in North Beach, though each writes from a very different point of
view.

Kerouac's San Francisco is valued for its embodiment of a certain type
of pulsating American energy that both enlivens and alienates at the same
time. Like Whitman, he lovingly chronicles the "felaheen" people who
live at the city's margins – bums, bohemians, blacks – and the street that
is their common province. He identifies the street with the people who
inhabit it – vital, moving, changeable – and establishes, thereby, his own
distance from it and them:

> But it was that beautiful cut of clouds I could always see above the little
> S.P. alley, puffs floating by from Oakland or the Gate of Marin to the
> north or San Jose south, the clarity of Cal to break your heart. It was the
> fantastic drowse and drum hum of lum mum afternoon nathin' to do
> ole Frisco with end of land sadness – the people – the alley full of trucks
> and cars of businesses nearabouts and nobody knew or far from cared
> who I was all my life three thousand five hundred miles from birth-O
> opened up and at last belonged to me in Great America.[33]

The city's beauty, rather than joining Kerouac to the world, reminds
him of his distance from it. He is far from his birthplace in Lowell,
Massachusetts, and seeks to find in the western city another kind of
womb that will protect him from the "end of land sadness" of daily life.
Elsewhere in this story he describes himself as a "big plump longhaired
baby waking up in the dark trying to wonder who I am."[34] If the city is
alienating, it can be negotiated by a visit to a local watering hole or by an
excited conversation with friends. When Kerouac goes off by himself –
as he does when he becomes a forest lookout in the Cascades or when he
stays alone at Ferlinghetti's Big Sur cabin – the results are catastrophic.

The immensity of nature, the power of solitude, overwhelms him, and he must flee to the safety of the city and the "railroad earth" of human connections and intersections.

Lawrence Ferlinghetti, though certainly more at home in the wilderness than Kerouac, also cherishes the city as a capacious window on a various world. His poems resemble leisurely mental strolls through the market district of the American mind (as Ferlinghetti might say). The things he encounters are synecdochic for larger, sometimes ominous patterns in American life: He pauses to investigate a piece of fruit or read a headline and sees the vast American capitalist universe stretching out before him; he takes his dog for a walk and encounters the police state; he watches the "champs of the Dante Billiard Parlor" playing pool and remembers his American boyhood as a Boy Scout, reading the *American Boy Magazine,* delivering newspapers, eating hotdogs at the ballpark. But gradually this Norman Rockwell portrait incorporates other, less typical elements:

> I landed in Normandy
> in a rowboat that turned over.
> I have seen the educated armies
> on the beach at Dover.
> I have seen Egyptian pilots in purple clouds
> shopkeepers rolling up their blinds
> at midday
> potato salad and dandelions
> at anarchist picnics.[35]

The catalogue continues in this manner, mixing nostalgia with irony, apple-pie America with anarchist history, American idealism, and American imperialism. Holding all together is the repeated declarative, "I did this I did that," combined with an occasional reference to the quiet life at Mike's Place that provides an ironic distance on his reflections. Ferlinghetti's "Autobiography" becomes less a history of the poet's life than a history of the conflicting sources (historical and literary) that produce the American character, an individual whose "quiet life" at a North Beach pool hall is the result of a considerably noisier series of contradictions. San Francisco is nothing in itself but provides the requisite cultural scenery that will support a moral argument.

It becomes clear that, for all of these authors, a poetry of place quickly becomes a theology. The particulars of landscape give way before the moral landscape discovered in it by its inhabitants. "The city redefined becomes a church," as Jack Spicer says, would not have been such an odd idea to a Dante or Baudelaire, for whom Florence or Paris offered a flawed, secular version of the divine. And for many poets who came of age in San Francisco, the city provided the possibilities for a new social or theological order. These possibilities, however indebted to the "spirit of place," could not be realized without the sustaining fact of community – the circles, salons, and bars in which artists could invent out of the earthly city a heavenly city of fulfilled potential. This tendency to turn place into allegory can be felt among all of the poets we shall study, and it exerted no small effect on the development of their poetics.

POETICS AS PERFORMANCE

> The actual world speaks to me, and when it comes to that pitch, the words I speak with but imitate the way the mountain speaks. I create in *return*. In the structures of rime, not "I" but words themselves speak to you. (Robert Duncan)

> Hello says the apple
> Both of us were object.
> (Jack Spicer)

To some people, the idea that the San Francisco Renaissance had a "poetics" might seem absurd. A bearded poet shouting poems to jazz in a dimly lit coffeehouse or raving on a street corner has become the popular image of what poetry amounted to during this period. John Hollander is representative of most early critics who saw in a work like "Howl" the "ravings of a lunatic fiend" and imagined it being read "before audiences of writhing and adoring youths."[36] It was an image popularized by the media but given validation by the poets themselves. Lawrence Ferlinghetti, for example, characterized North Beach poetry in distinctly populist terms:

> The poetry which has been making itself heard here of late should be called street poetry. For it amounts to getting the poet out of the inner esthetic sanctum where he has too long been contemplating his complicated navel. It amounts to getting poetry back into the street where it once was, out of the classroom, out of the speech department, and – in fact – off the printed page.[37]

Although this describes at least one version of the scene – the work of someone like Bob Kaufman, for example – it was by no means the dominant mode. Like other contemporary movements, the San Francisco Renaissance drew broadly on romantic and postromantic sources, but even here the antecedents are difficult to chart. How are we to compare the bardic utterances of Ginsberg's "Howl" with the hermetic lyrics of Jack Spicer or the personalist musings of Joanne Kyger? Could "romanticism," as a label, accommodate the more Eliotic side of William Everson or the neoimagism of Gary Snyder? And how could these two styles coexist alongside lines like these by Helen Adam:

There was a man who married a maid. She laughed as he led her
   home.
The living fleece of her long bright hair she combed with a golden
   comb.
He led her home through his barley fields where the saffron poppies
   grew.
She combed, and whispered, "I love my love." Her voice like a
   plaintive coo.[38]

Clearly, in the words of A. O. Lovejoy, we need a "discrimination of
romanticisms" here.

One could make such a discrimination by seeing several prominent
directions that San Francisco poets took from their romantic forebears.
There had been, since the 1940s, a strong impulse toward the apocalyptic
and bardic through the influence of Blake, Whitman, and, to a lesser
extent, Robinson Jeffers. A more immediate influence, however, came
from British poets like Dylan Thomas and George Barker, whose rolling
blank verse cadences, mannerist rhetoric, and oracular tone can be heard
in the early work of Duncan, Everson, and Rexroth. In addition, Thomas's oratorical style, as witnessed during his reading tours during the
early 1950s, inspired a tradition of poetry readings that has continued to
the present day.[39] Lawrence Ferlinghetti popularized a kind of French
boulevardier, or cafe poem, that had a biting, satiric quality one might
associate with Apollinaire (or, more appropriately, Jacques Prévert,
whom Ferlinghetti translated). Nature poetry, modeled on Chinese or
Japanese poets as well as the British romantics, can be seen in the work of
Rexroth, Snyder, Welch, and Whalen. The personalist lyric of introspection as manifested in a work like Coleridge's "Dejection" ode or "Fears
in Solitude" can be seen in many of the poets concerned, notably in
McClure, Whalen, and Duncan. One may also identify the strong "medieval" mode of Keatsian or Blakean ballad in the work of Helen Adam,
James Broughton, Madeline Gleason, and Robert Duncan. Surrealism –
one of the most pervasive traditions among San Francisco poets – makes
its appearance in the work of Philip Lamantia, Robert Duncan, Jack
Spicer, Lawrence Ferlinghetti, George Hitchcock, Bob Kaufman,
Michael McClure, and many others. And certainly jazz exerted a powerful influence on the rhythms and phrasing of much Beat poetry.[40]

Whatever the significant predecessors and influences, it is clear that the
San Francisco poets represent a subset of a much larger group of writers
attempting during the 1950s to provide an alternative to the rhetorically
dense metaphysical lyric advocated by the New Critics, and my subsequent chapters will often refer to individual ways in which this occurred.
For purposes of simplification, one could say that the poetry of this
generation has been characterized by a poetics of presence, or what
Charles Altieri, using a more theological rhetoric, calls "immanence."[41]

In its baldest form, such a poetics assumes the poem to be a direct, unmediated extension of the author. Language, rather than imitating or representing the world, becomes transparent before the numinous potential it discovers *in* the world. Form is "discovered" in the act of writing, not imposed from without. In Altieri's terms, the New Critical definition of poetic incarnation as the synthesis of local texture and transcendental values gives way to Keatsian "negative capability," or at least to the poet's ability to remain "in uncertainties, mysteries, doubts, without any irritable reaching after fact and reason."[42] Value does not depend on the synthetic imagination's ability to unite oppositions – as in Coleridge and, later, in symbolism – but rather in the poet's ability to remain open to a world of immanent value. Like Wordsworth in the preface to the *Lyrical Ballads,* the postmodern poet attends to "laws in nature and to the way the movements of the mind are linked to those laws."[43]

Altieri has provided the best overview of those epistemological tensions in the nineteenth century that have led to the poetics of our modern era, but his aesthetic genealogies are just that: aesthetic. They do not account for the historical moment in which a certain reading of romanticism became a necessary response to cultural attitudes prevalent in the society at large. The New Critics may have represented a literary conservatism, but it was as much their social and cultural philosophy – particularly in its southern agrarian manifestation – that a poet like Rexroth found so offensive. And the use of certain theological terms to define aesthetic acts ("immanence," "numinous") obscures the powerful influence of historical events – World War II, the transformation of the intellectual Left, global shifts in power brought about during the Cold War – which "produce" the poetics of an era as much as do the literary and philosophical crises of the past. And they produce the "subject" as well, not only the one who writes but the one who reads.

A poetics of immanence relies for its formulation on the ideal of a passive subject through whom a presumably more vital universe flows in Emersonian transparency. The poet's essential openness before the world, the refusal to edit or embellish, the cultivation of spontaneity and improvisation are taken by many contemporary critics as values in their own right. By emphasizing passivity and receptivity, criticism has neutralized the poet's ability to respond to historical events. This is especially true of hermeneutic criticism, which has seen in the open-ended, processual nature of contemporary poetry a corollary to Heidegger's notion of unconcealedness (*aletheia*) by which is discovered "the temporality of being that a recollective metaphysics covers over and forgets."[44] This recovered temporality, one entirely circumscribed within existential terms, represents the horizon of the poet's historicity.

Whereas the dominant discourse on contemporary poetry has been made in aesthetic and existential terms, the actual discussion among the poets has almost always been cast in political terms. Kenneth Rexroth, to take one example, constantly equated the political disaffiliation of San Francisco poets with literary disaffiliation from the academic marketplace. He was roundly dismissed for making such invidious comparisons, but his observations coincide with the vast majority of writings by the poets of the period, who saw the creation of a new personalist, oral style of poetry as part of a larger cultural upheaval. One has only to turn to Robert Duncan's landmark essay, "Towards an Open Universe," or William Everson's "Dionysus and the Beat Generation" or any number of Gary Snyder's essays to see the close alliance between aesthetic and cultural change.

It is a given of Altieri's "immanentist" position that postmodern poetry "captures in its own processes the basic forces or presences which give human existence its meaning."[45] Putting aside, for the moment, what such terms as "basic forces" and "human existence" might mean, I would like to extend this remark in a different direction, one that leads outward to the community rather than inward to the epiphanic moment. Although there is little continuity among the San Francisco poets, there are points of general agreement that derive from the activist position I have outlined above. Those points of agreement concern the poet's desire to reach a community by means of an operative or heightened language that can be experienced in nondiscursive ways. The rhetoric used to describe such communication is often cast in terms of transcendence, to be sure, but the necessity behind this rhetoric is, I will contend, social. Consider the following quotations:

> Working in words I am an escapist; as if I could step out of my clothes and move naked as the wind in a world of words. But I want every part of the actual world involved in my escape. I bring the laws that bound me into an aerial structure in which they are unbound as outlines of a prison unfolding. (Robert Duncan)

> The selves that comprise our whole being may play over this poem [*Rare Angel*], as if it were a tape, and make prints and new codings. The selves can reach out and speak as the pages move past. The book gives birth to itself from the substrate by writing out muscular and body sensations which are the source of thought. (Michael McClure)

> Dear Lorca, I would like to make poems out of real objects. The lemon to be a lemon that the reader could cut or squeeze or taste – a real lemon like a newspaper in a collage is a real newspaper. I would like the moon in my poems to be a real moon, one which could suddenly be covered with a cloud that has nothing to do with the poem, a moon utterly independent of images. (Jack Spicer)

Begin not from preconceived idea of what to say about image but from
jewel center of interest in subject of image at MOMENT of writing,
and write outwards swimming in sea of language to peripheral release
and exhaustion – Do not afterthink except for poetic or P.S. reasons.
(Jack Kerouac)[46]

In my separate sections on Duncan, McClure, Spicer, and Kerouac, I will
point out some of the disparities between such passages and the writers'
individual practices, but for the moment these four quotations will suggest a certain continuity among San Francisco poets. What differentiates
the positions of these poets from those of their peers elsewhere in the
United States is the degree of emphasis on performance, on the way that
the poem enacts in its own realm forces (whether psychological or physiological) that structure the natural world. By performance, I mean both
in the Burkean sense of a dramatistic agency of language in "making
something happen" (as in Spicer) and in the sociological sense of "acting
out" in a public sphere.

In its most basic form, this performative impulse can vividly be seen in
the important role assigned to poetry readings in San Francisco.[47] The
poetry reading is an occasion on which to place the poet physically before
his or her readers – in Ferlinghetti's words, to get off the page and into
the street. The reading also foregrounds the oral impulse of so much
contemporary poetry in which the poem draws from physiological and
muscular resources (Olson's "breath" line) and engages the reader as a
collective whole or tribe. The reading styles favored by San Francisco
poets – the vatic tone, heightened rhetoric, use of musical accompani-
ment, and so on – combined with certain notational strategies to structure pauses and operational juncture, must be set beside the oral style of
East Coast poets like John Ashbery, Frank O'Hara, and Denise Levertov, who, though they are accomplished readers of their own work, have
a considerably more conservative platform style. Whereas during the
1940s and 1950s, the poet had been exiled from the poem through Eliot's
impersonality or through New Critical ideas of irony and distantiation,
he or she reemerges in the most physical way in the poetry reading.

This public performance is matched by a form of operational rhetoric
in which the poet attempts to engage the reader in a more interactive
role. The often lush, overrich, even naive diction of many poets during
this period represents an attempt to bypass discursive modes and speak
directly to perceived sources of feeling and response. Similarly, the surrealist influence, with its unexpected conjunctions of images, its use of
automism, its celebration of the unconscious, represents a similar desire
to reach submerged, passional states. Jack Spicer, in his letter to Garcia
Lorca above, is not interested in finding an "image" that would represent
Lorca's tree but to find a corresponding language event analogous to

objects like lemons or trees. His is a symbolism divested of its meta-physical trappings. In his later writing, Spicer extends this theory of correspondences to a theory of dictation in which the poet empties him-self and "receives" the poem.

In this one respect, Spicer's dictation has some affinities with Ker-ouac's ideas of spontaneous prose, which represents an analogous at-tempt to capture the very contingent and occasional nature of reality without representing it. Kerouac's prose in works like *Visions of Cody* incorporates the swirl and confusion of conflicting perceptions during a single moment of heightened attention. Language serves to dramatize a mood rather than to depict an outline. And in his poetry – the choruses from *Mexico City Blues,* for example – language seeks to capture the sensual surfaces of perceptions as they swirl around him:

> The blazing chickaball
> Whap-by
> Extry special Super
> High Job
> Ole 169 be
> floundering
> Down to Kill Roy[48]

In these lines, Kerouac represents the sound of the train running down the tracks, the talk of the switchmen ("Ole 169 be / floundering / Down to Kill Roy"), and his own enthusiasm all in one compact stanza. The function of poetic language here is to keep things moving and give some sense of the intersecting planes of sensory experience in an abstract, musical frame.

I have used the terms "performance" and "performative" interchange-ably, but I should distinguish the latter a bit more precisely. The term is used by J. L. Austin to describe those speech acts in which a statement "performs" an event. Certain types of utterances – promises, oaths of office, wagers, marriage vows – do not describe or represent anything so much as they inaugurate events.[49] I have adapted Austin's term (and taken it rather out of context) to describe the attempt to create a poetry that "performs" what it describes, that effects a change in the reader beyond the mere reception of information – in short, that uses language to go beyond language. Whereas Austin speaks of more conventionalized utterances whose linguistic structure is not in question, the literary ap-plication of the performative uses a heightened linguistic context, nota-tion, or oral delivery to accomplish its ends.

Admittedly, my use of the performative utterance is metaphorical, but it does draw on several features of that speech act that directly pertain to literature. A crucial component of the performative – as opposed to constative or denotative – utterance is its function as an act. A vow of marriage or a court edict does not simply narrate or testify; it empowers something to happen. As Emile Benveniste says, "A performative utterance that is not an act does not exist. It has existence only as an act of authority."[50] And this act is possible only so long as the one delivering the utterance is in a position to do so. That is, only a designated judge or legislator may order a criminal to jail or open a session of Congress. This highly context-specific quality of the performative removes it from a realm of linguistic universals and emphasizes the uniqueness of the speech act situation itself.

It is this dual nature of the performative – its status as an act and its self-referentiality – that bears most strongly on our concerns here, for the emphasis in the speech act and in the poetics under consideration is on the pragmatics of poetry – its relation to an audience. The poetic act does not stand in a specular relation to reality but creates new relationships between author and reader and, ultimately, between reader and reader. Lest this sound like another version of Coleridge's "secondary creation" or its New Critical variants, the emphasis in a performative poetics is on the contingent nature of the poet's address and upon the reader's active participation with that address. A performative poetics stresses less the ontology of the speech act itself ("A poem must not mean but be") and more the dialogue established between poet and audience. When Allen Ginsberg says, "I have seen the best minds of my generation destroyed by madness," he means that he *has* quite literally seen these things and that, by attending to his testimony, his readers will be in a position to see things differently in the future. Ginsberg's readers are not meant to receive the poem passively but to grapple with its implications in their own lives. That Ginsberg's "vision" has, to some extent, altered our perceptions of American culture suggests that a performative poetics has succeeded as an "act."

The impulse toward orality and performance that serves as a unifying feature of San Francisco poetry is, as I have said, a subset of an immanentist poetics that pervades all of contemporary verse. Analyses of the origins and possibilities of this poetics have been made by such critics as Charles Altieri, Robert Pinsky, Ralph Mills, and Cary Nelson.[51] And though the "ground of postmodern poetics," to use Altieri's subtitle, is certainly to be found in the conflict over romanticism's ability to synthesize fact and value, too often the search for such origins is done unreflectively in the same terms as the poets themselves offer, terms that, as subsequent chapters will show, often exist in conflict with actual practices. Allen Ginsberg's most fervent gestures toward a Whitmanian unity and participation are often conducted in a rhetoric as unstable and insecure as that social nexus envisioned in "Howl." I see the performative aspect of the San Francisco poets as an attempt to open a dialogue with the reader, to establish a sense of community missing from American society at large. The terms in which this address is made – "spontaneity," "permission," "immediacy" – are foils for a more profound anxiety, one that the poems silently memorialize while they declare their independence. And often, because the address may strive too hard to perform where it might reflect, the poem fails altogether. This is its risk, but to a generation growing up in an era of consensus and moderation it is also its great advantage.

COMMUNITY AND PERFORMANCE

In the spiritual and political loneliness of America of the fifties you'd hitch a thousand miles to meet a friend. Whatever lives needs a habitat, a proper culture of warmth and moisture to grow. West coast of those days, San Francisco was the only city; and of San Francisco, North Beach. (Gary Snyder)

In a 1958 issue of *Esquire* magazine Jack Kerouac summarized the philosophy of the Beat generation:

The Beat Generation, that was a vision that we had, John Clellon Holmes and I, and Allen Ginsberg in an even wilder way, in the late Forties, of a generation of crazy illuminated hipsters suddenly rising and roaming America, serious, curious, bumming and hitchhiking everywhere, ragged beatific, beautiful in an ugly graceful new way – a vision gleaned from the way we had heard the word *beat*, meaning down and out but full of intense conviction.[52]

In the essay's most poignant image, Kerouac envisioned his fellow Beats as "solitary Bartlebies staring out of the dead wall window of our civilization." The reference to Melville's alienated copyist seems rather ironic when one considers that Kerouac's article appeared in *Esquire,* a slick, uptown magazine, designed for the young executive on his way up the corporate ladder. In fact, this ideal reader is represented in an advertisement that fills most of the page adjacent to Kerouac's column. The ad is for a new kind of all-weather mohair suit "that knows no season." The model who wears it epitomizes the new, positive-thinking corporate official: young, smiling, short-haired. "Dress right," the ad urges. "You can't afford not to."

The juxtaposition of Kerouac's antiestablishment Beat bum with what William H. Whyte, in a popular book of the period, called "the Organization Man," offers a felicitous image of the tensions faced by the Beat writer. Was he an alternative to mass culture, or a product of it, court jester to the Fair Deal society? Kerouac was, more than other writers of his generation, caught between two realms: the romance of the lumpen underclass and the myth of the professional writer, able to field questions on the David Susskind Show or carry on cocktail party conversation at Lionel Trilling's home.

By the late 1950s, it became common among Left critics to use Kerouac as an example of political apathy among the new bohemians, and because Kerouac helped them along by turning increasingly against his leftist friends and espousing right-wing causes, the attacks gained some justification. Measured against the politics of the 1930s, the early stages of literary bohemia might well seem apathetic. The Beats, in rejecting all official, institutionalized forms of social protest, naturally rejected group and party affiliations. Their political beliefs stressed individual conscience over group action, personal testimony over ideology, anarchism over collectivism. What offended critics was less the Beats' opinions on political questions than the fact that they lacked a program. Worse yet, they insisted that their apolitical, disengaged attitude was inherently political. It was the first stage of what was to become the countercultural politics of the New Left that saw social responsibility not as a matter of class struggle but as cultural change at all levels of society.

The cries of apathy coming from the Old Left often sound like confessions of impotence as well. The possibilities for radical activity had been severely curtailed abroad and at home as a result of the recently ended "hot" war and the rapidly escalating "cold" one. The publication of transcripts from the Moscow Trials, the Hitler–Stalin pact, and the coup in Czechoslovakia in 1948 had effectively closed off whatever residual enthusiasm was left for Soviet-style Marxism. At home, the defeat of the Wallace candidacy in 1948, the conviction of Alger Hiss, the execution of Julius and Ethel Rosenberg, and the witch hunts of the HUAC and McCarthy committees had caused much of the domestic Left activism to wither. The McCarren Act of 1950 imposed severe restrictions on organized political activity, and Taft–Hartley legislation struck a blow at union organizing. Eisenhower's defeat of Stevenson badly damaged the possibilities for what liberal Democrats called an "intelligent alternative" to the period's anti-intellectual, anti-Left attitude. As Daniel Bell summarizes, it was "the end of an age, . . . part of the time which has seen the end of ideology."[53]

The "agony of the American left," as one critic has called it,[54] was matched by the triumph of the middle class. The postwar period was marked by unprecedented prosperity. House buying, helped by FHA loans, increased at a phenomenal rate, and housing construction kept up with demand, providing Americans with an entirely new kind of landscape: prefab, suburban sprawl. Industrial production was up; wages were increasing; employment was at an all-time high; consumers were buying at unheard of rates. Businessmen became national heroes, eventually filling most of the major positions in Eisenhower's cabinet. And the traditional distinction between blue-collar and white-collar jobs gradually diminished to produce what appeared to be a classless society – a vast middle class whose main tasks were to consume and conform. Sociologists of the period wrote extensively about the new, "other-directed" individuals, their boring round of work, consumption, and routinized social intercourse. According to Vance Packard, their consumption was controlled by "hidden persuaders" built into advertising; their sex life and dating habits were scrutinized by the Kinseys; their loneliness became the subject of works like *Death of a Salesman* and *The Man in the Grey Flannel Suit*. "Both rich and poor avoid any goals, personal or social, that seem out of step with peer-group aspirations," David Reisman said.[55] It was this individual and these aspirations to which the Beats directed most of their scorn.

One of the claims against the Beats was that they had no formal critique of the class they attacked. Where their modernist predecessors had attempted to educate the bourgeoisie, the Beats preferred simply to satirize or reject it altogether. Even if the political views of Eliot or Pound were hierarchical and elitist, so the critics argued, at least they had values. Irving Howe was not alone in finding that, because the Beats lacked such a perspective, they must be mirror reflections of the class they rejected:

> These writers, I would contend, illustrate the painful, though not inevitable, predicament of rebellion in a mass society: they are the other side of the American hollow. In their contempt for mind, they are at one with the middle class suburbia they think they scorn. In their incoherence of feeling and statement, they mirror the incoherent society that clings to them like a mocking shadow.[56]

Howe failed to realize that it was precisely because they were "a reflex of the circumstances of mass society" that the Beats exerted such an effect. They may have lacked a formal critique of the expanding middle class, but they did not presume to stand above or beyond that society and judge from some "higher" cultural vantage as many of Howe's colleagues did. Rather, they acted out or celebrated certain alternative mythic possibilities already present in American life – the alienated James Dean hero, the Huck Finn adventurer, the oppressed Negro, the fast-talking Jewish comic. It was a time when drama and excess were kept in short supply, and the Beats were one of the better shows around. Kerouac was an easy target, and his critics used him to expiate their own feelings of inadequacy and guilt during a dark time. This is not to say that the criticism of Kerouac and company was entirely wrong, only that it was narrow in its interpretation of what constituted a political stance.

There are three frames by which this stance can be viewed, each of which contains elements of the others. The first frame refers to social practice (what writers did and thought), the second to cultural practice (what writers represented as a collective sign), and the third to aesthetic practice (how writers' poetics embodied the tensions and possibilities of contemporary history). Since I have already spoken about the last and since subsequent chapters will deal with the political implications of avant garde literary practice, I will discuss here only the first two. By focusing initially on Kerouac, I do not mean to generalize the politics of the San Francisco poets in terms of the Beats, only to see them as the most public instance of a countercultural tendency among all of the poets discussed here.

My first frame, the activist dimension, must begin with Kenneth Rexroth. He had long been involved in Left political activities, working as a labor organizer, civil rights activist, and journalist. His writing was a barometer of the changing political weather among American intellectuals, from whom he received little praise and much scorn. Although he had not been a member of the Communist Party (he claims to have become disaffected from official Soviet policy sometime around the end of the Bolshevik Revolution, when he was still a teenager), he was active in groups like the Randolph Bourne Council (an anarchist group), the John Reed Club, the Libertarian Circle, and the Waterfront Workers Association in San Francisco and participated in various WPA projects. For writers who gathered at his Friday evening "at homes" during the late 1940s and early 1950s, Rexroth represented a continuation of a much older radical tradition that was part of San Francisco's heritage. He served as an important model for poets like Gary Snyder, William Everson, and Robert Duncan, who were searching for a socially as well as intellectually committed poet.

The dominant politics of the Rexroth group took the form of anarchopacifism. A number of writers who met under this banner found themselves in conscientious-objector camps during World War II, most significantly that at Waldport, Oregon, where William Everson was interred. One of the first important small presses, the Untide Press, was established at Waldport under Everson's supervision and produced numerous early books by conscientious objectors during the war. Important early magazines of the period, like George Leite's *Circle*, *Ark*, *Goad*, *Inferno*, and *Golden Goose*, also reflected anarchist views. The anarchist position of many Bay Area writers during the war and after did not sit well ideologically with most Marxists and certainly not with reconstructed Leftists of the *Partisan Review* variety, but it had a decisive effect on the structure of political life in the West.

In another area, that of sexual politics, the San Francisco movement made its mark on the larger society. Robert Duncan's essay "The Homosexual in Society," printed in *Politics* in 1944, was one of the first discussions of the political role of the gay individual, identifying him with other oppressed groups. It was a daring essay to write, since it expressed the position of an openly homosexual writer, and a daring essay to print, even by today's standards. The same could be said for the publication of Allen Ginsberg's "Howl." Its censorship trial brought national attention to a work of art that is explicit about sexuality and about the structures that seek to suppress or control it. Ginsberg's was not the first censorship trial, but his open acknowledgment of homosexuality in the poem (as well as its appeal for sensitivity in dealing with drug addiction and its attack on the treatment of mental patients) opened the door for more frank and honest treatment of such matters in subsequent literature.

As the 1950s moved into the increasingly activist 1960s, the charge of apathy seemed patently absurd. Poets became increasingly involved in the civil rights movement, the Vietnam War protest, and the ecology movement. Gary Snyder was – and remains – much in demand as a spokesperson on environmental matters, and both he and Michael McClure have written at length on ecological politics. Allen Ginsberg was at the forefront of almost all forms of sixties protest, from anti–Vietnam War demonstrations to civil rights protests to gay rights activism. Lawrence Ferlinghetti has been a major spokesperson against issues involving American foreign policy, particularly those relating to Latin America. The same activist posture can be found in almost all writers on the San Francisco scene.

The poetry reflected this activist stance by its often polemical – even strident – tone and its political themes. Many of the period's most important individual works – Duncan's "Poem Beginning with a Line by Pindar," Ginsberg's "Howl," Snyder's *Myths and Texts,* and most of Rexroth's long poems – are harsh criticisms of American political life, and the magazines and anthologies in which many of these poems first appeared often were not the usual literary quarterlies but were devoted specifically to environmental, antiwar issues or at least had a strong editorial stance in these directions.

It is this level of activism that most people mean when they refer to "political poetry," the assumption being that the "political poet" is one who has convictions and incorporates them into poetry. Although this defines one area of political art, it is only the narrowest dimension of a socially critical art. There is a second area in which the San Francisco writers made their impact in the political arena, and that is in their collective role as a kind of oppositional sign.

At the 1982 Jack Kerouac Conference held at the University of Colorado, William Burroughs spoke of the Beat phenomenon as creating a "cultural revolution" in America:

> Once started . . . the Beat movement had a momentum of its own and a world-wide impact. In fact, the intelligent conservatives in America saw this as a serious threat to their position long before the Beat writers saw it themselves. A much more serious threat, say, than the Communist party. The Beat literary movement came at exactly the right time and said something that millions of people of all nationalities all over the world were waiting to hear. You can't tell anybody anything he doesn't know already. The alienation, the restlessness, the dissatisfaction were already there waiting when Kerouac pointed out the road. [57]

One way in which the Beats exerted this impact was through their creation of alternative forms of community. As I will develop in later chapters, the creation of a literary avant garde depends on complicated forms of bonding and self-definition that establish authority within the group. To the outside, such bonding may seem exclusive and narrow, but to the initiates it is essential for survival. Literary infighting and warfare, rather than undermining the sense of community, are important components in strengthening resolve and developing a strong platform. If this creates insularity, it also forges important types of opposition since by controlling who is "in," the community may also legislate who is "out." This was certainly the case with the Beats, who developed a private argot, dress code, and pattern of behavior designed to affirm group solidarity and, at the same time, keep out the "squares." Likewise, the largely homosexual circle around Jack Spicer maintained an almost medieval sense of loyalties and hierarchies that would secure a sense of community in a homophobic society. These communities were based on shared literary interests, to be sure, but they also reflected sexual and social preferences as well, some years before the sexual and gay liberations. And because sexual preferences often led to (or derived from) alternative theories of family and group, they prefigured the communalist "lifestyle" movements of the late 1960s.

The insularity of literary bohemia during the 1950s and 1960s may offend our sense of American egalitarianism and democratic institutions, but we should remember that this very American ideology was founded on the idea of an "elect" with a special theological dispensation, doctrinally mandated, that set itself off from the uninitiated. The antinomian tendency that critics such as Roy Harvey Pearce, Perry Miller, and Sacvan Bercovich have seen as formative for the American character not surprisingly reemerges in a group that identifies strongly with the self-reliant ethos of Emerson and Thoreau and that celebrates the "beatitude" of the individual. That this individualism was expressed within a small group, with its own structures of inclusion, should be seen not as a desire to withdraw and exclude but a need to find an alternative mode of communal organization within American mass society. As Gary Snyder says in the epigraph to this section, "In the spiritual and political loneliness of America of the fifties you'd hitch a thousand miles to meet a friend."[58]

The attraction of such community has to do with its ability to synthesize matters of art, politics, and social theory into lifestyle, which can then be inherited and extended to the larger culture. Allen Ginsberg was – and remains – the most recognizable version of this synthesis. To some extent his influence on a younger generation has had more to do with his role as a counterculture guru than with "Howl," although the two are obviously intertwined. He was present at rallies, marches, and television talk shows throughout the Vietnam War period, and he had an uncanny ability to be at the right place at the right time, whether it was the Human Be-In in Golden Gate Park, the Prague spring uprising, or the Chicago convention of 1968. His appearances on talk shows were particularly important because he disarmed even the most recalcitrant host or hostess by his humor as well as his knowledge of contemporary politics. At the same time, his poetry offered a daily account of contemporary history, full of specific information about who owned what and who was exploiting whom. One of his most important books was titled *Planet News* to suggest the informational role poetry was supposed to take during a period of crisis.

Ginsberg's politics, like that of many during the early 1960s, was a kind of *bricolage* made out of the swiftly changing cultural values of that period, each element quickly adapted to others as the implications of larger social constellations became clear. As early as 1958, Ginsberg was arguing with his father over the need to reject monolithic solutions to world problems in favor of more personal transformations:

> To get America into a situation and sense of understanding that would actually provide peace would be a complete change of values – I'm not talking of moral or political values – those are just ideas – but a change of inward understanding of themselves on the part of masses of individuals – a sort of breakdown of our habit of identifying ourselves with property, external property, and realization that value is inside and needs no excuses or properties to prove it – and this would amount to a series of personal changes as violent as a nervous breakdown.[59]

Whether or not one agrees with Ginsberg's prescription for a national "nervous breakdown," it is clear that Ginsberg made the fate of American culture a fact of his personal life. He saw himself in Whitmanian

terms as a representative figure through whom a generation could measure itself. The fact that he put his "queer shoulder to the wheel"[60] of
history gave his response to political events a degree of humor and
playfulness that an earlier political poetry had never dared to adopt.

Ginsberg is the most obvious case of my second frame for viewing the
politics of the San Francisco scene, and many of his friends followed his
lead. Like Ginsberg, Lawrence Ferlinghetti, Michael McClure, Philip
Whalen, Gary Snyder, and Jack Kerouac gained the public eye in ways
that had previously been reserved for politicians and media figures. They
became associated with jazz performers and rock musicians, and their
poetry could be found well outside the usual literary venues. In this role,
they most resembled their nineteenth-century counterparts, Emerson,
Thoreau, and Whitman, in seeing their personal lives in cultural terms.
They made poetry readers out of nonliterary citizens and political activists out of other poets. William Burroughs's sense that the Beats posed a
greater threat to conservative America than the Communist Party may
seem hyperbolic, but when measured against the inroads made by both
groups since 1955, his point seems well taken.

In this debate over political poetry, the term "postmodernism" emerges
in its most useful sense as describing cultural production in a period of late
capitalism. I have already spoken of the term's strictly literary application
to describe the transformation of modernist aesthetics, but it has come to
be used by historians and social critics to define the paradigmatic shift
between the market economics of the industrial revolution and the new
global economics of multinational corporations. Jean-François Lyotard
has defined this shift as one between modernist society, dependent on
certain legitimating master narratives that structure all of life (among
which would be the Old Left politics with its dependence on ideas like
class struggle, totalization, and dictatorship of the proletariat), and
postmodern society, which he characterizes as embodying an "incredulity
toward metanarratives."[61] Using Wittgenstein's language games,
Lyotard goes on to characterize modernist society – and its dependence on
scientific knowledge – as one based on the denotative utterance in which
the criterion of "truth value" determines its acceptability. This means that
the legitimation of institutions, whether social, scientific, or religious,
depends on a narrative that orders all of the parts. Postmodern, postin-
dustrial society is based on the performative utterance, a speech act that
inaugurates some human action and that can be uttered only by the
"legitimate" authority; it is not defined by any truth value intrinsic to the
statement itself.

Lyotard's argument is much more concerned with the legitimation
crisis surrounding scientific knowledge, but his deployment of a prag-
matic analysis, one that sees historical knowledge in linguistic and rhe-

torical terms, is useful for thinking about how one might link political with literary discourse. For our purposes it would be possible to see the San Francisco poets as offering not only a performative poetics, as I have already described it, but a critique of "master narratives." By refusing to propose an institutionally "correct" ideology and by celebrating an essentially plural society, these writers distinguish themselves from earlier political poets like Auden and Spender, who adhered to a single humanist ideal and a series of accompanying institutional and doctrinal supports (Marxism, the Catholic church, existentialism). At the same time, their qualities of self-projection, their use of popular culture, their exploitation of the media allowed them a kind of public exposure that turned them, as writers, into signs. If they were assimilated by the public imagination, they also willfully appropriated it to their own uses. This is an oppositional and critical stance that must be mentioned in any discussion of the period.

ELEGY OR UTOPIA

I began by discussing the "enabling myths" of the San Francisco Renaissance, the production of a literary movement out of a certain romantic ideology. This ideology is not confined to Bay Area writers by any means, but has influenced the assessment of contemporary poetry in general. Such criticism has seized upon the poetics of process, subjectivity, and orality as representing a rejection of high modernist formalism and impersonality. By contrast, cultural critics like Fredric Jameson and Jean Baudrillard have seen contemporary literature against the backdrop of the "degraded landscape" of popular culture in a period of late capitalism.[62] Postmodernism to them means the work of art in an age of information systems, spectacle, and simulation. The age is dominated not by a concept but by a prefix – postcapitalist, post-Marxist, postnarrative – when art has lost its ability to speak from an authoritative, critical perspective. Art has become subsumed by the "culture industry," which reduces all individual productions to simulacra, empty of any ability to refer.[63] These two versions of postmodernism – Altieri's neoromantic immanence and Jameson's Frankfurt school critical theory – conflict in important ways, one finding literature's historicity through the romantic subject, the other through the dissolution of the subject in various forms of ideological reification.

The poets to be studied in this book illustrate the limitations of both versions of the term "postmodern." Though it is certainly true that San Francisco writers tended to foreground the personal and autobiographical, they did so in distinctly historical, political terms. They were politically active from the outset, and as counterculture figures, they brought attention to alternative modes of community. At the same time, they developed an expressivist poetics less by linguistic transformation (the evolution of avant garde formal strategies) than by the revision of certain forms of romanticism (the ballad, vatic or rhapsodic rhetoric, surrealist juxtapositions, the cult of innocence, primitivism). Thus it is difficult to think of the movement as "postmodernist" when so much of it hearkens back to "premodern" sources. The postmodernism of the San Francisco Renaissance, ironically, is its primitivism.

This same movement forward by means of the past was performed by means of what Jameson calls an "aesthetic populism" in contemporary life, and it is here that our second definition of postmodernism may apply. Kerouac's cult of the American lumpen hero, the Chaplinesque satire of Ginsberg or Corso, the comic book superheroes and villains of Michael McClure's plays, the Gothic ballads of Helen Adam, Jack Spicer's pinball and martians, the neoprimitivism of Gary Snyder – these are the primary means and subjects by which the new poetry made its appeal. But whereas Jameson sees this landscape as essentially mediated by the postmodern commodity production, I see such cultivated naiveté as serving a critical function, directed as much "at" the production of myths as "by means" of it. When Lawrence Ferlinghetti celebrates his "quiet life" at Mike's Place, it is a foil for an implicit criticism of what innocence means: "I landed in Normandy / in a rowboat that turned over." "I see where Walden Pond has been drained / to make an amusement park / I see they're making Melville / eat his whale."[64] Though this is not the most sophisticated form of criticism, it tempers its nostalgia by the debunking power of satire.

Rather than worry over whether the poets of the San Francisco Renaissance are authentically post- or premodern, we should see their work as a collage of sources, both romantic and modernist, that attempts to revive some sense of community destroyed by the war. It is a utopian dream, a "glorious mistake," as Robert Duncan says, and yet it is necessary if the "naked string / old Whitman sang from" is to be revived.[65] The loss of this potentiality produced a need for a new bohemia, an Arcadian community of poets, in which something that was being lost could be identified and preserved. This sense of loss produced, among the poets of the 1940s, an "elegiac mood" that projected the future Arcadia while mourning the loss of those democratic vistas envisioned by Whitman. The San Francisco Renaissance begins here, at the convergence of elegy and utopia.

1

The Elegiac Mode
Rhetoric and Poetics in the 1940s

Our survey of the San Francisco Renaissance begins and ends with war. World War II and Vietnam, with Korea in the middle, provide the background for a literary movement that served as a sustained commentary on a political landscape in crisis. Kenneth Rexroth characterized the tone of poets living in the Bay Area during this period as elegiac, and Robert Duncan agreed. In a letter to Rexroth discussing a proposed anthology of local poets Duncan described their common ground:

> Well, [William] Everson calls us the "Libertarian" poets; but you are more right I think in seeing some kind of unifying principle in the elegiac tone. I feel, nine years now of correspondence underlies it, a kind of contemporaneousness to Everson – yet what other than that mode of the Elegy can link my contrivances with his so direct art?[1]

Like an earlier generation of postwar writers – that of Auden, Spender, and Day-Lewis – the poets who found themselves in the Bay Area after World War II were faced with creating an art within the context of massive human and psychological devastation. Support for the war among poets had been fitful; many were pacifists, several interred for long periods of time at conscientious-objector camps in the West. And whereas for the Auden generation there were soldier-poets like Wilfred Owen and Rupert Brooke to mourn, for the poets around Rexroth the devastation of World War II was too vast to focus on individuals. Instead, there was the incomprehensible carnage of the Holocaust, the bombed-out husks of European cities, the millions of soldiers and civilians who had died in those cities, and, finally, the specter of Hiroshima and Nagasaki looming over the future. What had begun as a valiant attempt to stamp out fascism had turned into a race to ensure military might *after* the war. The elegiac tone that Rexroth saw in local poets was directed not only at what had been lost within the human community but what would never be recovered now that the bomb, as William Carlos Williams put it, had "entered our lives."[2]

However much the elegiac tone responded to the historical context of the war, it was also a reaction to the dominant literary climate of the day. By the mid-1940s, the extraordinary achievements of the early modernists had been assimilated, and rather than extend the more innovative aspects of Pound, Williams, Stein, Eliot, Moore, and Stevens, poets of the mid-century retrenched, turning to more formal modes of versification while retaining the older generation's culture concerns. Delmore Schwartz spoke for many of his peers in this regard:

> What was once a battlefield has become a peaceful public park on a pleasant Sunday afternoon, so that if the majority of new poets write in a style and idiom which takes as its starting point the poetic idiom and literary taste of the generation of Pound and Eliot, the motives and attitudes at the heart of the writing possess an assurance which sometimes makes their work seem tame and sedate.[3]

The general thrust of this retrenchment arose from a careful – perhaps too careful – reading of T. S. Eliot's criticism, particularly those famous remarks from "Tradition and the Individual Talent" on the nature of personality. Eliot's Flaubertian notions of artistic distance and detachment were turned into critical imperatives against which the new poem could be assessed. The more expressive side of Williams or Pound was to be avoided in favor of properly bracketed personae, masks, or dramatic monologues. Formal experimentation, the hallmark of an earlier period, was now regarded with a certain skepticism, even downright hostility. As David Antin points out, "The loss of meter [for Eliot, Tate, and Lowell] . . . is equivalent to the loss of a whole moral order. It is a 'domino theory' of culture – first meter, then Latin composition, then In'ja."[4]

This attitude toward composition was institutionalized through critical works like Cleanth Brooks's *The Well Wrought Urn* and John Crowe Ransom's *The World's Body,* which projected an ideal of poetry as a self-closed, internally coherent structure, a "pattern of resolved stresses," as Brooks says. The New Critical ethos was given pedagogical force through the publication of Brooks and Warren's famous textbook, *Understanding Poetry,* which served both as an anthology of approved texts and as a critical method. The effect of this conservative impulse, from the writing of poems to their dissemination in the academic marketplace, was to neutralize much of the insurgent force behind the mod-

ernist enterprise, leaving behind a poetry of brilliant surfaces and technical virtuosity.

It would be inaccurate to say that poets in the San Francisco region
were unaffected by such developments. It might be better to say that
most were *disaffected* by the literary discussion appearing in the academic
journals. Certainly Yvor Winters, who taught at nearby Stanford, and
Josephine Miles at Berkeley were sympathetic to many of the New Critical tenets, and their students carried on that tradition. But for the poets
with whom I am concerned in this chapter – Kenneth Rexroth, Robert
Duncan, William Everson – the literary discussion of ambiguity, tension, irony, and paradox seemed an elegant and irrelevant distraction.
Where the Lowell generation absorbed the lessons of Eliot, Auden, the
metaphysical poets, and the French symbolists, the Rexroth circle feasted
broadly on the European modernist tradition – particularly surrealism
and the British "apocalyptic" movement (Dylan Thomas, Henry
Treece, George Barker) as well as more regional writers like Robinson
Jeffers and Henry Miller. A weekly discussion series of "modern masters" coordinated by Duncan and held at an off-campus communal house
featured lectures on Edith Sitwell, Gertrude Stein, James Joyce (particularly the Joyce of *Finnegans Wake*), H. D., and Ezra Pound – figures
hardly at the center of the academic curriculum during this period.[5] And
at a point where writers elsewhere in the country might imitate Donne or
Marvell, poets in the Bay Area were rediscovering the romantic tradition
in its most vatic forms. Regional distinctions are too schematic to cover
local variations, but it is safe to say that the forces leading to *Life Studies*
or *The Dream Songs* were not the same as those that formed Duncan's
"Venice Poem" or William Everson's "The Residual Years."

What Kenneth Rexroth saw as the "unifying principle" of the elegiac
will help us understand some of the differences between these forces and
will suggest the origins of what would later develop into the renaissance
of the 1950s and 1960s. At the heart of the elegy is a sense of personal
loss, but the object – whether the love of a friend or the "best minds" of
a generation – varies. For the poets who came of age during an earlier
elegiac period – that of the 1920s – that object was a constellated world
of accepted values and institutions that World War I had shattered. The
poet was left with what Eliot called "the immense panorama of futility
and anarchy which is contemporary history."[6] Eliot provided a significant model for the next generation of poets in the form of *The Waste
Land,* in which fragments of a broken world could be linked by myth and
thematic repetition. As Samuel Hynes notes, the significance of *The
Waste Land* upon the generation of Auden and Spender was pervasive,
both for its formal solution to the problem of social fragmentation and

for its humanist imperative.[7] For poets in postwar San Francisco, however, there was no single poem around which to focus a new poetics, nor was there a unified set of hierarchical beliefs or institutions whose loss could be mourned. And, to continue my parallel, there was no ideological solution in Marxism, as there was for Auden and Day-Lewis, that might assume the burden of the elegiac and transform it into social action or utopian vision.

What unified the forties writers in the Bay Area was their faith in personal statement and confession. The poetry was openly rhetorical – occasionally sentimental and pompous – in an attempt to register the affective qualities of a given mood. "What a time I had finding speech for the feeling I wanted," Robert Duncan complains, ". . . and how often I seem to have found speech for feeling I did not want at all."[8] For William Everson this rhetorical impulse is central to the West Coast poet's openness to experience, the ability to treat language as gesture or act rather than as narrative:

> The vatic commitment must break through the object we call the poem. An icon has to lose its nature of instrumentality in the reality of the thing it is registering. It becomes transformed by something greater than instrumentality, and that, when it happens, is what I call rhetoric.[9]

Rhetoric, in the minds of the forties poets, was related not to figurative language or logic of argument but to the dramatic enhancement of subjective states, a quality we shall find abundantly in Allen Ginsberg and Michael McClure.

The other unifying characteristic of this group is its thematics of loss and nostalgia. That which can never be recovered is often replaced by a grand projection of natural beauty (in Everson and Rexroth) or an unearthly, visionary reality (in Duncan, Spicer, and Lamantia). In the former case, the poet finds in enduring natural forms some alternative to his hopelessly time-bound state. In the latter case, the poet projects a distant world – Arcadia, Renaissance Venice, medieval Provence – by which a hidden potentiality might be revealed in the local environment.

This movement between nostalgia and projection occurs again and again in the work of the period, whether in Jack Spicer's Arcadian reveries over a "poetic paradise" or in Philip Lamantia's dream landscapes or Robert Duncan's idealized Berkeley. It is especially prevalent in Kenneth Rexroth's synthesis of classical and contemporary histories:[10]

And I,
Walking by the viscid, menacing
Water, turn with my heavy heart
In my baffled brain, Plutarch's page –
The falling light of the Spartan

Heroes in the late Hellenic dusk –
Agis, Cleomenes – this poem
Of the phoenix and the tortoise –
Of what survives and what perishes,
And how, of the fall of history
And waste of fact – on the crumbling
Edge of a ruined polity
That washes away in an ocean
Whose shores are all washing into death.

For these contemporary elegists, the contemporary scene is a "grave and lovely fire"[11] projected into a wished-for Arcadia. Such examples give the illusion that modernism never happened; a young man mourning the loss of his innocence or creating an allegorical landscape out of personal despair seems a regression to premodernist sentiment and nostalgia. And although Rexroth's language is a bit more tempered, his rather grandiose picture of himself walking by water while reading Plutarch lacks the imagistic and rhetorical crispness of his masters, Williams and Pound. The tedious alliterations and clichéd diction ("heavy heart," "shores . . . washing into death") could use some of Pound's editorial red pencil.

Such gestures, however awkward, prefigure some of the characteristics of what was to appear later as "open" or "field" verse, in which writing assumes the extremities of emotion, whatever the tone. If there is an absence of craft or artisinal polish in these poems, they at least strive to establish a mood, to capture in their irregular iambics, long vowels, and archaic diction a certain reflective sadness. Such poems are on the verge of a poetics, drawing from unfashionable literary modes and heightened diction some approximation of psychological states that, like Spicer's Arcadia, is "fathomless and deep."

The elegiac, as these examples make clear, is not a genre so much as a tone or mood. Its subject is the disappearance of some primary relationship among individuals or between the individual and a more vital form of social life, a relationship that is firmly reestablished in the poetry of the 1950s and 1960s. However personal, the loss is often that of a radical political tradition. As we shall see, many of the poets came together under the agency of Kenneth Rexroth, who, as I described earlier, had been influential both as a political and as an aesthetic adviser. The Arcadian retreat envisioned by Duncan, Lamantia, and Spicer must be read in the context of their anarchopacifist political stances and not strictly as the futile yearning of aesthetes for a new Eden outside of history. That yearning is present, to be sure, but it is for an immanent potentiality and not a Paradise lost. In order to understand the varieties of this mode, it might be well to understand something of the Bay Area poetry scene as it surfaced in the late 1940s.

CIRCLES AND CENTERS

If Auden or the New Critics or Eliot served as early models for writers on the East Coast, Kenneth Rexroth occupied a similar position in the West. He was the focal point for practically every poet who came to the Bay Area. His evening "at homes" provided a much needed occasion for conversation and community as well as a forum for the reading of new work. Poets associated with the Rexroth circle included Robert Duncan, Philip Lamantia, Jack Spicer, William Everson, James Broughton, Thomas Parkinson, Madeline Gleason, and Richard Moore. As Thomas Parkinson remembers, the focus of evening discussions was often political and theological. Modern literature was "seen in the perspective of Schweitzer, Buber, Berdyaev, Kropotkin, Emma Goldmann, Toynbee, Gill, Boehme, Thoreau, Gandhi."[12] The group was made up not only of writers; many of Rexroth's friends included political activists of various sorts: former conscientious objectors, Wobblies, local anarchists, longshoremen, and radical journalists.

Rexroth himself typified the eclectic nature of the western poet, mixing a kind of frontier bluster with enormous erudition. During his long and varied career, he was a dockworker, mountain climber, farmhand, forestry lookout, hospital attendant, labor organizer, muckraking journalist, and painter, in which roles he provided a distinct alternative to the image of the genteel poet. As a writer, he was no less eclectic, working in most modern literary modes, beginning with a kind of literary cubism in the 1920s, changing to a spare objectivism during the 1930s, and working later in more discursive, syllabic verse. He wrote in all literary genres and translated from the French, Chinese, Greek, Spanish, Latin, and Japanese. He read poetry to jazz in Chicago long before the Beat movement made it a popular mode. His erudition was enormous, and he was able to discourse on Eastern religion, French poetry, medieval church history, politics, jazz, modern painting, existentialism, and eroticism with the cracker barrel style of a southern sheriff. His sexual gossip was famous, and he was able to tell the most obscene jokes in the politest company – and get away with it.

Rexroth's various personae are best viewed through his *Autobiographical Novel,* a fabulous mixture of personal history and fiction in which the author's acquaintance with practically every major intellectual figure and movement of the modern period is chronicled. As Thomas Parkinson observes, "[Rexroth] had a trick of imaginative projection that allowed him to suggest he was a contemporary of Lenin, Whitman, Tu Fu, Thoreau, Catullus, Baudelaire, John Stuart Mill – they were all so real to him."[13] Whether or not Rexroth's accounts are true is beside the point. He thrust himself into current events and transformed them entirely to his own purposes, leaving behind a series of apocryphal stories in which he was the central actor. For the poets who gathered around him during the 1940s Rexroth represented a connection both with the earlier modernist movement and with the West itself. He had lived in San Francisco in the 1920s (arriving, prophetically, on the day that George Sterling committed suicide)[14] and had placed his faith in the city's potential to spark a literary ferment. If it took some years for the fire to start, it was that much brighter for Rexroth's efforts.

The two major magazines in which poets of the Rexroth group published were George Leite's *Circle* and the Anarchist Circle's publication, *The Ark*. Both expressed anarchist editorial views and printed experimental work. *Circle* maintained strong ties with European surrealism and printed the work of many expatriated Europeans then in New York. *The Ark*, which began in 1947, was more political, devoting pages in its first issue to excerpts from Kenneth Patchen's *Sleeper's Awake*, essays on anarchism by Ammon Hennacy and George Woodcock, in addition to poetry by Robert Duncan, e.e. cummings, Paul Goodman, William Everson, Philip Lamantia, Sanders Russell, and Thomas Parkinson. Both magazines served as important liaisons with circles in New York and to some extent were the centers of the nascent artistic community in the Bay Area.

There were other literary circles in the Bay region besides that presided over by Rexroth, although they were not to exert quite the same effect on the San Francisco Renaissance. To the south at Stanford, Yvor Winters presided over another literary group, formed largely by his students, many of whom became well known in their own rights.[15] For them, Winters was the defender of neoclassical aesthetics and formal versification, but in his earlier career he had been regarded as an experimentalist and writer of free verse. His early work, published in innovative magazines like *Broom* and *The Little Review*, was much closer to the imagist mode. Winters later converted from this free-verse mode to more strict forms, using as models poets like Fulke Greville and Sir Walter Raleigh, at which point he began a vigorous (some might say cranky) campaign against most modernist trends.

In Berkeley another group, the "Activist Poets," formed around a teacher at the University Extension, Lawrence Hart. Included in this group were Rosalie Moore, Robert Barlow, Marie Wells, and Jeanne McGahey. For them, "Activism" implied less a political stance than an aesthetic posture. They developed a systematic poetics of the image that emphasized the importance of associational or connotational meaning. As Hart explained, "The poem is not the sequence of words, but the sequence (or pattern) of emotions which the words produce."[16] Using Benedetto Croce's aesthetics as a base and Dylan Thomas, Hart Crane, and W. H. Auden as poetic influences, they stressed the controlled use of connotation toward an affective theory. Their aesthetic derives to some extent from symbolism and Eliot, but the actual poems seem a good deal more contrived – as though written to illustrate a theory:

> The chrysalid of bells across the breast
> (Marie Wells)

> We watched the old men go home
> With a candle of wet in our bones.
> (Jeanne McGahey)

> And the broom-flit shakes
> Over the eyed lawn of your mind.
> (Robert Barlow)[17]

Despite the overburdened, clotted quality of such lines, the Activists had a program that, for someone like Duncan, exerted its own interest insofar as it stressed the possibilities of indirection and psychological association.

Another important group in Berkeley was that surrounding Robert Duncan, Jack Spicer, and Robin Blaser, who, as students of English literature and medieval historiography, formed a circle of sectarian adepts. Duncan and Spicer studied with the German historian Ernst Kantorovicz, who, in addition to being a great scholar of medieval jurisprudence also represented a connection to the Stefan George circle in Germany. The "George-kreis" was a homosexual cult devoted to art and beauty, and to some extent the Duncan–Spicer–Blaser circle modeled itself on that earlier tradition. The three poets extended the lore of medieval and Renaissance culture into their own lives, creating a spiritual and artistic brotherhood out of shared homosexual experience, occultism, and the reading of modern literature.

The "Berkeley Renaissance" (which included, at times, Thomas Parkinson, Leonard Woolf, and Landis Everson) conducted its own series of readings and discussions in the manner of the Rexroth evenings. The group maintained an uneasy relationship with the university's English department and particularly with its major poet, Josephine Miles. As graduate students, both Spicer and Blaser worked with Miles and often acknowledged her importance,[18] but Duncan always maintained that the official campus literary program worked to undermine their literary (and sexual) influence. Whatever the actual conflict, the small group of Berkeley poets gained a certain momentum from their feelings of opposition to official literary culture and saw themselves as a "fraternity of despair" in a "defiled country."[19] This oppositional spirit became increasingly important in the formation of their poetics.

Each of these poetic circles operated somewhat independently of one another, occasionally crossing where Rexroth was concerned. In a sense we can find in the variety of Bay Area poetry a cross section of poetry in the country in general during this period: a neoclassicism deriving from aspects of Eliot and Auden, a new romanticism built out of British and Continental models, and an American regionalist spirit based on writers like Jeffers and Frost. I have used the term "circle" to define literary fellowship during this early period since the word connotes a kind of insularity and sectarianism that characterized the period. As I will point out later, such ideas of community were formative in generating the group affiliations of North Beach, and it was within such enclaves, with their shared social and sexual programs, that a new poetics emerged. We can see this poetics in its early form by looking at three long poems of the period: Rexroth's "The Phoenix and the Tortoise," Everson's "Chronicle of the Division," and Duncan's "The Venice Poem." Though not specifically elegiac in form, they exemplify that sense of loss and anxiety that I have been describing. And through their projection of social and cultural despair, these poems envision alternative forms of community yet to appear.

KENNETH REXROTH, "THE PHOENIX AND THE TORTOISE"

For Kenneth Rexroth, as for most of the writers around him, the elegiac signified the loss of a radical tradition. The Stalinist period dashed any hopes for a socialist alternative that the Bolshevik revolution might have offered, and Rexroth chronicled this failing in almost everything he wrote. His political choice was anarchism, particularly that defined in Kropotkin's *Ethics* and *Mutual Aid* and as practiced in religious and social communities – what Rexroth calls the "alternative society."[20] From the Krondstadt revolt of 1921 to labor uprisings in the 1930s and on to Vietnam War resistance, gestures of civil disobedience signal, for Rexroth, the enduring spirit of opposition within monolithic culture. The history of this oppositional spirit becomes *his* history, and to read Rexroth is to witness the entire post-Bolshevik period through one man.

Rexroth's tendency to absorb history into his own autobiography is matched by his ability to read history against the backdrop of the natural landscape. His elegiac mode is best viewed through those numerous poems in which he muses on the fate of political reality while surrounded by natural grandeur. His most common persona is that of a wandering Chinese philosopher for whom the natural world – a mountain peak, a waterfall, a trail – is an inverse reflection of the human condition. In the landscape he discovers laws of mutuality and ecological balance out of which an ethical order may be generated. Rexroth's task in the poems is to measure this ecological paradigm against current history, a task that seldom yields positive results.

"Climbing Milestone Mountain, August 22, 1937" is the most obvious example of what I have been describing. It begins, characteristically, with a description of the poet in his surroundings:

> For a month now, wandering over the Sierras
> A poem had been gathering in my mind,
> Details of significance and rhythm,
> The way poems do, but still lacking a focus.
> Last night I remembered the date and it all
> Began to grow together and take on purpose.
>   We sat up late while Deneb moved over the zenith
> And I told Marie all about Boston, how it looked
> That last terrible week, how hundreds stood weeping
> Impotent in the streets that last midnight.
> I told her how those hours changed the lives of thousands,
> How America was forever a different place
> Afterwards for many.[21]

The two landscapes, the Sierras of 1937 and Boston on the eve of Sacco and Vanzetti's execution ten years earlier, are combined in the single date: August 22. The star Deneb still moves "over the zenith" as it had in the ancient past, providing an image of stellar continuity in contrast to the fragmentations of modern history. The poem follows the contours of the poet's meditation, back and forth between these two periods. Its easy discursiveness suggests that we are in the presence of that very poem "gathering" in his mind – not the final product but the process of thinking it. This processual quality becomes more important as he reflects back to an earlier time when he visited Vanzetti in his cell before the execution, but these flashbacks are counterpoised to his gradual ascent of Milestone Mountain:

> Climbing the chute, up the melting snow and broken rock
> I remembered what you said about Sacco,
> How it slipped your mind and you demanded it be read into the
>   record.
> Traversing below the ragged arete,
> One cheek pressed against the rock
> The wind slapping the other,
> I saw you both marching in an army
> You with the red and black flag, Sacco with the rattlesnake banner.
> I kicked steps up the last snow bank and came

To the indescribably blue and fragrant
Polemonium and the dead sky and the sterile
Crystalline granite and the final monolith of the summit.
These are the things that will last a long time, Vanzetti.

(CSP, 90)

In these lines we see the suspended arch that extends from the "Simplon Pass" episode of *The Prelude* to the poetry of Gary Snyder. Rexroth's are the "forests unapproachable by death" against which backdrop Wordsworth measured the triumph (and later failure) of the French Revolution. "Climbing Milestone Mountain" offers a similar form of natural supernaturalism as it invokes Sacco and Vanzetti, mountainous in their martyrdom:

I think men will be remembering you a long time
Standing on the mountains
Many men, a long time, comrade.

(CSP, 90)

What distinguishes these lines from Rexroth's best-known inheritor, Gary Snyder, is the degree of statement – even sentiment – allowed. Rexroth's scenic mode is severely mediated by a need to establish relationships between the landscape and the human order, relationships that are ultimately hierarchical. Snyder's best work sustains the same relationship between natural and social orders but insists on the landscape's autonomy beyond its ability to reflect human concerns.

Rexroth's tendency to read the landscape allegorically can be seen in long poems like "The Phoenix and the Tortoise" and "The Lion and the Unicorn," in which the meditation on history is given focus by reference to an as yet untouched (but threatened) landscape. Whether the scene is a campsite by the ocean or a trail in the mountains, the backdrop is history as seen through "the pandemic destroying Europe" of World War II in which history is a "chronicle / of the more spectacular failures / To discover vital conflict" (CLP, 68).

"The Phoenix and the Tortoise" could be seen as a meditation on the sources of these failures. Its theme is clearly stated in the poem's opening section as Rexroth, "Walking by the viscid, menacing Water," meditates the "fall of history / And waste of fact" occurring in Europe at the height of the war. He selects the phoenix and tortoise as images of the transcendent and temporal, "what survives and what perishes," and searches among classical authors for other evidence of this polarity. His first example is taken from Plutarch's *Lives,* of Agis and Cleomenes, two Spartan leaders who, through strong and virtuous leadership, restored a demoralized state. The two leaders, in a political vein congenial to Rexroth's own, redistribute the wealth of the state and gain popular support

by attending to the public's needs. But in doing so, they incur the wrath
of aristocratic citizens, who arrange to have them assassinated. Their
tragic demise in the "late Hellenic dusk" mirrors the contemporary condition of the modern world, "on the crumbling / Edge of a ruined
polity."

As a contrast to Plutarch's tale of civil authority and historical tragedy
stands Shakespeare's narrative poem "The Phoenix and Turtle," which,
although never directly mentioned, may have inspired Rexroth's title.
This strange allegory elegizes the death of ideal love, personified by the
phoenix and the turtle dove. Their marriage embodies a Pascalian reason
that challenges all attempts to codify and explain:

> Reason, in itself confounded,
> Saw division grow together,
> To themselves yet either neither,
> Simple were so well compounded;
>
> That it cried, 'How true a twain
> Seemeth this concordant one!
> Love hath reason, reason none,
> If what parts can so remain.'
>
> (ll. 41–8)

Shakespeare's celebration of love as a form of existential mutuality
(". . . the turtle saw his right / Flaming in the phoenix's sight") con-
forms to Rexroth's closing lines, in which the historical tragedy of the
war is rescued by the appearance of the poet's wife, emerging from the
sea. Rexroth has reinforced the contrast between transcendent and mortal love by transforming Shakespeare's "turtle dove" into a tortoise,
perhaps to emphasize the contrast between the overreaching phoenix and
the considerably humbler reptile. The earlier poem is, in part, an elegy
for the loss of an ideal love, whereas Rexroth's holds out hope for a
phoenix-like *aufhebung* from the ashes of war.

The poem is a philosophical dark night of the soul, covering the period
of one night during the war, ending on Good Friday morning. Rexroth
uses this duration to study the central paradox of anarchist thought: the
coexistence of mutuality and individual volition. He finds that the paradox cannot be solved, if by this is meant the isolation of one term over
the other. Mutual aid means the coexistence of individual action in a
pluralistic universe. But all around rests the sad alternative evidence:

> Endurance, novelty, and simple
> Occurrence – and here I am, a node
> In a context of disasters,
> Still struggling with the old question,
> Often and elaborately begged.
> The atoms of Lucretius still,

Falling, inexplicably swerve.
And the generation that purposed
To control history vanishes
In its own apotheosis
Of calamity, unable
To explain why anything
Should happen at all.

(CLP, 71)

Such failures of vision, the loss of value to a world of fact, leave Rexroth alone with the wheeling stars overhead and the constant reminder of human fallibility in the form of low-flying "night patrol planes." As he wakes throughout the night, lying next to his wife in her sleeping bag, he senses the disparity between these two aerial dramas and awaits the morning.

If there is a redemptive fact beyond this dehumanized world it is the idea of heroic self-sacrifice, figured, on the one hand, in the Christian Easter drama, against which the poem occurs, and, on the other hand, by the self-actualized individual who accepts responsibility for his acts:

He who discriminates structures
In contingency, he who assumes
All the responsibility
Of ordered, focused, potential –
Sustained by all the universe,
Focusing the universe in act –
The person, the absolute price,
The only blood defiance of doom.

(CLP, 89)

The tone here is that of the later Eliot, for whom self-action is asked within the specifically Christian incarnational context. But Rexroth challenges doctrinal definitions of action by appealing to conscience, believing that one's "capacity for recollection and transcendence is developed by a kind of life rather than by manipulation."[22] Although he was an Anglo-Catholic from his early years, he placed his ultimate faith in the "self-determining person" and his power of choice. Rexroth's religious existentialism derives as well from a characteristic Yankee belief in self-sufficiency that we more readily identify with Emerson and Whitman.

The "self-actualizing man" confronting the meaninglessness of war or the incomprehensible ways of his creator takes solace in nature, but not as a place of escape. Rather, nature is where that confused self may measure itself against more enduring forms:

This is not the first time this shingle
Has been here. These cobbles are washed
From ancient conglomerate beds,

> Beaches of the Franciscan series,
> The immense layer cake of grey strata
> That hangs without top or bottom
> In the geological past
> Of the California Coast Ranges.
>
> (CLP, 63)

Rexroth mourns the loss of this essential organic measure to the cash nexus, the state bureaucracy, the "worship / Of history as demonic will." Against these are pitted irresolvable paradoxes of natural process and coexistence. He searches out ancient and modern texts for illustrations of a rapprochement between process and reality, endurance and novelty, accident and necessity. He finds such sources in Aristotle, Zeno, Plato, Jesus, the Greek tragedians, Marx, Darwin, and others, but notes how their remarks become caught in a vertiginous spiral of contradictions and restatements:

> Was it Carnot who said, "The end
> Justifies the means?" Or was it Marx?
> Or Adams? "As teleology
> Subsides to a minimum, achievement
> Rises to a maximum." "The sum
> Of conflagration is tepidity."
> The infinitely cool, Virgin
> Or Dynamo; the term: entropy
> Or fecundity; the bleak Yankee
> Purposiveness always gnawing:
>
> (CLP, 76–7)

For Rexroth, the solution to this babel of seductive binaries must be found through a certain type of individual who is able to see through all reifying tendencies and act independently for the common good. Anarchists, mountaineers, ancient Chinese sages, laborers, classical poets, union activists – all serve as reminders of a tough, iconoclastic spirit that endures, and Rexroth summons them like shades. They live by what he calls a "transcendental empiricism," a faith in the everyday world to yield transcendental rewards. In a preface to his *Collected Longer Poems,* he elucidates this idea:

> I have tried to embody in verse the belief that the only valid conservation of value lies in the assumption of unlimited liability, the supernatural identification of the self with the tragic unity of creative process. I hope I have made it clear that the self does not do this by an act of will, by sheer assertion. He who would save his life must lose it. (CLP, iii)

This "assumption of unlimited liability" can be found most vitally in sexuality. "The Phoenix and the Tortoise" ends with a potentially erotic

moment that casts off the night's historical reflections and rejoins the
poet and his wife to a more vital nature:

> My wife has been swimming in the breakers,
> She comes up the beach to meet me, nude,
> Sparkling with water, singing high and clear
> Against the surf. The sun crosses
> The hills and fills her hair, as it lights
> The moon and glorifies the sea
> And deep in the empty mountains melts
> The snow of Winter and the glaciers
> Of ten thousand thousand years.
>
>   (CLP, 91)

Whether this Lawrentian moment of apotheosis and vision is adequate to
the historical dirge that precedes it is worth pondering. A good deal of
what occurs in Rexroth's poems, from his early cubist experiments to his
later epigrams, concerns the creation of some philosophical bridgework
between an earlier time of vital conflict and the present heroic, if tragic,
solitude. As a result, the poems tend toward the discursive, allowing for
occasional moments of epiphanic clarity: the sight of his wife's naked-
ness, the play of sunlight on her hair and on the landscape. Such moments reflect that "liability" mentioned earlier, but they are subservient
to a rhetoric of loss and self-consciousness that severely limits any
powers of participation.

The generalized rhetoric of Rexroth's long poem is perhaps a risk of
the elegiac: that something mourned must, by definition, be absent and
unformed. No language can be adequate as replacement. This is the
problem with the Good Friday morning beach scene that closes "The
Phoenix and the Tortoise," a passage that attempts to collapse incident
into cosmic rhythm by positing an observer who stands at the center,
interpreting. The problem is that Rexroth is too much an observer and
too little a participant; he demands that *he* be the one making all connections, finding the "figure in the carpet," so that he may never enter the
"tragic unity of creative process" he so values. He may eschew the will
as a terrible inheritance of postlapsarian acquisitiveness, but he everywhere signals his own failure to escape it.

WILLIAM EVERSON, "CHRONICLE OF DIVISION"

In 1935, Kenneth Rexroth received a pamphlet of poems from a
young man who at that time was growing grapes in the San Joaquin
Valley. The book was *These Are the Ravens,* and the man was William
Everson. Speaking of this early book, Rexroth remembers that the
poems

weren't much like the poems being written in those days, either in the *New Masses, Partisan Review,* or the *Southern Review.* They were native poems, autochthonous in a way the fashionable poems of the day could not manage. Being an autochthon of course is something you don't manage, you are. It was not just the subjects, the daily experience of a young man raising grapes in the Great Valley of California, or the rhythms, which were of the same organic pulse you find in Isaiah, or Blake's prophecies, or Whitman, or Lawrence, or Sandburg at his best, or Wallace Gould, or Robinson Jeffers. This, it seemed to me, was a young fellow out to make himself unknown and forgotten in literary circles.[23]

Rexroth goes on to say that his last remark was proved untrue, but his equation between the autochthonous spirit and literary anonymity was certainly accurate for the prewar period. If the poetry was unfashionable at the time, so was the tradition with which Everson identified, but it was precisely because of people like Everson that a new appraisal of Whitman, Jeffers, and Blake was made.

What Rexroth would have appreciated in this first book was some of his own tendency toward self-dramatization (he says as much in his introduction) and the same interest in a Lawrentian sexual mysticism. Like Rexroth, Everson senses the latent power of the western landscape; in "Muscrat Pruning" he stops in his work to testify to its stark beauty:

> All these dormant fields are held beneath the fog.
> The scraggy vines, the broken weeds, the cold moist ground
> Have known it now for days.
> My fingers are half-numbed around the handles of the shears,
> But I have other thoughts.
> There is a flicker swooping from the grove on scalloped wings,
> His harsh cry widening through the fog.
> After his call the silence holds the drip-sound of the trees,
> Muffling the hushed beat under the mist.
> Over the field the noise of other pruners
> Moves me to my work.
> I have a hundred vines to cut before the dark.
>
> (RY, 6)

The "dormant fields," "scraggy vines," and "broken weeds" offer the suggestion of a Williams-like objectivism, but the iambic cadence, the musical clustering of alliterations and broad, open vowels, the active intervention of the first-person pronoun, and the quality of dramatic brooding take the poem away from the world of *Spring and All* and place it more in the tradition of Jeffers or Roethke.[24] Where Rexroth treats nature as a theater against which human dramas may be measured, Everson sees it as a reflection of one's inner life. Powers latent in the earth are similarly to be found in the self, and this potentiality is released in the poet's interaction with his locale. When William Everson became a lay brother in the Dominican Order in 1949, that latency was given form and intention, but in these poems of the 1930s and 1940s, he is content to watch and witness.

Everson represents a pervasive sacramental impulse among San Francisco poets. Unlike Lowell, whose early Catholicism involved acceptance of doctrinal definitions of God's incarnation, Everson's gradual struggle with the "crooked lines of God" (as he titled one book) was agonized and difficult. Part of this agonizing is tied to his native pantheism in which the sacred is part of biological and natural forces. The sacraments are as fleshly as they are spiritual, and belief is formed as much through sexual intercourse as through Christ's living witness.

In his early poetry, this sacramentalism was inspired by Lawrence and Jeffers, the former admired for his "affinity to nature and the celebration of sex as the central archetype of the natural" and the latter for his "celebration of nature as divine, the divine made concrete."[25] Everson's conversion to Catholicism was by no means a rejection of this secular incarnationalism but a heightening of that sexual relationship to nature within a doctrinal frame. In his pantheist phase, as Albert Gelpi points out, Everson surrendered "to primal experience until at last it yielded him the Christian mystery," but by so thoroughly accepting the church he was given over to "that dark area, at once the center and circumference of psyche, where passion and spirit reveal themselves as personhood incarnate."[26]

In all of his writings, Everson stresses a certain Nietzschean vulnerability before experience, a need to remain open to the plenitude of feeling. He characterizes this "giving over" as the Dionysian aspect of poetry, which manifests itself formally in heightened rhetoric and thematically in sexual and confessional subjects. The Dionysian – which he later links to the new American poetry embodied by the Beats – exists in opposition to an Apollonian precisionism associated with high modernism: "My view of the Dionysian is that you gain more through a certain quality of imprecision . . . a certain openness or vulnerability to sensation."[27] We shall see these terms reappearing in other poets as the central tenets of "open" or "field" verse. In its early phase, however, this impulse leads to a poetry of dramatic witness and testimony.

Something of this vulnerability can be felt in a short lyric, "Invocation":

> Year going down to my thirtieth autumn,
> Year through the spring and the soaring summer
> To the equinoctial season of my birth,
> Yield me the breadth and the crowning measure;

> I now have need of your last bestowment:
> The deferent strength,
> Nurtured through many a somnolent season.
> Bold in the formed and final bloom.
> Yield me that blossom.
>
> (RY, 98–9)

Like many of his poems of the 1940s, "Invocation" yearns for communion, a mystical synthesis of self and nature. Its inverted syntax, its alliterations, its archaic diction ("equinoctial season," "last bestowment," "deferent strength") and its irregular dactyls strain toward a richness in concert with its subject. His search for a "deferent strength" cannot be fulfilled by naming the things of the world; he yearns for an incarnation among the "shy and outcast weeds," and his rhetoric attempts to capture that yearning by its sheer extravagance.

Everson's poetry of the 1940s might be called, in M. H. Abrams's terms, a "theodicy of the private life,"[28] a chronicle of the self's engagement with an elusive spiritual purpose. Unlike Christian spiritual autobiography, of which Augustine's *Confessions* would be the model, the romantic theodicy is secular, recording one's gradual coming-into-awareness of divine relations as reflected in the natural world. Everson's early poetry is a theodicy of divisions, ruptures, self-doubts, illuminated against the backdrop of the war and, alternately, against the poet's own spiritual confusions as he moves closer to the church. The landscape that had been such a powerful source in the 1930s becomes more and more schematic by the time of the war, and in the late 1940s that landscape is almost entirely one made up of men and women in their difficult, trying relationships.

The representative poem of this attitude and period, "Chronicle of Division" (1943–6), could be usefully compared with "The Phoenix and the Tortoise," since both speak of the personal and spiritual destruction brought about by the war and since both appeal to nature for some form of apotheosis. But where Rexroth stays within the grand theater of history, Everson studies the individual subject and its negotiations with others. "Chronicle" deals with the breakup of his marriage to his first wife, Edwa, and since much of the poem was written while Everson was interred at the conscientious-objector camp at Waldport, Oregon, the themes of sexual infidelity and loneliness fuse with that large, social and historical division occurring in Europe.

The opening sections of "Chronicle" detail the conflicts in the author's marriage, which are exacerbated by his physical distance from his wife.[29] The tension between the ideological decision that brought him to Waldport and the ambiguous personal relationships within the camp becomes a central issue in the poem's opening section. In setting out this conflict,

Everson notes that the injunction "Thou shalt not kill" may unify members of the camp, but it does not efface the loneliness of men "struck from the woman." Hence "deep cruelties and secretive hurts" breed an ethos contrary to the communality implied by pacifist ideals.

Within this more generalized loneliness, the poet turns to the rift in his own marriage, beginning with his receipt of a "Dear John" letter and continuing through the agonized self-accusations that ensue. He searches for some source of his wife's disaffection, "the harsh word, / The injurious act that turned her away," but the rift cannot be reduced to simple causes. His attempts to resolve the conflict during the couple's awkward and painful meetings do little to alleviate the crisis. These meetings are set against an autumnal landscape, the darkening season illustrating the couple's condition as well as that larger global drama, the war, that separates the couple physically and emotionally. Unlike Rexroth's antiwar poem, Everson's "Chronicle" does not foreground the war as the central drama against which human temporality might be measured. For Everson the war is an archetype of human and psychological conflict of which the broken marriage is but one example.

Gradually Everson's stoical loneliness in the poem yields another view of the event – one more coincident with his ethical beliefs and one that rejoins him to the common humanity that adultery and the war have violated. "He will be given again to the indifferent world, / Go south to a city" where sights of human sadness and misery present alternative challenges to his solipsism. He will

> . . . see the blind veteran enter,
> Bearing his unrejectable cup;
> And will then understand
> How the gnarled event must be weighed in its world,
> Under the havoc-holding sky,
> Under the iron,
> Under the catapulting dead,
> Who grin in the metallurgic grip
> And eat their answer.
>
> (RY, 150)

The possibility of human sympathy, the ability to weigh an event "in its world" and not subordinate it to one's personal concerns, allows Everson to break away from the inward-directed, self-accusatory tone of the earlier sections. He becomes open to the world again.

This change occurs in section 5 with its long, Whitmanian chant. Standing at the sea's edge with the terrible division behind him, the narrator looks to the sea and to the world of natural process for some "mnemic speech" that he might interpret for himself. Like Whitman in

"Out of the Cradle Endlessly Rocking," he listens to the sea's voice, "Probing its weftage for what it could mean, / For what was in it, / What it held for him" (RY, 152). The answer is all the more difficult to interpret given the terrible price paid for the recently achieved peace in Japan:

> Now that the old volcanic hurt,
> In its black upheaval,
> Buried the civilization of the past?
> Now that the Peace,
> Breached in the air over Nagasaki,
> Lays its ash on the world?
>   (RY, 153)

The answer, interpreted out of the sea's speech, is to "Dip down" beneath the world of will and explanation, beyond the "divisible selves, / Ill-eased with each other." There he will find a repressed speech that links him to the cosmic order. Like Whitman, who in section 38 of "Song of Myself" realizes that he must never look "with a separate look on my own crucifixion and bloody crowning," Everson comes to understand his own suffering as that of the world. The war that had caused a "chronicle of division" can never be separate from the one who discovers his alienation in its folds.

In "Chronicle of Division," Everson wants to discover a language that exists in some ratio to that crude, "mnemic speech" latent in the landscape. He must free archetypes of the unconscious while recognizing their origins. Defending Jeffers against a critic's accusation of excess, Everson speaks as well for himself: "The initiating locus of energy (the archetype) must determine the configuration of its effect."[30] These same ideas appear in a modified form in projectivist aesthetics – form as extension of content, poetry as process – here used to define a certain extremity of speech and self-presentation. In "Chronicle of Division" the event – a division between man and woman – is revealed to be part of a larger violence in the world, and only vatic, exalted language might penetrate to this primordial realm. It is this value that Everson later recognized in the Beats, who "revolted against the poem as an object in order to reassert that the vatic commitment in the poet's unconscious is the thing and not the aesthetic object."[31]

What we usually call rhetoric – the application of figural language, the control of affective response, the role of persuasion – is turned by Everson into a term for the transcendence of instrumentality. It is this heightened, rhetorical language that marks Everson's contribution to Rexroth's "elegiac" impulse. In writing his own postromantic secular theodicy, Everson realized that personal testimony would have to discover the terms for its own transcendence in the act of writing. This act, while attempting to chronicle a division in the poet's biographical life, became the agency of transformation and the ultimate mirror of a creative process in the natural world.

ROBERT DUNCAN, "THE VENICE POEM"

In a notebook entry for March 18, 1947, Robert Duncan responded to a recent reading by Everson of "Chronicle of Division":

> He has a hovering tone over the refrain in the *Chronicle,* a declamatory exalted voicing of credo passages, and a most moving agony of expression – mouth as in a tragic mask – almost a musical voice at these times. [He seems a] poet in search of the deepest suffering, the external drama in which the inner drama can find its proper manifestations and the poet be fulfilled.[32]

From this discussion of Everson, Duncan goes to his own developing poetics:

> Demands of a new poetry push from within; the rushing sense of new thresh-hold and a presence to be realized. I have too, not time to let it lie, to gather force and necessity. As I study, I read there of the world in which I live. To dream greatly, to adore, to give oneself to the sacramental.[33]

Within a page of these entries, Duncan launches into what would become the major poem of his early period, "The Venice Poem." "To dream greatly, to adore, to give oneself to the sacramental" could easily serve as the strong imperatives of that poem and of the constellation of Berkeley poets for whom Duncan was a central figure.

For Duncan, as for Everson, the sacramental was as much sexual as spiritual, and in the notebook containing "The Venice Poem" can be found diary entries chronicling the extent to which Duncan had indeed "given himself" to and suffered the agonies of such sacraments. He lived in a charged intellectual and personal environment where writing was quite literally "performed" in the atmosphere of a seance table at which lovers and friends attended. Duncan's first major poem, "Medieval Scenes," was written in such company, the individual sections "received" while others looked on.[34] His communal house at 2029 Hearst Street, as Ekbert Fass says, was the center of the nonacademic poetry scene at that time, and to a large extent it was there – in the seances and sexual magics of young homosexual writers – that the idea of a poetic renaissance took form.[35]

The "demands of a new poetry" were very much on Duncan's mind during this period, and though he answered them with his friends at the

evening round table, he pursued them as well through his medieval and
Renaissance studies at the university. The new poetry would involve a
revival of earlier traditions at the same time that it would extend the
contributions of certain modernists. As I point out in Chapter 4, Duncan's modernism is by no means the one we usually think of when we
look to the origins of contemporary verse. His period style of the 1940s is
an odd pastiche of sources, influenced as much by Edith Sitwell or St.
John Perse as by Pound or Williams. His penchant for long, highly
subordinated sentences and rocking iambic meters derives from British
poets like George Barker as well as seventeenth-century poets like Herbert and Milton:

> Already ere I wake I hear that makes disturbing
> all this dear and pleasant world about me so devised
> in harmonie where we would, fallen, see
> in garden chaos – I hear the clamor of that bell
> ring rathe upon my ears like iron.[36]

In other poems of the period, one can find Duncan experimenting with
surrealism, the "magic of perspectives and definitions of reals and unre-
als," which he derived from Sanders Russell. St. John Perse's *Anabase* in
Eliot's translation provided some of the qualities of "nostalgia and por-
tent, of evocation and hallucination"[37] that contributed to Duncan's dramatic rhetoric. The lyrics of Laura Riding and Edith Sitwell found their
way into the poet's songs and nursery rhymes:

> This is the Heaven-House Everyday Do
> that Mr Responsible Person God
> built in a day.
>
> This is Mr Responsible Who
> looks out for the welfare of me and you,
> of Eve, of you, of Adam, of me.
>
> (FD, 19)

All of these sources represent stages in an apprenticeship as Duncan
sought to find his own voice. The single characteristic throughout is
what in a later poem he calls the "verdant rhetorical,"[38] a language rich
in suggestion and nuance, a language that in its sheer excess replicates
charged emotional states.

   "The Venice Poem" synthesizes all of these various voices and adds an
overall structural complexity that characterizes his later work. As I have
already pointed out, the fact that it emerged out of the specific context of
a poetic coterie informs its larger thematics of betrayal and jealousy.
Duncan had lost his lover to a rival, and the poem attempts to render the
"empire" that jealousy creates. The sexual rage of that conflict is figured
through references to Shakespeare's *Othello:*

The cry I heard upon the water
might have been Othello's song
who sang:

> Why is the house so still?
> Where have you gone?

> My knowing now will never be still.
> My loving now will never be still.
> I am like an empty shell
> tortured with voices.

(FD, 83)

Like Othello, Duncan sees himself as both king and fool, secular ruler
but ruled himself by the domain of his passions. His jealous fears circum-
scribe his world, and he seeks to find "another world of man and beasts /
taking their own fabulous color beyond [his] hand" (FD, 88).

The poet's cry of loss is set against the backdrop of two cities, one
ancient the other contemporary. Renaissance Venice, which Duncan
knew only through art history slides, represents an unearthly city of
gilded domes and ageless monuments. Contemporary Berkeley represents the other side of Venice, the historical city whose campanile bells
mock the poet's desire for transcendence:

> Damn the persistent tolling of the hour
> Damn the actual brute time.
>   I hug my hurt and
>   fixing mind away from my heart
> describe the sea-wed timeless
>   city.

(FD, 84)

This double city appears in earlier poems like "Heavenly City, Earthly
City" and "Medieval Scenes," but in "The Venice Poem," the duality is
rooted in the specific context of sexual jealousy. Venice becomes a
"monument of all desire and fear / for mind's anxiety to feed upon."
The fact that it is known only through "lantern-slides" reinforces this
point: that the city is largely a projection in which the poet reads his own
life. Unlike Rexroth or Everson, Duncan does not escape the city in
order to understand himself but lives within the deceptions and illusions
of an urban environment. Rexroth and Everson treat the city as a place of
corruption, despoiler of nature, and symbol of all that the war has
wrought. By contrast, Duncan sees the city as a paradigm for his own
dualistic nature:

> I saw the City of Venice in that poem as my own and the history of its
> empire as the history of an imperialism in Poetry in which I saw my
> own dreams expand. . . . And in my vision of Empire in *The Venice*

Poem I saw again the power and the Accumulation of Wealth, the grandeur and domination, as a poetry established in a pathos, a pathetic claim having . . . knowledge of the remains of Venice, of today.[39]

The opposition between two cities is but one of many pairs of contrasts around which this poem occurs: Venus/Venice, Byzantium/Europe, Othello/Shakespeare, the Venus of Lespuges/Aphrodite, Berkeley/Venice. Each pair contrasts ideas of originality and innocence with ideas of belatedness, sexual violation, and knowledge. The many references to Venus and her avatars in primitive and modern forms suggest the plural nature of love in its divine and secular forms. Duncan works through these oppositions in order to understand his own lovesick state, seeing in the lustrous golden domes and glittering pomp of Venice the insistent falseness and possessiveness that he calls empire. And equally, he sees in the primitive figure of the Venus of Lespuges − a small statue viewed in an art book − an atavistic reminder of the cult of love:

> I return to first things: Her image looms
>   wherein lies the universe
>   of felt things; from which
>   the spirit is flung outward,
>   born out of the fat fruit.
>
>   (FD, 96)

These "first things" stand as alternatives to the "mock gold glories cut from paper." Their endurance comes as an optimistic challenge to the poet's own narcissistic revery on loss. He attempts to look more deeply into the world for signs of his inner state and finds, at the same time, a poetics: "This is the first proposition: / in the poem as a mirror − the whole world, / an instruction" (FD, 88). The mirror that had reflected himself wrapped in the empire of loss now turns outward onto the world for instruction. The poem reflects and creates a world at the same time. He traces this idea to Dante's *De Monarchia:* "The universe 'speaks to us and in us, and we but imitate in what we call our language the real speech which surrounds us, out of which, indeed, we are born.' "[40]

This idea of rebirth through art becomes the subject of the poem's final section, a "Coda" in which Duncan seeks to return to a world of impulse and feeling that he associates with the Venus of Lespuges. From jealous Othello, ferocious in his adulterous rage, he becomes a "Little cross-eyed king held / secure in the center of all things," and what had been the monotonous cadence of the campanile's bells reminding him of loss becomes a charm for the child: "Ring, then, ring clear! / Fatherly towers in the air!" The child that is born from these "Fatherly towers" is a part of the poet himself, an "infant emperor in his autistic universe," as he says elsewhere. Duncan sees in his own possessiveness an image of the

greed of the world and comes to understand poetry's role in this duplicity. He does not seek to transcend this knowledge but to witness its
effects in the process of writing. If the birth is a thematic resolution to
"The Venice Poem," it is also a transformation of Duncan's sense of
what poetry has to do.

Three poetic guides appear in the poem to indicate the way: "Saint
William Shakespeare," canonized for his complete projection of the complex workings of love; Ezra Pound, who, though never mentioned by
name, provides instructions for composition; and Igor Stravinsky,
whose ideas of musical form inspired the shape of the poem. Shakespeare
is valued not only for his thorough elaboration of jealousy but for incorporating himself as subject and object of his own creations. All three
artists provide models for how the "earthly city" in history can be given
narrative form. Duncan is less interested in previous thematic representations of Venice (Shakespeare's depiction of the city in *Othello* or Pound's
in "Canto XVII," for instance) than he is in finding formal solutions for
embodying extreme psychological states.

Although Pound deals with Venice several times in the *Cantos*, his
main importance for Duncan's poem is his advice to the younger poet on
matters of poetic composition. Quotations taken from letters written to
Duncan while Pound was at St. Elizabeth's appear at various points,
urging the poet to "understand what is happening" and "watch 'the
duration of syllables / 'the melodic coherence, / 'the tone leading of
vowels,'" instructions that have become central to Duncan's poetics.
Pound's insistence on vowel music can be felt throughout "The Venice
Poem" in the way that sounds echo and resonate against each other,
blurring distinctions between words much as, at the thematic level, Venice becomes Venus.

Stravinsky provides inspiration for the larger structure of "The Venice
Poem" through works like the *Symphony in Three Movements,* written
during the war, and his lectures on music, published as *The Poetics of
Music.*[41] Whether or not there are structural parallels between poem and
symphony would be hard to say (Stravinsky's work is in three movements, whereas Duncan adds a fourth to his), but it is clear that the work
gave the poet some notion of how to organize large units. "The Venice
Poem" proceeds by sudden shifts and contrasting moments – from sections written in short lines of regular accents to long, prosaic lines,
continually varying and changing the pace. And beyond any structural
influence, Stravinsky's writings on music appear within the poem (as do
Pound's) to instruct the poet on general problems of composition:

> "These natural sounds suggest music
>   but are not yet themselves music;
>   Pleasing in themselves

they are but promises of music.
It takes
a human being to keep them."
(FD, 86)

This meditation on art and its principles strongly differentiates "The
Venice Poem" from both "The Phoenix and the Tortoise" and "Chronicle of Division." Although all three poems deal with personal and cultural fragmentation, Duncan's poem is unique in realizing the interrelationships between fragmentation and poetic language. "The Venice
Poem" is the most formally complex of the three, combining in its four
sections a wide range of poetic styles, from short lyric passages to prose
quotations from other writers to long, Whitman-like rhapsodies. In such
variety we see an early instance of Duncan's later collage style as found in
"Passages." And although Pound is acknowledged as the source of such
patterning, the rhetoric and tone of the poem derive from earlier romantic sources. Those "sources" are only partially literary; they are part of an
ideal of community that found its voice in a revival of the romantic
tradition within Duncan's poetic circle.

Such a rhetoric was hardly fashionable in 1947, but for Duncan it was a
necessity if a poetry of intense personal states was to be written. The city
of Venice could not simply serve as a metaphor for the poet's emotional
condition, nor could it merely symbolize the vulgar wealth of civilization. It had to be evoked in the luxurious language of an equivalent
emotional excess, one that Duncan noted in Everson's work. Like the
lions of Venice, mentioned in the opening lines, language is "suppliant to
the ringing in the air," willing to risk the unfashionable for passion's
lure.

"THE RHETORIC OF AN EARLY MODE"

In attempting to describe the origins of the San Francisco Renaissance, I have chosen three poems that illustrate varieties of what
Rexroth called the "elegiac mode." Obviously there were other important tendencies operative at the same time – Philip Lamantia's surrealism
and the masques and children's rhymes of Madeline Gleason and James
Broughton, for example – but these three long poems display an impulse
toward the sacramental that would be a central feature of the next two
decades in the Bay Area. This impulse stemmed from a need to discover
some sort of vital contact in the aftermath of the war. For Rexroth, this
contact involved new forms of liability and mutual aid. Whereas Rexroth
looked to the entire field of history for examples of this mutuality,
Everson looked to the cathartic moment in which horizontal, linear time
was transformed into vertical, salvational time. For both poets, the natural world provided a model for the organic cohesion and durability that

human society lacked. For Robert Duncan, the unity of flesh and spirit was possible only within the play of meanings that poetic language inaugurates.

The search for vital contact was not simply a matter of developing a private theology or aesthetic position; it involved discovering forms of community that would link the disparate parts of an emerging bohemia. It would also provide a viable political nexus for an increasingly disaffiliated Left. The three poets discussed here shared an ideological commitment to anarchopacifism that found its communal basis in Rexroth's Libertarian Circle, the Waldport conscientious-objector camp, and Duncan's and Spicer's Berkeley round tables. Within the latter group something more than conversation and exposure to new art was possible: the development of a collective voice for homosexual writers living in a homophobic society. Not all members of the Duncan–Spicer circle were gay, but an important component of their self-conscious aestheticism was a defense against a hostile outside for which the creation of an insular fraternity was necessary. Duncan's gilded rhetoric must be read within the frame of that social milieu.

In a later poem, remembering the "Berkeley Renaissance," Duncan, in the voice of Dante, addresses Robin Blaser:

> Robin it would be a great thing if you, me, and Jack Spicer
> Were taken up in a sorcery with our mortal heads so turnd
> The life dimmd in the light of that fairy ship
> *The Golden Vanity* or *The Revolving Lure*[42]

Duncan goes on to say that as worshipers of the cult of Eros, the three would "be glad / To be abroad from what he was." These lines describe very well the spirit of the earlier period in which young poets, on the verge of a poetics, sought a "sorcery" in poetry that might transport each far "from what he was" only that he might discover "who" he was. They sought such a magic in an evocative, brooding rhetoric and a thematics of loss and division. Within a short time, however, elegy became vision, and the bohemia so fervently desired by all Bay Area poets during the 1940s became a reality.

2

"The Darkness Surrounds Us"

Participation and Reflection among the Beat Writers

BEFORE BEATITUDE

To most readers the "San Francisco Renaissance" and the "Beat movement" are synonymous. To be sure, the Beats provided the most public demonstration that some sort of literary ferment was occurring in the Bay Area. San Francisco was the city in which Lawrence Ferlinghetti first published many of the Beat generation writers through his City Lights editions and sold their books through his bookstore of the same name; it was the city in which Allen Ginsberg's "Howl" was written and where the book's subsequent censorship trial took place; it was the focal point for many of Jack Kerouac's novels; it was the site of bars and coffeehouses like The Cellar, The Place, and The Coexistence Bagel Shop, where poetry was read to jazz; and, finally, it was the city in which many members of the Beat generation lived for periods of time during the 1950s. Allen Ginsberg, Jack Kerouac, Lawrence Ferlinghetti, Michael McClure, Gary Snyder, Philip Whalen, Philip Lamantia, and others found themselves in San Francisco at some point during the crucial period of the 1950s.

Despite the obvious centrality of the Beat movement to the San Francisco literary scene, it was, as my other chapters will indicate, only one strand in a much more diverse and eclectic movement. Although poets like Jack Spicer, Robert Duncan, and Kenneth Rexroth at various times supported the Beats against the attacks of journalists and official censors, they often – and in print – expressed animosity toward the more excessive gestures of Ginsberg and company. And the Beat scene was by no means restricted to San Francisco. It had its inception in New York during the late 1940s when Allen Ginsberg, William Burroughs, Jack Kerouac, and others met in the cafeterias and bars around Columbia University. Most of the poets associated with the Beat generation in San

Francisco came from elsewhere, and few stayed for any extended length of time. It might be more accurate to say that San Francisco, with its long tradition of literary bohemia, provided a hospitable theater for the Beats at a point when the political and literary conservatism of postwar America was at an all-time high.

Like many literary movements, the Beat generation was largely the projection of the media, albeit aided by its participants. At the height of the period, the *San Francisco Chronicle* dressed one of its columnists in beard, beret, jeans, and workshirt and sent him undercover into the pads and jazz clubs of San Francisco's North Beach to report on the strange habits and sexual mores of these social misfits. And it was the *Chronicle's* feature columnist, Herb Caen, who added the suffix "nik" to the term "Beat," making a connection with the recently launched Russian satellite, *Sputnik*. The Beat*nik*, then, could be associated in the public mind not only with antisocial behavior but with things subversive and anti-American. For a while it was essential for comedians to have an arsenal of Beatnik jokes, and many of the television sitcoms of the day had a resident bearded bohemian. Adopting the period's red-baiting rhetoric, *Life* magazine announced that the Beat generation was under the direct influence of a few neurotic poets:

> This is not to say that the bums, hostile little females and part-time bohemians of the Beat Generation would not have been bums, hostile little females and part-time bohemians anyhow. But without the slightest missionary intent the poets have provided them with a name, the fuel of self-justification and attitudes guaranteed to "bug the squares."[1]

Beatniks, the article goes on to say, are "talkers, loafers, passive little con men, lonely eccentrics, mom-haters, cophaters, exhibitionists with abused smiles and second mortgages on a bongo drum – writers who cannot write, painters who cannot paint, dancers with unfortunate malfunction of the fetlocks."[2] Such vituperative language, in the context of a major journalistic exposé, did little to diminish the public ardor for a new fad and no doubt did much to bring about the very enthusiasm it lamented.

If the major tabloids' critical reception of the Beat generation was less than friendly, it was at least predictable. A more disturbing criticism came from writers of the Left, who might be thought to have shared some of the Beats' antiestablishment sentiments. These critics, writing in magazines like the *Partisan Review* and the *Nation,* saw in the Beat movement an apolitical and naive attempt to substitute for social commitment and activism a policy of retreat and egocentric self-absorption. Norman Podhoretz was representative of those critics who made invidious comparisons between the new bohemians and the "authentic bohemians" of the 1920s and 1930s. "The Bohemianism of the 1920's," according to Podhoretz,

> represented a repudiation of the provinciality, philistinism, and moral hypocrisy of American life – a life, incidentally, which was still essentially small-town and rural in tone. Bohemia, in other words, was a movement created in the name of civilization: its ideals were intelligence, cultivation, spiritual refinement.[3]

The bohemia of the 1950s, in contrast, "is quite another kettle of fish altogether."

> It is hostile to civilization; it worships primitivism, instinct, energy, "blood." To the extent that it has intellectual interests at all, they run to mystical doctrines, irrationalist philosophies, and left-wing Reichianism. The only art the new Bohemians have any use for is jazz, mainly of the cool variety. Their predilection for bop language is a way of demonstrating solidarity with the primitive vitality and spontaneity they find in jazz and of expressing contempt for coherent, rational discourse which, being a product of the mind, is in their view a form of death. To be articulate is to admit that you have no feelings (for how can real feelings be expressed in syntactical language?), that you can't respond to anything . . . and that you are probably impotent.[4]

It is not that Podhoretz was necessarily wrong about specific attributes but that he was invoking these qualities negatively against such official abstractions as civilization, coherent discourse, and feelings. And one wonders how the bohemians of the 1920s would have responded to Podhoretz's sunny picture of their "intelligence, cultivation, [and] spiritual refinement." The implication is that if one is going to reject the status quo, there is a series of self-evident standards by which one may do so.

To some extent this media coverage of the Beats, whether from the Luce organization or the *Partisan Review,* reflected a need, in the midst of the Eisenhower doldrums, to have a scapegoat for the anxieties facing mass society. The McCarthy committee had already provided a steady stream of such misfits, and the Beats became a more theatrical extension. And rather than repudiate their role as outsiders, they accepted it – even reveled in it – finding in the word "Beat" an immanent "beatitude" that would transform what critics saw as nihilism into a religious ideal. In doing so, they became projections of the very society they rejected – a fact that ultimately made life difficult (witness Jack Kerouac's sad later years) and that continues to make it almost impossible to untangle their writing from the fictions their writing created.

One of the most pervasive fictions surrounding the Beat writers is their cult of energy, a tendency to exalt the present over the past, action over reflection, movement over stasis. "Whooee," yells Dean Moriarity in *On the Road*.

> "Here we go!" And he hunched over the wheel and gunned her; he was back in his element, everybody could see that. We were all delighted, we all realized we were leaving confusion and nonsense behind and performing our one and noble function of the time, *move*.[5]

In Beat argot, to "move," to be "hip," to "groove" are ways of participating with – not reflecting upon – the "natural" rhythms of life. Movement is not a means to an end but an end in itself. This cult of energy is buttressed by an Emersonian belief in the identity between natural forces and the mind, a relationship that may be activated by writing at great speed, without constraints and without revision. The correspondence between text and world is sustained by what Levy-Bruhl calls a "participation mystique," in which the linguistic sign partakes directly of the natural sign in a relation of synecdoche. The word does not represent but incarnates powers latent in the world.[6]

Though many remarks by Allen Ginsberg, Jack Kerouac, and Michael McClure would seem to support this view, one finds in their works a corresponding anxiety or self-consciousness about the difficulties of attaining such participation. For every Emersonian affirmation of the holiness of all being, there is a Poe-like skepticism about its realization in contemporary American life. In its extreme form, this anxiety turns into the bitter cynicism of William Burroughs, whose novels chronicle the various addictions of a society bent on authoritarian control.

If one wanted to characterize the tension between a "participation mystique" and reflectiveness in Beat poetry, one might look at Robert Creeley's well-known lyric "I Know a Man." Although Creeley is not usually associated with the San Francisco Beats, he was close to all of them, and his poetry of the period embodies much of what could be called a Beat "ethos."

> As I sd to my
> friend, because I am
> always talking, – John, I
>
> sd, which was not his
> name, the darkness sur-
> rounds us, what
>
> can we do against
> it, or else shall we &
> why not, buy a goddamn big car,

drive, he sd, for
christ's sake, look
out where yr going.[7]

The speaker is caught between two conflicting positions: whether to
solve his existential despair by escaping from the world (by buying a
"goddamn big car") or by paying a greater attention to what is immediately in front of him. Despite the poem's title, he cannot truly *know*
anyone – either himself or another – because he is constantly talking and
thus avoiding recognition of the other. He does not really know the
other's name, nor is he able to differentiate himself from his interlocutor.
His despair is generalized ("the darkness sur- / rounds us"), and to drive
and thus escape such despair is an inadequate solution to a problem of
much greater proportions.

The poem's last tercet introduces a voice of reason that urges the
speaker to pay attention to what is happening: "for / christ's sake, look /
out where yr going." But the terse and enjambed lines, the highly subordinated quality of the syntax, and the confusion of speaker and interlocutor conspire against the ostensible solutions these lines proffer.
Adding to the general instability of the lines is the fact that the word
"drive" could equally be a continuation of the previous lines (Why not
buy a car and drive somewhere?), or it could be the beginning of an
imperative spoken by "he" ("drive . . . look out where you're going").[8]
Such ambiguities enact at a structural level the very conditions that pre-
vent the "I" from "knowing" anyone. The poem, then, demonstrates
one kind of attention – poetry's power to embody contradictory states of
feelings and emotion – while denying another.

Creeley states in compressed form some of the dilemmas that can be
found in the work of many Beat writers. The world is perceived as alien
and hostile, an undifferentiated "darkness" created and maintained by
forces beyond the individual's control. The hipster's endless talk becomes a tentative way of countering that darkness and of acknowledging, if inadequately, the need for dialogue. Another solution, one found
in many another American literary work, from *Huckleberry Finn* and
Moby Dick to *On the Road,* is to take the open road, "drive" away from
Aunt Polly or the Man in the Grey Flannel Suit toward some indefinite
freedom. Most accounts of the Beat myth stop here, at the edge of the
highway, where the vast spaces of the West offer the illusion of escape.
But Creeley's conclusion offers a salutary warning to pay attention in the
midst of distraction and abstraction. This moment of self-consciousness,
however tenuous, represents a side of the Beat myth seldom acknowledged: the recognition of solitude and vulnerability despite the compet-
ing claims of participation and communalism.

In terms of *On the Road* this quality of self-correction is embodied in the figure of Sal Paradise, who takes both a literal and a figurative "back seat" to the voluble, sociable Dean Moriarity. Or in the case of Ginsberg, it is the quality of loneliness and insecurity that pervades poems like "In a Supermarket in California" or "Kaddish." What Creeley offers in "I Know a Man" and what the Beats in general offer in their work is a demonstration, through a highly charged expressive vehicle, of extreme psychological and spiritual states, *including the limitations of those states*. If this corrective aspect of the Beats' writing has not been discussed, it is perhaps because their work has been valued for extraliterary qualities.

The imperative to "drive" away from (or more deeply into) the moment is reflected in the poetics of all the Beat writers. "First thought, best thought" is Ginsberg's condensed statement, and Kerouac's "Essentials of Spontaneous Prose" carries a similar message: "Never afterthink to 'improve' or defray impressions, as, the best writing is always the most painful personal wrung-out tossed from cradle warm protective mind – tap from yourself the song of yourself, BLOW! NOW! – YOUR WAY IS YOUR ONLY WAY."[9] Kerouac seems to have carried his theory one step further by mythologizing his own compositional practice, just as he mythologized his life. According to an article he wrote for *Playboy*, *On the Road* was composed in "three weeks in the beautiful month of May 1951 while living in the Chelsea district of lower West Side Manhatten on a 100-foot roll" while taking ferocious amounts of benzedrine.[10] But as recent studies have shown, Kerouac's method was considerably more crafted than he admitted.[11] What we call *On the Road*, according to Tim Hunt, is actually the fourth version of his "road" book, the final and ultimate text being *Visions of Cody*. Portions of *On the Road* appear in some of his other novels, and discarded segments from the early manuscript can be found in later books. As Kerouac wrote his "road" book, beginning sometime in 1947, he discovered new modes of composition that allowed him greater flexibility in his narrative and greater immediacy in rendering individual scenes. The manuscript of *On the Road* finally accepted by Malcolm Cowley was a considerably edited and reworked version of the famous teletype roll. None of this disqualifies Kerouac's remarks on spontaneity in prose; it simply points out certain discrepancies between theory and practice that are inevitable with a poetics dominated by such an expressive ideal.[12]

The same could be said for Ginsberg's "Howl," the first section of which was composed, we have been told, "madly in one afternoon, a huge sad comedy of wild phrasing, meaningless images for the beauty of abstract poetry of mind."[13] James Breslin has pointed out that "Howl" was actually composed over a number of years, beginning as early as 1951 in notebooks in which were recorded the first catalogues of those destroyed "best minds" of his generation. In the Ginsberg archives at Columbia University, there are forty pages of worksheets for part II of "Howl" alone, in which "at some point [Ginsberg] went back and underlined those phrases [relating to Moloch] that struck him as most effective."[14] We can trace the painstaking evolution of this manuscript by regarding a facsimile edition of *Howl* in which it is clear that Ginsberg made many drafts of each section and made liberal use of his editorial pencil.[15] And when Ginsberg has discussed "Howl" publicly, he has always insisted upon the poem's formal structure. "It's built like a brick shithouse," he said to Richard Eberhart,[16] and Ginsberg devotes the entire opening segment of his *Paris Review* interview to identifying the metrical structure of his poetic rhythms in "Howl."[17] The fact that Kerouac's and Ginsberg's manuscripts reveal the kind of formal care that would seem to contradict their stated aesthetic beliefs indicates the difficulty of realizing a participation ethos without some of what Kerouac calls "afterthink."

This disparity between participation and reflection animates much Beat writing. In Kerouac's prose, it can be seen in his tendency to validate the present while secretly yearning for a state of permanent boyhood. In Ginsberg, it takes the form of an Emersonian involvement in the world mediated by a quality of loneliness and insecurity; and in the work of Michael McClure, it exists as a need to reach some primal, mammalian state while using traditional rhetorical modes. I would like to look briefly at these three writers and their attempts to deal with this tension between participation and reflection, between an idealization of the present and a desire for distance and detachment. I see this tension as both a limitation and a generative element of Beat writing, as something that animated much American writing during the hundred years between the first edition of *Leaves of Grass* and the publication of "Howl."

THE "TOO-HUGE WORLD VAULTING US": JACK KEROUAC

> Now events of this moment are so MAD that of course I can't keep up but worse they're as though they were fond memories that from my peaceful hacienda or Proust-bed I was trying to recall in toto but couldn't because like the real world so vast, so delugingly vast. (Jack Kerouac, *Visions of Cody*)

Jack Kerouac's presence may seem somewhat out of place in a book dealing largely with poets, but his importance to fellow Beat writers is seminal and his poetry, particularly that in *Mexico City Blues,* is significant in its own right. It was Kerouac's prose that initially influenced Allen Ginsberg's practice in poems like "Howl" and "Kaddish."

And it was Kerouac's prose, rather than his poetry, that obviously captured the imagination of a larger readership. Other writers like Lew Welch, David Meltzer, Michael McClure, Ted Berrigan, and Clark Coolidge have commented on the importance of Kerouac's short-lined poetry – its go-for-broke goofiness and immediacy – but it is the novels in which the full richness of his visual and auditory imagination is displayed. And especially in a work like *Visions of Cody*, Kerouac challenges the generic designations of "novel" and "poem" by writing in a variety of voices and styles that make him much more than an ephebe of Wolfe or Twain and very much a part of the international avant garde.

Much journalistic copy has been devoted to Kerouac's invention of the term "Beat," a term that combines the hipster's qualities of existential malaise and world weariness with a "beatific" or angelic potentiality latent in that generation. Kerouac, however, associates the origins of the term with things very secular and very American. In his 1959 *Playboy* article, he first talks about Beat spirituality and identifies the generation's alliance with Christ, Lao Tzu, and Muhammad but then moves more directly into his own childhood sources in popular media.[18] The Beat generation "goes back" to radio mysteries like "The Shadow" and to the comedies of W. C. Fields, the Three Stooges, and the Marx Brothers. Kerouac's central refrain, "it goes back," suggests that to be Beat is also to return to childhood. At this point "Beat" ceases to describe a religious or psychological condition and becomes a private signature for lost youth. It is this essentially boyhood state with its large-scale projections of danger, magic, power, and innocence that characterizes much of Kerouac's own work – the atmosphere of Tom Sawyer's gang with its secret signs, its antisocial nature (Kerouac later applauds the rascally Ignatz in the Krazy Kat cartoons), and fictionalized adventure. To be Beat, then, is to be innocent, to reclaim a time when the only danger is the maniacal sound of the Shadow's laughter on the radio.

The attraction of Tom Sawyer's gang is that it affords possibilities of community in a world dominated by authoritarian elders. If Kerouac's novels are "about" any one thing, it is the companionship of males and the pleasures of male bonding. Where fathers are noticeably absent, such fraternity replaces one kind of authority with another, one based less on filial than on sibling interrelationships. This bonding is particularly important for Kerouac as he seeks to find surrogates for his own brother, Gerard, who died at an early age. And just as bonding helps to create a sense of family, it also sanctions certain types of sexual experiences, whether hetero- or homosexual, that, as Catherine Stimpson points out, "have the intensity of family life without the threat of incest or the taint of biological destiny."[19] However liberated, the Beats often replicated many of the cultural stereotypes of power (passive–aggressive, master–

slave) that their sexuality seemed to reject. As Stimpson points out, they were "heroic protagonists in cultural drama about homosexuality who exemplify how much harder it is to be free and to extend freedom than to be sexual, and homosexual."[20]

This freedom is exemplified in Kerouac's novels by friends like Neal Cassady and Gary Snyder or by marginalized social types like the black jazzman, the skid row hobo, and the Zen eccentric. He projects these heroes as foils for his own confused relation to adulthood while he remains an endistanced observer:

> But then they danced down the streets like dingledodies, and I shambled after as I've been doing all my life after people who interest me, because the only people for me are the mad ones who are mad to live, mad to talk, mad to be saved, desirous of everything at the same time, the ones who never yawn or say a commonplace thing, but burn, burn, burn like fabulous yellow roman candles exploding like spiders across the stars. (OR, 9)

Kerouac's characteristic position, shambling after the "mad ones," allows him both a narrative and an existential distance from his own story: He may act as first and third person, subject and observer of his own story, even while the ostensible focus is the wild, spontaneous life of others. For a novelist who set such stock in the uses of immediacy, his own narrative strategy is curiously Jamesian.

Although Kerouac is best known for individual novels, he essentially wrote one long novel all his life, a "vast book like Proust's, except that [his] remembrances are written on the run instead of in a sickbed."[21] The name of this work is "The Legend of Duluoz" and it concerns the attempt by Jack Duluoz, alias Kerouac, to find a realm of vitality and comfort in the midst of modern, alienated American life. Occasionally he finds it among the "falaheen" people – the bums, Beat bohemians, blacks, and Indians – who live at the fringes of American life. The plot consists of a series of variations on incidents drawn from Kerouac's life (and, in the "road" book, from the life of Neal Cassady). The characters are projections of Kerouac's friends and family who represent the values and aspirations – and limitations – against which Duluoz must measure himself. If the "Legend" has a single social ethos, it is a blend of working-class, Roman Catholic, redneck American values combined, in the later novels, with ideals of compassion derived from Kerouac's idiosyncratic version of Buddhism.

The dominant theme of each novel is time – time passing and time regained: "Dreams of a kid and this whole world is nothing but a big sleep made of reawakened material (soon to reawake)."[22] Kerouac's work comprises the "visions of the great remembrancer," and if a given

passage seems familiar to us, it is usually because we have seen it recorded in another form in another novel or in an earlier passage. It is
Kerouac's gift that he can use and reuse his incidents again and again,
each time seeing them from different perspectives. Since incidents from
the past illustrate rather than move the plot forward, they may be re-
played again and again in order to intensify what are essentially timeless
values. In this sense Kerouac's novels resemble those of his modernist
predecessors, for whom time is cyclic, for whom the present is suffused
with the past. A novel like *Desolation Angels,* for example, is an anthology of incidents taken from previous novels (hopping freights, living
in San Francisco's skid row, hitchhiking cross-country with Cassady,
etc.), which Duluoz remembers once again as he sits alone in his watch-
man's shack on the top of Desolation Peak. He recalls these incidents to
sustain himself, just as Kerouac, the novelist, invokes them to cement
events distant in time.

Compassion might well be the central theme of the Duluoz legend
since it is the quality that the narrator most often admires in others, but
an even more pervasive theme in the novels turns out to be loneliness.
Kerouac "feels" for everyone but is terrified of solitude, of being un-
loved, of becoming swallowed by the void. Loneliness haunts his novels;
his best moments occur when he evokes the solitude of bus stops, of
wind in the trees, of winos on the skids, of a jazz saxophonist wailing in
the night, of foghorns over the bay, of empty space itself:

> What is that feeling when you're driving away from people and they
> recede on the plain til you see their specks dispersing? – it's the too-
> huge world vaulting us, and it's good-by. But we lean forward to the
> next crazy venture beneath the skies. (OR, 130)

The only recourse against the "too-huge world" is to drive on to the
"next crazy venture," although coming to the end of the road often
involves returning to his East Coast home and his mother, where Jack
can regroup and rekindle his restlessness.

On the Road is paradigmatic of Kerouac's thematics of youth and solitude. The narrator, Sal Paradise, respects and admires Dean Moriarity's
sexual prowess, wild conversation, and muscular abandon, but he also
recognizes in him vestiges of his long-lost brother and his own childhood
"in those dye-dumps and swim holes and riversides of Paterson and the
Passaic" (OR, 10). Being with Dean represents a regression to a more
immediate life, one free of adult cares and anxieties. But when Sal is on
the road alone, he experiences his first pangs of aging, a moment of
introspection that is associated immediately with the geography of
America:

> I woke up as the sun was reddening; and that was the one distinct time in my life, the strangest moment of all, when I didn't know who I was – I was far away from home, haunted and tired with travel, in a cheap hotel room I'd never seen, hearing the hiss of steam outside, and the creak of the old wood of the hotel, and footsteps upstairs, and all the sad sounds, and I looked at the cracked high ceiling and really didn't know who I was for about fifteen strange seconds. I wasn't scared; I was just somebody else, some stranger, and my whole life was a haunted life, the life of a ghost. I was halfway across America, at the dividing line between the East of my youth and the West of my future. (OR, 16)

Later, Dean's wild conversation and driving will distract Sal from such introspection. Dean invariably appears at a moment when Sal's life has become static, when he has been too long living at home or when a relationship threatens to tie him down. At this moment, Dean shows up and offers "the road" as a panacea.

But the road by itself is not enough. It provides adventure and change, but it also represents an escape from conditions that Sal is not willing to face. Before one trip with Dean, Sal tries to convince himself that he is going along only for the ride. His friends interrogate him about the reasons for his trip. Carlo Marx (Ginsberg) demands, "Now I'm not trying to take yo hincty sweets from you, but it seems to me the time has come to decide what you are and what you're going to do" (OR, 107). And when the gang arrives at Old Bull Lee's (Burroughs) in New Orleans, Lee asks, "Sal, what are you going to the Coast for?" Sal's answer is oblique: "Only for a few days. I'm coming back to school." Even the ordinarily voluble Dean lacks a sufficient answer:

> Then a complete silence fell over everybody; where once Dean would have talked his way out, he now fell silent himself, but standing in front of everybody, ragged and broken and idiotic, right under the light-bulbs, his bony made face covered though tremendous revelations were pouring into him all the time now. . . . He was BEAT – the root, the soul of Beatific. What was he knowing? He tried all in his power to tell me what he was knowing, and they envied that about me, my position at his side, defending him and drinking him as they once tried to do. Then they looked at me. What was I, a stranger, doing on the West Coast this fair night? I recoiled from the thought.
> "We're going to Italy," I said, I washed my hands of the whole matter. (OR, 161)

Sal has relied too much on the road as a value in itself and on Dean's energy as a sustaining power. In this passage Sal tries to force a kind of spiritual presence on his "beat" friend, implying that Dean's silence betrays a kind of cryptic truth. But Sal's slightly hysterical answer – "We're going to Italy" – indicates how inadequate that projection is. The story of *On the Road* is not, as the book blurb describes, "an explosion of consciousness – a mind-expanding trip into emotion and sensation, drugs and liquor and sex," but a qualification of the limits of detachment. Kenneth Rexroth characterized the art of the Beat generation as "disengagement,"[23] but Kerouac's novels often point to the psychic toll that such disengagement takes.

In his essay on Walt Whitman, D. H. Lawrence comes to a similar conclusion about the American writer's tendency to become absorbed in the world.[24] He complains that the end of Whitman's desire to penetrate all things, his amorous "ache," is death. The price of absorption is fragmentation and dissolution, and something of the same realization occurs in all of Kerouac's novels. In *On the Road* this realization is thematized in the dream of the "Shrouded Traveler," in which Sal Paradise encounters the mortality at stake in his desire to penetrate the world:

> Something, someone, some spirit was pursuing all of us across the desert of life and was bound to catch us before we reached heaven. Naturally, now that I look back on it, this is only death: death will overtake us before heaven. The one thing that we yearn for in our living days, that makes us sigh and groan and undergo sweet nauseas of all kinds, is the remembrance of some lost bliss that was probably experienced in the womb and can only be reproduced (though we hate to admit it) in death. (OR, 103)

The dream of the road, the lure of escape and motion is reseen as a metaphor of mortality. And instead of the romantic traveler in Dean, Sal suddenly sees in himself, like Blake's Mental Traveller, a figure hopelessly locked within the cyclic nature of life.

As Kerouac described in a letter, *On the Road* was a "horizontal account of travels on the road," presumably because it followed a more traditional, diachronic narrative. He thought of his next novel, *Visions of Cody,* as a "vertical, metaphysical study of Cody's [Cassady's] character in its relation to the general America."[25] In order to achieve this "vertical" form, he developed a technique that he called "sketching," whereby he would render an incident on the spot, writing quickly while gaining as much particularity as possible. As he wrote to John Clellon Holmes:

> What I'm beginning to discover now is something beyond the novel and beyond the arbitrary confines of the story . . . into realms of revealed Picture . . . *wild form,* man, wild form. Wild form's the only form holds what I have to say – my mind is exploding to say something about every image and every memory. . . . I have an irrational lust to set down everything I know . . . at this time I'm making myself sick to find the wild form that can grow with my wild heart.[26]

In practice, sketching allowed Kerouac the freedom to describe Cody from a number of vantages without providing the usual rhetorical connectives. He could finally dissolve the distance between Jack and Cody, narrator and subject, into one multiple consciousness.

Kerouac's new "wild" narrative moves paratactically from one observation to another with a breathless, improvisatory quality. Unlike surrealist automism, sketching keeps the focus steadily on the scene − its shifting patterns of light, its ambient noise, its distractions:

> An immense plate glass window in this white cafeteria on a cold November evening in New York faces the street (Sixth Avenue) but with inside neon tubular lights reflected in the window and they in turn illuminating the Japanese garden walls which are therefore also reflected and hang in the street with the tubular neons (and with other things illuminated and reflected such as that enormous twenty-foot green door with its red and white exit sign reflected near the drapes to the left, a mirror pillar from deep inside, vaguely the white plumbing and at the top of things upper right hand and the signs that are low in the window looking out, that say *Vegetarian Plate 60 cents, Fish Cakes with Spaghetti, Bread and Butter* (no price) and are also reflected and hanging but only low on the sidewalk because also they're practically against it) − so that a great scene of New York at night with cars and cabs and people rushing by and *Amusement Center, Bookstore, Leo's Clothing, Printing,* and *Ward's Hamburger* and all of it November clear and dark is riddled by these diaphanous hanging neons, Japanese walls, door, exit signs. (VC, 16)

In this passage Kerouac describes the way that various surfaces in a brightly lit cafeteria − a plate glass window, neon lights, walls, a mirror pillar, signs − reflect each other so that inside and outside are constantly confused. The "enormous twenty-foot green door" across the street from the cafeteria suddenly appears to be inside among the "Japanese garden" wallpaper and neon lights. Menus hanging in the window itself seem to project outside among the "cars and cabs and people rushing by." Everything hangs tentatively in the air like a giant urban mobile while Kerouac adds to its "diaphanous" quality by intruding into his description with parenthetical remarks and qualifications. Duluoz is juxtaposed to this plethora of details as both observer and as object of observation. To some extent the constant shifting of perspective from near to far, inside to outside, mirrors the larger problem of subjectivity in the novel itself as Duluoz seeks to gain a perspective on his main character while understanding his complicity in Cody's life. Although this is but one sketch among many in the novel's opening two sections, it functions to create the character of Duluoz by studying *how* as well as *what* he sees.

At a larger structural level *Visions of Cody* makes use of this distortion of perspectives in five separate sections, each of which captures Cody from a different angle and by means of a different narrative strategy. The first section consists of sketches like the one above, which relate, as Gerald Nicosia observes, "the narrator's psychological preparation to meet the hero."[27] In the second, Cody himself is introduced through a straightforward description of his youth in Denver. The third section changes the narrative once again by presenting transcripts of tapes made by Kerouac and Cassady in the early 1950s. These tapes were originally made to provide material for a novel that Cassady intended to write, but Kerouac appropriates them as another level in his own narrative. The fourth section, "Imitation of the Tape," parodies many of the narrative techniques already developed and imitates (or mocks) a wide range of modern literary styles. The final section, subtitled "Joan Rawshanks in the Fog," takes many of the incidents encountered in *On the Road* but reframes them from the standpoint of an older and more self-critical Sal Paradise. By using the frame of the movie ("Joan Rawshanks in the Fog" parodies the Joan Crawford movie *Sudden Fear*), Jack Duluoz may suggest his own role in directing Cody's life as a fiction. All of these narrative techniques help to frame Cody not as a fictional character but as the site of Duluoz's own speculations on himself and on "the general America."

Whereas in *On the Road* Cody's actions are valued in themselves as signs of primitive vitality, in *Visions of Cody* they are part of a phenomenological matrix that depends on Duluoz's role as interpreter. At one point he says, "So I not only took care of Cody's understanding but protected him from horrors which he, unlike me, was not capable of absorbing" (VC, 36). A remark such as this indicates that Duluoz's role in this novel will not be one of patient scribe but one of active agent in his friend's life. This position is very different from that of Sal Paradise, who trusts Dean's intuitions and perceptions without understanding his own complicity in fictionalizing them. Duluoz, unlike Sal, celebrates Cody's Faustian excesses but also qualifies them with parenthetical remarks – reminders that it is he, Duluoz, who is capable of providing a frame.

At times the sheer density and speed of sensations threaten to overwhelm him. He often complains that he cannot keep pace with the welter of events and wishes for a "peaceful hacienda or Proust-bed" from which to "recall in toto" (VC, 99–100). But such a position is too passive and hermetic for Duluoz, who becomes increasingly anxious when he has such a vantage. At one point Duluoz says, "I wish God had made me vaster myself – I wish I had ten personalities" in order to take it all in, but then he qualifies that he "must struggle to live it all, and *on foot* and in these little crepesole shoes."[28] This is a version of Creeley's warning that, however ambiguous or threatening the territory, one lives within certain economies; one still must pay attention to the road. Kerouac desires the scope of Whitman's "I" (or Proust's memory) while retaining the perspective of a single, historical individual.

The tension between participation and critical distance is most thoroughly apparent in section 3, in which the tape transcripts offer what appears to be the unmediated interaction between narrator and subject. Ostensibly, it is a chance to hear Cody's fast-paced, energetic speech, but it becomes a demonstration of the ways Duluoz appropriates that speech in order to "create" his friend. Part of this appropriation is performed by editorial remarks that Duluoz provides in order to establish the context of the conversation:

> JACK. How can I be eating on Benzedrine? (*eating at table*)
> CODY. (*laughs*) That tea'll overcome anything. (*pause*) . . . Why don't you let me read John's letter? (*playing whiny little boy*) (VC, 155)

Although we hear Jack's voice as the interlocutor, we also see him as editor, qualifying and shaping the conversation in its particular mood and tone by means of parenthetical stage directions. I see these editorial remarks not as refinements of Cody's speech but as introjections to indicate the narrator's role as transcriber.

As one can readily tell, much of the conversation and editorializing concern the drugs that are being consumed while the sessions are in process:

> JACK. See, did you dig this here? I didn't notice that till I played it back
> CODY. (*after long silence*) . . . (*laughing*) . . . It's like last night – ah damn thing
> JACK. Hmm boy that was good. That was a good one wasn't it? (VC, 132)

The "good one," of course, is a hit of pot, which the two consume in large quantities. Such references to pot – the rituals of lighting up, passing the joint, blowing out smoke – provide yet another frame to the entire section as Cody attempts to remember events from his past. And this attempt to "get it down" as accurately as possible is frustrated by distractions that are both chemically and rhetorically induced. The constant interchange between drug talk and Cody's memories creates a counterpoint of present and past, observation and reflection that make section 3 the most charged part of the novel.

As I said, the ostensible purpose of the transcripts is to provide an accurate record of Cody's speech, but the result, curiously enough, is a metadiscourse on the problem of representation. Jack poses as the faithful recorder, but it quickly becomes obvious that he is as interested in the difficulty of recording as he is in Cody's actual stories. Much of the conversation, in fact, concerns Cody's comments on previous transcripts. Rather than tell a story, Cody must also critique his own telling of it as it appears in Duluoz's typed version. At one point Cody describes his first visit to Old Bull Lee in Texas, a conversation that describes Lee's accidental shooting of his wife June:

> Here's this Bull, he's so high, he's just sittin there with his bad order high, see he can't see a hundred yards, y'know, that sonofabitch, no wonder he hit June and killed her, imagine, no shit, he can't see with them glasses. (VC, 122–3)

But Cody, whether or not because of the pot, quickly becomes involved with his difficulties in remembering the event clearly:

> Phew! naw, but man, what I'd tell you is, I didn't know that I'd appreciate remembering these things more, so therefore when I was there I didn't pay much attention to any of this, I was hung up on something else, you know so I can't remember, say, like for example, I can remember NOW for example, but now that I CAN remember it doesn't do any good, because . . . man . . . I can't get it down. You know . . . I just remember it, I can remember it well, what happened 'cause I'M not doing nothin, see?
> JACK. You don't have to get it down
> CODY. (*demurely downward look*) But I can't remember what happened there, man, except I remember certain things. . . . But I'm sayin like Huck [Herbert Hunke], me and Irwin [Ginsberg] goin out in the middle of the Louisiana bayou on a particular New York kick (VC, 123)[29]

This incident is discussed at the next session, at which point Cody begins to qualify phrases from the previous transcript like "bad order high" and "can't get it down." He is especially concerned with Duluoz's parenthetical description of him as looking "demurely downward":

> And, so – that's what I say when I say "I can't get it down," and then . . . "two minutes" – but you picked up on that, of all the different things I was sayin, and so you said, "But you don't *have* to get it down," you know, that's what you said . . . and so the demure downward look . . . was simply in the same tone and the same fashion . . . as my reaction and feeling was when I said the words "but you can't get it down" you know.(VC, 133)

Much of the third section consists of this kind of wandering interrogation of individual phrases. If Cody has trouble "getting it down," Duluoz is always present to help him remember, to goad him on, to fill in the gaps. And Cody recognizes the crucial role of his friend in articulating his thought:

> . . . because see that's what happened, see, and I'm describin now, see, nowhere I'm going through the process of telling *you,* and you're the

one who *wrote* it down, see, so I'm saying, you know, you know more
about it than *I* do –
JACK. I didn't punctuate it
CODY. No, you know more about it than I do . . . no – well, it *was*
unpunctuated talk anyhow (VC, 146)

Cody acknowledges that his "describin" depends on its textualization by
his friend. Jack's modest disclaimer, "I didn't punctuate it," claims a
kind of authorial neutrality – that he does not tinker with or modify the
recorded speech – but Cody understands what Jack's modesty conceals:
that to "know" more about an incident is to give it narrative shape.
Cody may be the hero of the novel, but he lacks this essential ability to
translate his life into a story, a failure that Duluoz quietly records while
placing his friend on a pedestal.

Kerouac described this novel as "visions of the great rememberer,"
and while certainly this applies to Cody, it also applies to Duluoz. The
novel presents visions (sketches) of Cody, but their accuracy depends on
the narrator's ability to see through his subject's eyes. Hence the novel's
title, *Visions of Cody*, contains the very problem with which its author
had to contend: how to fuse subjective and objective poles in a single
narrative. Kerouac seems to have realized that he could no longer represent his main character from a detached position but had to intrude
himself as mediator of that life. *On the Road* remained, as he said, horizontal and linear, lacking the crucial "wildness" that would transform a
historical chronicle of Cassady into what Allen Ginsberg, in his introduction to the novel, called "the sacramentalization of everyday reality"
(VC, viii).

Kerouac himself underwent the same fictionalization process to which
he subjected Cassady. He became the official representative of a certain
lifestyle that he was able to describe but was ultimately unable to live.
His depressed, alcoholic decline (perhaps like Cassady's anonymous
death near the Mexican border) testifies to the toll that society exacts
from the writer who reaches a wide audience. It also testifies to the
human toll exacted by the writer caught between a desire to be "on" the
road and to retain his ability to drive the car.

"INCARNATE GAPS": ALLEN GINSBERG

Kerouac, most of all, was the biggest influence I think – Kerouac's
prose. (Allen Ginsberg)

Allen Ginsberg was not so sanguine about *Visions of Cody* as one
might have anticipated. He complained to Kerouac that it "sounds like
you were just blowing and tacking things together, personally unrelating
them, just for madness sake."[30] He was also concerned about the book's

publishability: "I don't see how [*Visions of Cody*] will ever be published, it's so personal, it's so full of sex language, so full of our local mythological references."[31] Given Ginsberg's own commitment to personal confession, such qualms about Kerouac's explicit description of sex comes as a surprise. The letter in which these remarks were made was written in 1952 at a point when Ginsberg was trying to assimilate both the lessons of his current master, William Carlos Williams, and the more academic influence of Mark Van Doren or Lionel Trilling, with whom he studied at Columbia. It is a letter that expresses a side of the young poet that varies strikingly with the portrait of him that has been painted by the media. It shows a Ginsberg concerned with literary proprieties which, despite his own comments to the contrary, never left him. Kerouac's example was a challenge – perhaps even a threat – that pushed Ginsberg into his own highly autobiographical mode.

Crucial to this change from the early Williams-derived poems in *Gates of Wrath* and *Empty Mirror* to the more recognizable long lines of "Howl" and "Kaddish" was the example of Kerouac's sketching. Although Ginsberg had already seen a draft of *Visions of Cody* (at that point still called *On the Road*), he learned of its new compositional mode in a letter that Kerouac mailed from Mexico in May 1952.[32] In this letter Kerouac advocates a kind of verbal "sketching" in which the writer imitates the painter's rendering. Kerouac's ideas of honesty, spontaneity, and immediacy quickly became a model for Ginsberg, who likened Kerouac's method to the improvisatory style of jazz musicians.[33] This "spontaneous bop prosody" allowed Ginsberg to turn aside from his shorter-lined poems and "follow [his] romantic inspiration – Hebraic – Melvillian bardic breath."[34] And it was very much the matter of "breath" that attracted Ginsberg. In a letter to his father, Ginsberg described Kerouac's contribution as one of reinstating the speech base to prose:

> It has the same syntactical structure of fast excited spoken talking – this is an interesting event in prose development, and it's no less communicative to me than heard speech, mine, yours, his, – when you speak *you* also talk a little like that, especially when you're moved, excited, angry, or dizzy with happiness etc. etc. – heightened speech in other words.[35]

In more recent years, Ginsberg has elaborated his poetics of breath and speech to include Charles Olson's ideas of the breath line in "Projective Verse," mantric breathing, and chanting. What is central to all of his statements is a need to return language to the body, to the physiology and musculature of the writer. Poetry thus approaches the condition of mantra, which "refocuses mental and physiological activity right back into the present in a world of frankly physical sound, pure sound, body sound, a continuous humming body sound that wakes up the body to some extent."[36] The poem should not be a demonstration or description of states of consciousness, but should itself manifest the energies of those states.

Another necessary component of this poetics of the body is some agency that will circumvent traditional rhetorical and syntactic structures by which ideas are subordinated one to the next. While a student of Meyer Shapiro's at Columbia University, Ginsberg found such an agency in the paintings of Cezanne. Ginsberg studied the way that the painter recovered the "petites sensations" of the phenomenal field.[37] According to Ginsberg's account, Cezanne painted a landscape or object by recording the moment-by-moment impressions of his own optical field. Rather than synthesize a single Mt. St. Victoire in virtual, three-dimensional space, Cezanne painted the history of his individual perceptions of that mountain, registering each one separately so that the painting gained its own mass and volume equivalent to the landscape. With the aid of Cezanne's letters, Ginsberg saw a strong symbolist impulse in the painter's landscapes; the images Cezanne painted were not re-creations of actual mountains, card players, or apples but the outward surfaces of spiritual and eternal states. The reconstitution of "petites sensations" led to nothing less than a vision of *pater omnipotens aeterna deus,* a phrase that has become more familiar to us in the conclusion to part I of "Howl."[38] In these same lines, Ginsberg turns from his long catalogue of suffering individuals and invokes the verbal art, "the syntax and measure of poor human prose," by which his own poem is being written. It is an act of self-reflexiveness necessary if he is to move beyond the elegiac to some critical posture in relation to those "best minds." Ginsberg makes "incarnate gaps" in his text in which he – both as representative man and as poet – may stand before his readers, "speechless and intelligent and shaking with shame."

According to Ginsberg, Cezanne's ability to juxtapose two dissimilar images (or perspectives) creates a third image that partakes of the two but that is freed from the here and now. Such ideas are derived as well from Fenollosa's ideas of the ideogram and Pound's imagist tenets. In "Howl" this practice can be seen in the word clusters that make up Ginsberg's catalogues:

> who sank all night in submarine light of Bickford's floated and sat through the stale beer afternoon in desolate Fugazzi's, listening to the crack of doom on the hydrogen jukebox.
>
> (CP, 126)

A phrase like "hydrogen jukebox" makes use of the associations attached to the hydrogen bomb and combines them with something as ordinary as a jukebox to give the feel of anxiety and paranoia that pervades the lies of Ginsberg's generation. A phrase like "submarine light" helps create the vague, floating quality of mind that is felt while one sits all night in Bickford's cafeteria. Many of these word clusters resemble T. S. Eliot's slightly surreal metaphors ("sawdust afternoons," "a patient etherized upon a table") in his early poetry, an identification that, at least in 1955, would have made Allen Ginsberg wince.

If individual phrases resemble Eliot's, whole clusters of them, as used in Ginsberg's catalogues, create a rather different effect. Relations between parts of speech are dissolved, substantives are jammed together, adjectives and nouns become intermixed:

> Peyote solidities of halls, backyard green tree cemetery dawns, wine
> drunkenness over the rooftops, storefront boroughs of teahead
> joyride neon blinking traffic light, sun and moon and tree
> vibrations in the roaring winter dusks of Brooklyn, ashcan
> rantings and kind king light of mind,
>
> (CP, 126)

Majorie Perloff has pointed out that such clusters of substantives, however indebted they are to Whitman's catalogues, also resemble the dada styles of Apollinaire and Cendrars.[39] Their effect is to keep things in motion by linking powerful, percussive sounds ("kind king light of mind") with words from multiple semantic fields ("teahead joyride neon").

In a poem like "Sunflower Sutra," this use of noun clusters is particularly effective in rendering the specific incarnational moment that is the poem's subject. Ginsberg describes a walk with Jack Kerouac through a railroad yard when, all of a sudden, they come upon a sunflower covered with the grime of a thousand passing locomotives. This sad flower stirs memories of Ginsberg's Blake visions of the 1940s:

> – I rushed up enchanted – it was my first sunflower, memories of
> Blake – my visions – Harlem

> and Hells of the Eastern rivers, bridges clanking Joes Greasy
> Sandwiches, dead baby carriages, black treadless tires forgotten
> and unretreaded, the poem of the riverbank, condoms & pots,
> steel knives, nothing stainless, only the dank muck and the
> razor sharp artifacts passing into the past –
>
> (CP, 138)

Here the detritus of the contemporary wasteland combines with the detritus of memory; there is little difference between the Harlem of the 1940s and the railroad yard of the present, though the sunflower has provided the first step in what is to become a visionary awakening. Ginsberg then addresses the sunflower, urging it to forget its grime and poverty and see itself as a living, growing thing. And because it has taken Ginsberg back in time, it provides him with an opportunity to regard his own "sunflower existence" beyond the quotidian moment. In the poem's last (and longest) line, Ginsberg uses his substantive clusters to create the visionary moment:

> We're not our skin of grime, we're not our dread bleak dusty
> imageless locomotive, we're all beautiful golden sunflowers
> inside, we're blessed by our own seed & golden hairy naked
> accomplishment-bodies growing into mad black formal
> sunflowers in the sunset, spied on by our eyes under the
> shadow of the mad locomotive riverbank sunset Frisco hilly
> tincan evening sitdown vision.
>
> (CP, 139)

This vision recorded in the poem is not of an airy world beyond this one; it is made out of things – locomotives, riverbanks, sunsets, San Francisco, hills – that in themselves have a spiritual potential. Only through their "incarnation" in Ginsberg's vision can they lose their isolation and become part of a single experience. Ginsberg links them, without the usual syntactic connectives, to both enact and invoke their common universe.

To recover the body in poetry through a return to speech rhythms, through the disordering of conventional syntax, through a lineation based on the breath, we now recognize as pervasive features of postwar poetry. Charles Olson's inaugural formulation of these qualities in "Projective Verse" in 1950 was only the first of many statements advocating a poetics of "embodiment." But if his gesture seemed unique in 1950 or 1955 it was only so against the backdrop of the then-reigning New Critical orthodoxy that valued detachment and ironic distance. We see from a later vantage that it was less a new direction than a recuperation of certain aspects of romanticism that could be found in Blake, Wordsworth, Shelley, and Whitman. Ginsberg, like Olson, Duncan, Creeley, and others, was aware of this heritage and invoked such predecessors often and loudly.

However anxious Ginsberg may have been to develop a purely physical poetry, he was no less anxious to ascribe intention to his procedures. The burden of his essays on poetry and poetics, his interviews, and his correspondence is to clarify his knowledge of formal prosody and poetic structure. In doing so he reveals some ambivalence about the source of his inspiration: Although poetry presumably emerges from the poet's physiology, it often appears in the trappings of Greek classical meters.

The distinction he makes is between a poetry written from a pre-established pattern and one discovered in the process of writing that may, after the fact, have a recognizable form: "Nobody's got any objection to even iambic pentameter if it comes from a source deeper than the mind; That is to say if it comes from the breathing and the belly and the lungs."[40] By appealing to concepts like depth and surface, mind and body, Ginsberg reinstates their opposition while appearing to dissolve their boundaries. Iambic pentameter is permissible so long as its source lies in the internal organs and not in the regular count of a metronome.

The return of, and to, the body in poetry arises out of a more profound desire to rejoin the larger body of the world:

> yes, yes,
>   that's what
> I wanted,
>   I always wanted,
> I always wanted,
>   to return
> to the body
>   where I was born.
>   (CP, 112)

This participation carries with it the attendant dangers of solipsism and self-consciousness that proved so troubling to Wordsworth and Shelley. Ginsberg most often identifies this crisis of participation with Whitman:

> I saw you, Walt Whitman, childless, lonely old grubber, poking
>   among the meats in the refrigerator and eyeing the grocery
>   boys.
> I heard you asking questions of each: Who killed the pork chops?
>   What price bananas? Are you my Angel?
>   (CP, 136)

This vision of a latter-day Whitman rummaging among the cornucopia of foods available in a modern supermarket is wonderfully funny and tragic at the same time. Whitman becomes an alter ego for Ginsberg, who himself is "self-conscious" and "shopping for images." Ginsberg's invocation of Whitman (and perhaps of Garcia Lorca) "eyeing the grocery boys" emphasizes that this loneliness is also the historical lot of the homosexual who is denied the opportunity to participate in the bounty of "normal" American life. The sight of Whitman in a modern-day supermarket reminds Ginsberg of the "lost America of love" in which Whitman could fervently believe:

> Ah, dear father, graybeard, lonely old courage-teacher, what
>   America did you have when Charon quit poling his ferry and

> you got out on a smoking bank and stood watching the boat
> disappear on the black waters of Lethe
>
> (CP, 136)

Whitman is placed in Hell, curiously enough, not by his disbelief but
because of his extreme faith. But if Whitman lives among the shades, his
realm may still be glimpsed by the poet who inherits his mantle.

The price of participation is loneliness, and Ginsberg has been anxious
to point out the importance of this theme to those who see in his poetry
only a wail of despair or else a celebration of oneness. In a letter to John
Hollander, who had written a review condemning *Howl* (a "dreadful
little volume"), Ginsberg attempted to set the record straight:

> . . . and some jerk named Brustein who TEACHES at columbia writ-
> ing . . . drooling on about how I express every degradation but the one
> human one loneliness – I mean some completely inaccurate irrelevant
> piece of journalism! ignoring big queer lonely lyrics about Whitman
> and Moloch in whom I sit lonely cocksucking.[41]

Ginsberg is referring to part II of "Howl" in which he catalogues the
collective force that has appropriated and neutralized the creative spirit of
his generation. If "Brustein" were correct, if "Howl" were simply an
enumeration of certain members of society who "purgatoried their tor-
sos night after night," it would not have the power that it has. But as
Ginsberg observes, Moloch gains its power not because it lives beyond
human will but because we willingly, if blindly, participate in its
authority.

At the beginning of part II, Ginsberg asks "what sphinx of cement and
aluminum bashed open their skulls and ate up their brains and imagination." He then answers his own question: "Solitude! Filth! Ugliness!
Ashcans and unobtainable dollars!" But at the point where this decalogue
threatens to remain a list of Moloch's attributes, Ginsberg turns the
poem on himself:

> Moloch in whom I sit lonely! Moloch in whom I dream Angels!
> Crazy in Moloch! Cocksucker in Moloch! Lacklove and
> manless in Moloch!
> Moloch who entered my soul early! Moloch in whom I am a
> consciousness without a body! Moloch who frightened me out
> of my natural ecstasy! Moloch whom I abandon! Wake up in
> Moloch! Light streaming out of the sky!
>
> (CP, 131)

The imperative is Blakean: to "wake up" within the "mind forged man-
acles" of an absolute devouring power and recognize one's complicity in
the very systems in which one is bound. Here Ginsberg is not the happy

bard, piping songs of visionary delight, but a more troubled poet who recognizes that the road to "natural ecstasy" is paved with self-deception. The consciousness, once separated from the body, creates specters that in turn become accusers. Only by first identifying with Moloch can the speaker truly "wake up" and alert others.

We can see the workings of Ginsberg's participation ethos best in a poem like "Wales Visitation," in which the poet, in order to testify to the unity of all things, must first separate himself from nature and address himself as another: "Bardic, O Self, Visitacione, tell naught / but what seen by one man in a vale in Albion" (CP, 480). The rhetoric is exalted and the diction archaic in order to give a tone of lofty seriousness and depth to what is, in actuality, an acid trip on a hillside in Wales. Ginsberg establishes kinship with his romantic precursors in order to collapse historical time into poetic eternity: "the lambs on the tree-nooked hillside this day bleating" are the same "heard in Blake's old ear." The clouds become "the silent thought of Wordsworth in eld Stillness" of Tintern Abbey. And Ginsberg even establishes kinship with himself, now "160 miles from London's symmetrical thorned tower," where recently he had appeared on television. He remembers the television screen "flashing bearded your Self" and addresses himself from the standpoint of a viewer. These gestures, while removing Ginsberg from historical time, also tend to distance him from any specific location so that he may literally "visit" where he is.

Aided by LSD, the poet observes a nature quivering with life:

> All the Valley quivered, one extended motion, wind
> undulating on mossy hills
> a giant wash that sank white fog delicately down red runnels
> on the mountainside
> whose leaf-branch tendrils moved asway
> in granitic undertow down –
> and lifted the floating Nebulous upward, and lifted the arms of the
> trees
> and lifted the grasses an instant in balance
> and lifted the lambs to hold still
> and lifted the green of the hill, in one solemn wave
>
> (CP, 480)

Ginsberg, like Wordsworth, hears in this wind a "correspondent breeze" pertaining to himself; he cannot simply remain "Crosslegged on a rock," observing nature; he must embrace the landscape physically; he must "Fall on the ground," "Stare close . . . ," "Kneel before the fox-glove . . . ," "look in the eyes of the branded lambs." Each of these admonitions suggests that although he experiences a great affinity for the

land and seeks to participate with it, he still remains an observer, addressing himself as another.

When he speaks for the first time in the first person, it is as if he is
answering the prophetic bard's injunctions:

> I lay down mixing my beard with the wet hair of the mountainside,
>   smelling the brown vagina-moist ground, harmless,
>   tasting the violet thistle-hair, sweetness –
> One being so balanced, so vast, that its softest breath
>   moves every floweret in the stillness on the valley floor,
>   trembles lamb-hair hung gossamer rain-beaded in the grass,
>   lifts trees on their roots, birds in the great draught
>   hiding their strength in the rain, bearing same weight
>
>   (CP, 481)

The problem with passages like these is that Ginsberg must assert affinities that he finds in nature instead of letting them grow naturally out
of the physical circumstance. He must name "One being so balanced, so
vast" at the point where he had successfully "created" an omnipotent
vantage. Another way of stating this limitation is to say that once
Ginsberg fully inhabits his "I," he loses sight of the problematics of
observation that dominates the first half of the poem.

The conclusion of "Wales Visitation" is a kind of coda, written from
the vantage of London a week later, a vantage that is now informed by
his new awareness:

> What did I notice? Particulars! The
> vision of the great One is myriad –
> smoke curls upward from ashtray,
>   house fire burned low,
> The night, still wet & moody black heaven
>   starless
> upward in motion with wet wind.
> *July 29, 1967 (LSD) – August 3, 1967 (London)*
>   (CP, 482)

The dating of the poem becomes an important dimension of the experience described: that he wrote the poem in two places, LSD and London,
the sacred (or at least psychedelic) and secular combined much as the
poem unites the particulars of the Welsh landscape with a reincarnated
Albion. The smoke curling "upward from ashtray" in London is now
invested with the same upward drafts of air that he had observed during
his psychedelic trip. And just as Wordsworth revisited Tintern Abbey
while living " 'mid the din / Of towns and cities" far from that enriching
landscape, so Ginsberg will be able to revisit Wales, not as place but as
visitation.

"Wales Visitation" is not Ginsberg's best poem, but it illustrates his awareness of the double self that mediates participation in the largeness of nature. One side of him "sees" with great accuracy while the other observes himself seeing. It is as though he has adopted the role of bardic poet in order to see at all, to become "one man in a vale in Albion." Ginsberg adds an interesting twist to the romantic pastoral ode that sets it off from its predecessors: his use of LSD. But the poem is not so much about the drug experience as it is about the "wisdom of earthly relations" glimpsed through a particularly heightened sensory moment. This moment is the product of specific images, recorded by a local "eye" willing to "Stare close." The moment is expanded when Ginsberg filters his observations through his visionary "I," which recognizes "no imperfection in the grass."

What links "Wales Visitation" to all of his other poems is its quality of testimony, its sense of witness and observation. Throughout his career, Ginsberg has asserted his participation in all aspects of American life, and in his best poems this assertion is combined with wry humor and self-deprecation. Whatever the tone, however, the poem is invariably about Allen Ginsberg being present at events that his presence ultimately affects. During the 1960s he became a sort of populist chronicler, providing, as he titled one book, "planet news" of contemporary history: the Chicago convention, the Human Be-In, various antiwar marches, May Day in Prague. Ginsberg was both the reporter and the antennae through which these events were received; his physical body (and, by extension, his physicalized long line) was the instrument on which history played, and his romantic rhetoric acted, in part, to dramatize the importance of the music. But Ginsberg has suffered the same difficulty as all romantic poets – that of participating so much in the world that he often lacks a vantage from which to speak. At its best, Ginsberg's work recognizes the vantage as well as the field before him.

"ABSTRACT ALCHEMIST OF FLESH": MICHAEL MCCLURE

Every man has his treasure. It's inside him. It's called meat. (Michael McClure)

One of the most remarkable films made by National Educational Television in its "Poetry USA" series features Michael McClure reading his *Ghost Tantras* in the lion house of the San Francisco Zoo. While the big cats pace back and forth in their cages, McClure is seen pacing himself, reading in a rich, resonant voice. *Ghost Tantras* is written partially in what the poet calls "beast language," a language somewhere between human speech and animal sounds. As McClure reads, the lions become increasingly animated and begin roaring – whether in response or annoyance – to the poet's own voice:

I LOVE TO THINK OF THE RED PURPLE ROSE
IN THE DARKNESS COOLED BY THE NIGHT
We are served by machines making satins
of sounds
Each blot of sound is a bud or a stahr.
Body eats bouquets of the ear's vista.
Gahhhrrr boody eers noze eyes deem thou.
NOH. NAH-OHH
hrooor. VOOOR-NAH-GAHROOOOO ME.
Nah droooooh seerch. NAH THEE!
The machines are too dull when we
are lion-poems that move & breathe.
WHAN WE GROOOOOOOOOOOOOOOR
hann dree myketoth sharoo sree thah noh deeeeeemed ez.
Whan eeeethooze hrohh.[42]

Obvious precedents for this kind of poetry – and its performance – could be found in futurist and dadaist sound poetry, although McClure maintains a closer bond to some source language than do poets like Vladimir Khlebnikov or Kurt Schwitters. If one could speak of the "diction" of beast language, one might point to its incorporation of Anglo-Saxon and Middle English words. When McClure reads *Ghost Tantras* in public performances, he often prefaces his reading by quoting the opening lines of Chaucer's *Canterbury Tales* to suggest the origins of his poetry in early English verse. Beast language oscillates back and forth between modern and archaic speech, between recognizable words and expressive utterances.

Besides the language, another distinctive thing about the poem above is its presentation on the page. Like most of McClure's poems, it obeys a center margin, its lines built around a central axis. McClure compares the physical shape of his poems to biological organisms. "[The poems] look like a little whirlwind or a gyre. They have the bilateral symmetry, of an organism. . . . I've come to intuitively think in terms of the centered line. We are centered organisms, in the sense that we're bilaterally symmetrical, so poems come out that way with ease and naturalness."[43] Not only does the poem imitate beast sounds (or hypothesize the beast sounds that humans might make) but it replicates on the page the skeletal structure of vertebrates. The center "spine" emphasizes, as well, the line as a physical entity on the page. Instead of returning to the left margin, the line asserts itself boldly as a free image, connected to the other lines like ribs to the spinal column. Instead of the line as a score for the voice, it becomes a separate object among other objects.

McClure's formulation of poetry as beast language and as bio-graphological grid represents the most radical example of a physiological or "embodied" poetics that we have seen so far. Where Kerouac and Ginsberg base their remarks on an appeal to speech rhythms and breath, McClure carries poetry further back to the cellular and genetic basis of human life. He wants a poetry that lives at the borders of articulate speech, a poetry that manifests in its structure the nature of all organisms. For McClure, humans are meat, and one's expression – in its ideal state – is an incarnation of one's mammal nature. We are part of a biological, not a logical or rational, universe and our intercommunication involves the sharing of our biological heritage: "The biological energy of ourselves is extensions or tentacles of the universe of meat."[44]

McClure's biological poetics is linked to the idea that every organism bears the imprint of its entire genetic history. Words are like DNA in the sense that they derive from the earliest human communication as well as from childhood babble. To speak is to gesture from a primordial position, one locked inside rationality. Since we have lost sight of this mammalian and genetic heritage, the only way to reclaim it is by testifying as directly as possible to our emotional states. And if this testimony takes the form of nonverbal expression, so much the better. To this end, McClure has always been interested in language at its most expressive – at moments when its semantic and performative characteristics merge. He devotes an entire essay, "Phi Upsilon Kappa," to the word "fuck" and to its liberating potential in poetry.[45] The characters in his plays often spend a good deal of their time giggling, shouting, groaning, and expostulating for the sheer pleasure of physical sound. "Part of a man is the words leaping from his lips. They are made by his real meat lips and throat and signalled by his real physical hands of spirit sending them on their way."[46]

McClure gained support for such ideas from poets like Blake, Shelley, and Artaud, but perhaps even more from the action painters whom he studied as an art student in the early 1950s. The big drip and splatter canvases of Pollock, de Kooning, and Kline gave McClure a sense of the importance of gesture and spontaneity in creation whereby the physical act of manipulating paint (or writing words on paper) was itself a psychologically cathartic act. His early poems often seem to be attempts to effect the same "gestural" style on the page that he admired in painters of the heroic period of abstract expressionism:

OH FUCKING LOVER ROAR WITH JOY – I, LION MAN!
I GROAN, I AM, UPON THE CONE SHAPED BREASTS
& tossing thighs!
. . . .
And I am some simple cub

with plump muscles, loving immortality!
THE SHEETS ARE WHITE.
THE PILLOW SOFT.
JESUS HOW I HATE THE MIDDLE COURSE![47]

The heavy use of upper-case letters, the prominence of exclamation marks, the presence of numerous expletives and imperatives provide signposts for feeling. If the reader has any doubts as to McClure's hatred of the "middle course," the bold typographic display will dispel them. At the same time, McClure eschews any rhetorical subtlety or irony by making direct assertions ("I GROAN, I AM . . . ," "And I am some simple cub / with plump muscles . . . ," "THE SHEETS ARE WHITE"). By wearing his heart on his sleeve, as it were, he attempts to recover a kind of Blakean drama of declaration.

Despite this appeal to the biological and gestural basis of poetry and language, McClure's own rhetoric is quite formal. The poems tend to proceed by declarative sentences and assertions with little subordination or modification. His lineation is most often end-stopped. The above "Ghost Tantra 51," for example, is based on five declarative sentences, spread out over fifteen lines. Only two lines are enjambed, and the meter is quite regular – iambic, with an occasional anapestic substitution. Given the mystery and strangeness surrounding the poem's subject, one would expect a considerably more broken syntax, but in fact the sentencing is relatively conventional. Each "nonbeast" sentence is a regular declarative period, and passive constructions tend to dominate. Even the "theme" of the poem seems rather civilized. The idea that if we recognize our "beast" nature we can conquer the inhuman world of machines is a timid version of what poets have been saying since the early eighteenth century. Blake found infinite variations on the theme, and it is a standard part of every romantic and Victorian poet's repertoire.

What *is* radical about McClure's poetry is his extreme faith in the power of bald statement and gesture. In his plays and his poetry, he explores the thematics of innocence and naiveté in ways that make Jack Kerouac's pronouncements seem Augustan in comparison. The impetus to move in this direction was certainly inspired by the poets in San Francisco who were searching for a more direct and personal statement, but McClure pushes an expressive poetics even further to suggest that naming and declaration are essentially animal acts:

> An animal does not specialize in a discipline. He puts the large chunks that will not pass through the sieve into an aggregate to ensure his survival. The wolf is not a wandering scholar but a wandering minstrel – with the whole prairie for an auditorium and world field to work upon. He can visualize a universe of sound as a field on which to conceive and topologize his personal statements.[48]

A statement such as this helps explain McClure's willingness to "name his states" in a fairly bald-faced manner and to do so with childlike gusto:

I AM MY ABSTRACT ALCHEMIST OF FLESH
made real!
I AM MY ABSTRACT ALCHEMIST OF FLESH
made real!
I AM MY ABSTRACT ALCHEMIST OF FLESH
made real!
And nothing more!
NO LESS THAN A STAR –
a chamber and a vacuole.
Without sense!   A Thing!   I feel![49]

The problem with this kind of statement is that the reader has no room in which to participate or evaluate. The entire poem depends for its authority on the poet's sincerity of expression, his gesture in saying rather than the specific words he uses. Words are only the outward signs of internal states even though they are foregrounded as objects on the page. The lack of semantic or syntactic complexity further frustrates the reader's participation by closing off all alternative or divergent readings. One is left with an assertion that must be accepted by its sheer intensity. The poems, despite their energetic surface and dramatic rhetoric, remain relatively static and two-dimensional. In the terms outlined in my introduction, McClure's is a performative poetics that stresses only the performance and not its reception.

It is in his plays that McClure has managed to diversify his poetics and provide a more complex arena for working out his mammalian poetics. In works like *Gargoyle Cartoons*, *Gorf*, *The Beard*, and *The Blossom*, he has created a kind of alchemical theater in which his biological and ecological concerns are given vivid – and often comic – form. Like his poetry, his plays represent a direct manifestation of organic life. He conceives of each play as a cell. "It has its organelles, its ribosomes, and its DNA and RNA, and a good enactment of it is harmonically and biochemically in balance."[50] McClure's early plays, now collected in *The Mammals*, tend to have some of the same static qualities as his poetry. "The Feast," for example, is written for thirteen actors who sit around a table drinking black wine and eating bread. They speak, for the most part, in beast language, and their interaction is limited almost entirely to expressive grunts and roars with an occasional interruption of "human" speech:

Thantar:
KRYBEKK ALL MEOOOOGRR GEOOWWW
GREEEEEAAKORRS KROOOOOOO
Yeorg:
. . . NOTHING AIR

/GROOMSHAKTARBYMETH! TORNTORP!! CEREMENT!
MARIGOLD
OF MAMMAL'S EAR. WE ARE BANNERS! . . .
Thantar:
AHH! EEEH OOOOH AKKKKORR! GROOOOOOOOO![51]

At this stage in his writing, McClure was strongly influenced by Artaud's "theater of cruelty" and with the possibility of using the stage as "projective verse turned to theater."[52] Characters do not speak so much as give testimony, retaining something of the hieratic posture of figures in religious allegory. With *The Beard* in 1965, however, McClure begins to give voices and identities to his obsessional world. The play's main characters, Billy the Kid and Jean Harlow, represent American folk heroes whose actions occur in some Elysian Fields of the wide screen. Their conflicts and sexual ecstasies resemble those of tragic theater or, more appropriately, modern westerns with their "high noon" shootouts and overdrawn characters. And in McClure's subsequent plays, giant penguins, comic book superheroes, odd forest creatures, and fairy sprites come to populate the stage in a theater that resembles, on the one hand, baroque masque and, on the other, the absurdist dramas of Beckett and Ionesco. Like the works of other experimental theater movements of the 1960s, McClure's plays attempt to break the frame of the proscenium by engaging the audience in some form of participation, whether through direct address or by extending elements of the dramatic mise en scène into the larger theater space.

McClure's plays extend and develop many of the themes of the poetry but do so with a degree of complexity that the poetry seldom approaches. And whereas in the poetry, claims for authority and participation depend on a unitary "I," the plays displace such claims among several characters. Billy the Kid's posturing and primping are always qualified by Jean Harlow's sardonic retorts. In *The Meatball*, McClure's tendency toward grand pronouncement is undermined by hysterical passages of nonsense, new-age language:

> YOWEEEEEEEEEEEEEEEEEEEEE! INCREDIBLE! [*Ecstatically*] YOWEE! WOW! [*Clasping hands together in a transport.*] OH WOW, WOW, WOW, WOW, WOW, WOW, WOW! [*Falls off chair. Rolls in joy.*] OW WOW WOW WOW! Look at it, man. It is a whole UNIVERSE! [*Getting up and staring into flowers.*] WOW! A UNIVERSE! A UNIVERSE! THE MAGIC IS GETTING STRONGER, MAN. SLEEK HEY, SLEEK . . . WE'VE GOT TO HAVE MAGIC MUSIC WITH THIS![53]

In *Spider Rabbit*, this debunking, comic spirit is combined with a powerful antiwar polemic. The play was written during the Vietnam

War at a point when political double talk allowed for massive human suffering under the neutral rhetoric of Washington bureaucratese. McClure's central figure – a cross between a blood-drinking spider and a soft, cuddly rabbit – embodies this duality by alternately endearing himself to the audience and pulling hand grenades, electric saws, and human organs from a sack. His standard refrain is "I HATE WAR!" but his actions (usually involving forms of torture and cannibalism) contradict his statements. The play sustains the tension between a rhetoric of childhood play and the considerably darker rhetoric of political genocide. In such plays, McClure reveals an awareness of the tone of hypocrisy found in the public sphere and yet uses the stage for all of its possibilities of entertainment, spectacle, humor, and display.

The most complex realization of McClure's biopolitical theater is found in *Gorf,* a multilevel spectacle that, on the one hand, resembles classical comedies like those of Euripides and, on the other, seems made out of television soap operas. Its star is a winged phallus named Gorf, whose function is to alert the world to the great "bump" – a kind of Atlantean shift into mythical time – and who helps to reunite the realm of the sacred to a scattered and secular world. The other principal characters, Mert and Gert, have lost their child – known as the Shitfer – to the cosmos, and they, with the help of Gorf, try to find him throughout the play. Mert and Gert represent the lumpen American couple straight out of "All in the Family" who lead unenlightened lives – until they are sat upon by, of all things, the hindquarters of a giant, hairy elephant. This mock apotheosis projects them into mythical time, in which they encounter figures like the Blind Dyke, a naked girl with fairy wings, a pair of dancing television sets, and the Giant Penguin, all of whom serve as comic guides through the astral realm.

If all this seems preposterous, it is not without its ethical point, provided by what I perceive as McClure's alter ego in the play, the Giant Penguin. This wonderful creation articulates the positive ecological ethos that will reunite the particles of the Shitfer that have been scattered throughout time and space in some gnostic dispersion. When the penguin invokes this reunification, he does so in McClure's favored Shelleyan rhetoric:

> JOY, JOY, JOY SUBLIME –
> FEEL THE NEARING OF TIME.
> JOY, JOY, JOY WITHOUT CRIME –
> SENSE THE PASSING OF SPACE.[54]

But when the penguin attempts to be interpretive – for example, when he tries to explain the transformation from real time to mythical time – his speech is slightly buffoonish:

> Before the sqwunch of Time and Space, before the abyss was
> Abyssinia. . . . [Pause] Before the giant hairy elephant sat on Mert and
> Gert. . . . [Pause] In the olden times that precede these days of myth.
> [Pause] When things were real. [Pause] When the snooty-rootian move-
> ments still jiggled in all the bumps that matter is made up of. . . .
> Then. . . . [Pause] Then the Shitfer was one. Then the Shitfer was just
> one thing. Everything else as well, and whole, and happy, and the olive
> grew, and the duck fell down with a heart attack at the foot of the
> hunter. (G, 61)

In some sense, the Giant Penguin represents McClure's own tendencies
toward cosmic statement and visionary pronouncement, but unlike the
voice in the poems the rather bombastic and portentous voice of the
penguin is treated with humor.

It is the Giant Penguin who recognizes that he, and the other characters
in the play, are all particles of the Shitfer. At the end, the entire cast
gathers with him in a huge "Tableau of the Shitfer," which represents
the lifting of mythical time and the return to a redeemed "real" time.
The allegory here resembles Gnostic and Orphic cosmologies (the story
of Atlantis, the Orphic theogony of Phanes) but its application to the
current ecological crisis tempers its metaphysical trappings and makes it
a particularly topical play.

Gorf, like McClure's other plays, provides an important polemical and
political dimension that, in the poems, is often handled by means of sheer
assertion:

> YES! THERE IS BUT ONE
> POLITICS AND THAT
> IS BIOLOGY.
> BIOLOGY
> IS
> POLITICS[55]

In those lines, the force of declaration and statement is spatialized into an
icon. An essentially prose statement is divided into a series of lines that,
however urgent the message, depend upon rather simple equations.
Gorf, by contrast, draws from a number of rhetorical frames (television
sitcoms, mystical literature, comic books) to give flesh to the political
and ecological dramas of our day.

Michael McClure's poetry represents all of the daring as well as some
of the limitations of the Beat ethos. He wants the poem to dissolve into
nature – to become transparent to the world of which it is a part. He
would like his individual words to free themselves from language and
attain an autonomous presence like so many protozoans on a microscope
slide. McClure's belief in the mammalian base of human consciousness
leads him to exceed the normal orthographic conventions of poetry and,

in the case of "beast language," normal semantic patterns. The result is a language act caught somewhere between physical gesture and shout, between act and object. At the same time, his sense of language remains essentially passive and static. In an attempt to personalize his poetry more radically, he relies on a two-dimensional concept of the subject whose identity is largely dependent upon the sincerity of his expressive gesture. In the plays, however, this problem of unitary subject is eliminated by the creation of multiple roles and qualities of self-reflection and self-mockery that make for a considerably richer surface.

OUR GANG AND THE CANON

"Do I contradict myself?" asked Whitman one hundred years before "Howl." "Very well then I contradict myself." The author of *Leaves of Grass* envisioned an art large enough to contain contradiction, and in a sense this was his great legacy to the Beat writers. They appeared on the scene at a time when contradiction was a matter of rhetorical tension rather than existential disclosure. However therapeutic their appeal to openness and spontaneity may have been, their practice risked calling into question its own status as writing. McClure's desire to write words of meat and spirit means that we are asked to accept his poem as a metaphor – that is, as other than a collection of words. When Ginsberg and Kerouac ask that writing have the speed and energy of consciousness, they unwittingly detach the mind from the body they are so anxious to rejoin. And when the Beat writers elevate personal testimony to a value in its own right, they limit their ability to assess and measure the nature of their testimony. I have defined this problem as one of participation in which the desire to make the poem transparent before the world often leaves the poet without adequate grounds for self-reflection. In their best work, the Beat writers were aware of the dangers of such participation and made *that* a generative element of their work.

When making qualifications about Beat writing, it is necessary to remember the literary climate circa 1950, when this personalist poetics made its first appearance. It was a time of careful, modulated responses to Eliot's famous "dissociation of sensibility," and any attempt to cut the Gordian knot of form and content by anything less than a sonnet in blank verse was considered bad form. The Beats did not make distinctions. They raised the unwholesome specter of romanticism to center stage, talked about their personal lives in distinctly nonmetaphoric terms, and appeared to live the lives that their writing described. Their impact was immediate – if grudgingly admitted – causing even the sons and daughters of Ransom and Tate to examine the "life" in their "life studies."[56] If we, in retrospect, find contradictions between their stated goals and their practice, it should not obscure the necessity of their attack.

The first intelligent critique of Beat writing *qua* writing occurred not in a professional journal or review but in Judge Clayton Horn's San Francisco Municipal Courtroom, where a half-dozen local academic critics and journalists (Kenneth Rexroth among them) testified in behalf of "Howl." It may have been the most appropriate forum.[57] Today "Howl" finds itself in rather odd company: It is taught in classrooms, discussed in journals, and printed in college anthologies complete with footnotes on arcane subjects like "Bickford's," "Bellevue," and the "Bowery." Ginsberg's poetry has been collected into a massive *Collected Poems* with appendixes and notes. The manuscript of "Howl" has been printed in an expensive facsimile edition, complete with scholarly apparatus, notes, and transcription. There is a Norton Critical Edition of *On the Road* with critical commentary appended, and Kerouac is now the subject of six biographies. Documentaries on the Beats have been made by public television and Hollywood studios. Michael McClure's plays have been produced all over the world by distinguished companies, and several have won prestigious awards. Gale Research has devoted a two-volume reference encyclopedia to the Beats, and university libraries pay lavish amounts of money for their papers. In Europe, the Beats are regularly invited to international conferences and symposia, and their books are translated into practically every language.

This accommodation to the canon should not come as a surprise. To some extent it is a belated response to the fact that the Beats were *from the outset* part of American culture, not alienated from it. Kerouac's identification of his "gang" with the Marx Brothers or Ginsberg's and McClure's appearances at rock concerts and in Bob Dylan's *Rolling Thunder* movie are but some of the manifestations of this tendency. If the Beats attacked American life, they certainly identified with its antinomian and individualistic spirit. In their eyes, the social "darkness" that surrounded everyone during the 1950s represented a betrayal of a Whitmanian democratic spirit gone astray. The Beats saw their function as modern Jeremiahs waking a populace too easily swayed by the rhetoric of consensus and accommodation.

"O but there are times SHAZAM is not enough," Gregory Corso reminds us. "There is a brutality in the rabbit / That leads the way to Paradise – far from God."[58] The darkness that surrounded Americans could not be solved by driving away from it. The Beats realized that there are no magic passwords to eternity, even though they often found them by accident in sunflowers, sutras, and the wind along the highway. In their permission to remain open to quotidean experience they most resembled Whitman and followed the lessons of Huck Finn.

3

"Spotting That Design"
Incarnation and Interpretation in Gary Snyder and Philip Whalen

A popular misconception about the Beats is that they were dabblers in esoteric religion, turning to Zen, cabala, or activist versions of Catholicism in order to discover new spiritual highs. John Ciardi, writing in the *Saturday Review* in 1960, claims that the Beats have "raided from Zen whatever offered them an easy rationale for what they wanted to do in the first place,"[1] and Herbert Gold, writing in *Playboy,* says that "Zen Buddhism has spread like Asian flu. . . . Zen and other religions surely have their beauties, but the hipster dives through them like a side show acrobat through a paper hoop."[2] Though it is certainly true that poets turned to alternative religious systems and practices during the 1950s and 1960s, it is demonstrably *not* true that this interest was in any way casual.

Consider the facts: Gary Snyder left San Francisco in 1955 to live in Japan on and off for the next twelve years while engaged in formal Zen training. During this time, under the tutelage of Roshi Oda Sesso, he took formal vows as a Zen monk. Allen Ginsberg has spent much of his time during the past fifteen years as a follower of Tibetan Buddhism, traveling extensively in India and the East as part of his spiritual training. During this period he was a disciple of Chögyam Trungpa at the Naropa Institute, where Ginsberg helped direct the Jack Kerouac poetics program. Philip Whalen has, until recently, lived at the San Francisco Zen Center, where, in 1973, he was ordained Unsui (Zen Buddhist monk), and later, in 1975, became Shuso (head monk) of the Zen Mountain Center at Tassajara Springs, California. In 1949 William Everson converted to Catholicism and soon after (1951) entered the Dominican Order at St. Albert's College in Oakland, California. He adopted the name Brother Antoninus and served as a lay monk until he left the order in 1969. Kenneth Rexroth was Anglo-Catholic for most of his adult life and in his last years converted to Roman Catholicism.[3] He was active in the Catholic workers movement during the 1930s and has written extensively on Western and Eastern religions, devoting an entire book, *Communalism,* to a history of alternative religious and political practices.[4] Most of the poets we shall encounter in this book developed the terms for their poetics out of specific theological concerns (Robert Duncan's theosophy, Jack Spicer's Calvinism, Michael McClure's animism, David Meltzer and Diane DiPrima's cabalism) that provided both the problematic of belief and the rhetoric by which that belief could be translated into aesthetic terms. Such religious activism was based not on a casual glance into a primer on comparative religion but on sustained study and research.

Given this active involvement in both Eastern and Western religious traditions, it is difficult to see how anyone could dismiss it as "dabbling." In fact, it is hard to think of any modern literary movement in which writers so actively yoked their poetic vocation to specific spiritual practices. Of course, what critics usually implied by their deprecations was not that the Beats were not interested in religion but that they were not interested in the *right* religion. While a poet like Robert Lowell was trying to solve the thorny question of incarnation within the doctrinal framework of Catholicism, poets of the San Francisco Renaissance turned increasingly to Eastern religions (Buddhism, Hinduism) and to various forms of pantheism to deal with many of the same questions. For Lowell in the early 1950s the supreme task of poetry was to render the complex logic of God's word through metaphors that would, by their rhetorical complexity and rigor, manifest something of the inconceivable quality of Deity itself. The poem was the site of what John Crowe Ransom called a "miraculist fusion" of particulars with some universal, nondiscursive order, presenting at the level of local texture an equivalent "supernatural" force.[5] The tough metaphysical conceit, yoking diverse ideas together, stood as a concrete universal, giving form to that which has no form and voice to that which cannot speak. As Charles Altieri has characterized it, incarnation for the New Critics provided "a doctrinal basis by which an essentially symbolist poetic can assert the value of the mind's orders while insisting that universals are not mere fictions but contain the actual structure and meaning of particular experiences."[6]

For poets like Gary Snyder, William Everson, and Allen Ginsberg incarnation is a matter not of reconciliation but of activation and energy. God is manifest in terms of Lorca's "dark and quivering Duende" or as Lawrentian sexuality, a force emerging from the earth and from the unconscious. Lawrence, in his preface to the American edition of *New Poems,* equates this power with an emerging free verse. "The seething poetry of the incarnate Now," as he calls it, participates directly with natural forces and, as such, is distinct from metrical verse. In free verse,

> we look for the insurgent naked throb of the instant moment. To break the lovely form of metrical verse and to dish up the fragments of a new substance, called *vers libre,* this is what most of the free-versifiers accomplish. They do not know that free verse has its own *nature,* that it is neither star nor pearl, but instantaneous like plasm. . . . The utterance is like a spasm, naked contact with all influences at once.[7]

For Lawrence as well as for his latter-day adherents, the poem does not reconcile opposites by sustaining rhetorical tension but provides examples of oppositions living in harmony in the natural world. Many of Gary Snyder's and Philip Whalen's poems consist of catalogues or lists of disparate things existing side by side as part of a "vast jewelled net" of interconnected elements.[8] God is present as process, revealed in physical labor, sexual ecstasy, and moments of visionary insight. The Kantian or Coleridgean view of the creative imagination as a repetition of the "eternal act of creation in the infinite I AM" is replaced by Wordsworth's view of the artist as one who need only "look steadily at the subject."[9] Pound's "natural object" replaces the "miraculist" objective correlative as the poet seeks to find – not represent – the interknit modalities of God's presence. What for the New Critics involved the imposition of order on flux becomes, for the Beat writers, the rediscovery of the creative potentiality of flux itself.

Within this "poetics of numinous presence," as Altieri has called it, we find a separation between the poets described in Chapter 2 (Ginsberg, Kerouac, McClure) from their Northwest counterparts, Gary Snyder and Philip Whalen. Though both groups have a common frame of religious beliefs, based largely on Buddhist tenets, they differ in the nature of their spiritual practices. Using two concepts from Buddhism, we could divide the poets of the Beat movement into two camps: those who take the direction of *karuna* (compassion) and those who follow the way of *prajna* (wisdom). These are by no means incompatible concepts; both encourage the pursuit of enlightenment, but they suggest different emphases. In more familiar terms, this division could be seen as that between Emersonian idealism with its belief in an unmediated relationship between phenomenal reality and spiritual life, and a more solitary, speculative form of transcendentalism like that practiced by Thoreau.

For Ginsberg, Kerouac, and McClure, Buddhist compassion for all sentient things is expressed through forms of worship (and embodied in poems) that are essentially passive and receptive. The individual attempts to become an empty vehicle, free of all material desires, through whom what Emerson called the "currents of universal Being" may flow.

Ginsberg's emphasis on mantric forms of poetry, on Hindu breathing exercises, and on communal chanting could be seen as gestures directed at achieving this emptiness by returning self to body and participating broadly in the creative powers of nature. His most formative experiences – his Blake visions of the late 1940s, his peyote and yage experiences of the 1950s, and his psychedelic trips of the 1960s – represent moments in which he literally *hears* "the voice of the Bard." He does not create a persona or mask through which a projected spiritual voice may speak, but directly transcribes the presence of that voice in his life. And in similar ways, Kerouac's and McClure's ideas of spontaneity, simplicity, and ecstatic testimony could be seen as alternative ways of transcending boundaries between temporal and spiritual realms, between secular vision and visionary potential.

For Gary Snyder and Philip Whalen, by contrast, the pursuit of enlightenment involves processes of intellection, discrimination, and observation that focus attention on the here and now. In describing why he chose the Rinzai sect of Zen Buddhism, Snyder quotes Yeats's lines, "The fascination of what's difficult / has dried the sap out of my veins . . . ," and elsewhere approves of the hard "Dharma combat" tied to Zen koan study.[10] Enlightenment is achieved not in a sudden flash of illumination but as a result of years of study and meditation.[11] Philip Whalen, though less inclined to celebrate the rigors of spiritual practice, tends toward the same intellectual position as Snyder. In his poetry, Whalen can usually be found negotiating the conflicting claims of ego identity and mindlessness. With a sardonic and often rueful humor he mocks his own self-consciousness while in pursuit of some unmediated, natural state.

When translated into poetics, these differences in spiritual practice can be seen in the opposition between a poetics of immediacy and improvisation, derived from Whitman or jazz, and a poetics of objectivist clarity and economy, associated with Pound and Williams. Certainly Ginsberg wrote many of his early poems in imitation of Williams, but the bulk of his post-"Howl" poems are modeled on mantra and chant. Snyder and Whalen and their Reed College roommate, Lew Welch, developed their poetics out of readings in modernists like Pound, Williams, and Stein as well as the Chinese T'ang dynasty poets, whom they read in translations by Arthur Waley. The result is a considerably more clipped, terse syntax and a shorter line. In some sense the two groups that I am describing here represent two strands of Eastern influence on American writing in general: the Indian, Vedic tradition that nurtured the American romantics of the mid-nineteenth century and the Chinese lyric tradition, focused in the haiku, that became the model for much of modernist lyricism in the early part of the twentieth century. That both traditions were tied to specific religious and cultural ideologies should not be disregarded in considering any of these poets.

If Gary Snyder and Philip Whalen can be paired by their shared commitment to the "wisdom–oriented line"[12] of Zen or by their common northwestern background, they can be differentiated according to the way each poet treats his own voice in the poem. Snyder typically removes himself, allowing the particulars of a landscape or the events of a day to constellate realms of value. When the first-person pronoun enters the poem, it is not the expressive "I" of romantic subjectivity but rather the "I" as interpreter who establishes relationships between local and universal. Charles Altieri sees a conflict between Snyder's early poetry, in which this "I" is content to see without interpreting, and his later poetry, in which the "I" is fully invested with its prophetic role.[13] Though I would agree with Altieri's sense of the limitations of the later work, I would say that even early poems like "Milton by Firelight" and *Myths and Texts* evidence the same prophetic intent.

Philip Whalen's poems often have the same objectivist surface as Snyder's but with far more investment of the mediating ego and with a greater range of tonal variation in the poet's voice. Whalen is invariably the subject of his poems, asking questions, worrying about his relations to others, and worrying about worrying too much. But instead of producing the ironic circularity one associates with John Ashbery or James Merrill, this self-consciousness dramatizes the difficulty of uniting a belief in natural process with complex dramatic and perceptual frames that create their own demands:

> Suzuki Roshi said, "If I die, it's all right.
> If I should live, it's all right. Sun-face Buddha, Moon-face Buddha."
> Why do I always fall for that old line?
>
> We don't treat each other any better. When will I
> Stop writing it down.[14]

These lines typify Whalen's meditational style: The Zen paradox must be tested within epistemological structures at the level of poem itself. "Why do I always fall for that old line?" is a recognition of the difficulties encountered in living *with* the difficulties posed by Suzuki Roshi's paradox, a resignation signaled in the poem's last line.

In a sense Gary Snyder and Philip Whalen represent two possible variations on the Buddhist notion of no-mind, the attempt to achieve an essentially egoless state necessary for illumination. In Western terms, we may see this impulse in terms of the romantics' desire for a state of "negative capability" or in Charles Olson's concern with avoiding the "lyrical interference of the ego." Certainly all of the Beats idealized various forms of mindlessness, whether enhanced by drugs and booze or by mantric chant and jazz. For Snyder and Whalen, however, the achievement of such a state is directly linked to a sense of community. Unlike their Beat colleagues who stress a kind of global inclusiveness or democratic ensemble, Snyder and Whalen advocate the tribe or family as models of social organization. The pursuit of personal enlightenment must be effected through the tribe, because spiritual activity is linked to other forms of group interaction. What Snyder calls the "communities of practice" are those tribal units that have existed since the Neolithic period within which work, prayer, childrearing and art are shared.[15] He feels that the tribe is still alive and well, even in urban America, and much of his writing has been devoted to celebrating its endurance.

In our attempt to differentiate the Beat writers, the idea of tribe as the synthesis of personal vision and social cohesion will become a major issue. Not only has it been a theme in Snyder's and Whalen's work; it became a reality during the 1960s as young people – often with Snyder as a model – turned increasingly away from state politics and official church religion to the commune and the collective. Snyder himself left for the foothills of the Sierras, where he lives in a semicommunal settlement, and Whalen spent fifteen years at the Zen Center. Their example is a logical outgrowth of that incarnationalist spirit I have already described, a desire to make spirit flesh not only in words but in social practice as well.

GARY SNYDER AND THE REAL WORK

Just as when I went to Japan I found out who *I* really was . . . an American pragmatist.

By "modern" I mean the last two thousand years. (Gary Snyder)

Strange to say, there are times when Gary Snyder bears an uncanny resemblance to T. S. Eliot. Like the author of "Tradition and the Individual Talent," Snyder believes that the poet's task is to provide links with cultural patterns and values from the past that may continue to inform the present – values achieved only by the extinction of personality:

> I think that poetry is a social and traditional art that is linked to its past and particularly its language, that *loops* and draws on its past and that serves as a vehicle for contact with the depths of our own unconscious – and that it gets better by practicing. And that the expression of self, although it's a nice kind of energy to start with, would not make any expression of poetry per se. (TRW, 65)

Of course, Snyder's cultural sources differ from Eliot's as do his views on how such traditions improve society. Snyder would hardly feel comfortable with Eliot's Anglican religious views or conservative politics. Nevertheless, the two poets have a common interest in reviving cultural models from earlier traditions that might help to reunite a sensibility sundered by the forces of collectivization and secularization.

Unlike the Europeanized Eliot or Pound, Snyder embodies distinctly American characteristics: a sense of tribal interparticipation that he derives from Amerindian cultures and a sense of Yankee self-reliance that he takes from his upbringing in the Pacific Northwest. Snyder's paradigmatic cultural model is the close tribal unity of Neolithic societies that developed a high degree of sophistication in artisanal, hunting, and agricultural skills at the same time that they maintained a good balance between population and natural ecology.[16] He identifies similar values among the American Indian cultures that he studied in his undergraduate days at Reed College and that became the focus of many of his early books. His other primary model is the self-reliant proletarian, whose independence and practical knowledge embody the ideal of Buddhist detachment as well as the Marxian ideal of a totally productive individual within society. Snyder learned from his own experiences as a mountain climber, woodcutter, trail blazer, and forest lookout, and has adapted them to his concerns as a poet: "I've just recently come to realize that the rhythms of my poems follow the rhythm of the physical work I'm doing and life I'm leading at any given time."[17]

For Snyder, the "rhythm of . . . physical work" develops intellectual and spiritual qualities that cannot be realized through institutional forms of religion or philosophy. "All the junk that goes with being human / Drops away" (R, 12) in the intense focus required to dig a trail, chop wood, or fix a car. And just as unalienated labor draws the individual into harmony with the materials of daily work, so the "common work of the tribe" draws one close to a vital social nexus. The rewards of individual labor are minimal in a material sense, but they afford insights of incalculable value. In a poem like "The Spring" Snyder describes the possibilities of personal vision within the context of back-breaking physical work:

> Beating asphalt into highway potholes
>   pickup truck we'd loaded
> road repair stock shed & yard
> a day so hot the asphalt went in soft.
>   pipe and steel plate tamper
> took turns at by hand
> then drive the truck rear wheel
> a few times back and forth across the fill –
> finish it off with bitchmo round the edge.
>
> the foreman said let's get a drink
> & drove through woods and flower fields

```
            shovels clattering in the back
       into a black grove by a cliff
           a rocked in pool
           feeding a fern ravine
                   tin can to drink
       numbing the hand and cramping in the gut
       surging through the fingers from below
           & dark here −
       let's get back to the truck
       get back on the job.
```

                                    (BC, 10)

Such a poem resists interpretation, lacking the usual rhetorical markers
that assign values and make connections. The first-person pronoun is
almost completely effaced, submerged in contractions: "we'd loaded,"
"let's get back." The indented line, "tin can to drink," swerves as far in
the direction of objectivity as it is possible to go, the infinitive turning
the act of drinking into a generalized function relating more to the cup
than to the drinker.[18] Snyder pares away all unnecessary verbiage to
provide language as hard and unrelenting as the difficult labor being
described. Almost all lines are end-stopped, each one describing a single
action. Reading the poem becomes a task akin to filling in potholes, a
gradual synthesis of disparate events until their terminus: "finish it off
with bitchmo round the edge." Now he − and his readers − may have a
brief respite.

With the same fragmented quality as the opening section, the second
stanza describes another kind of activity: that devoted to obtaining a
much-needed drink. The lines become increasingly disjointed, the verbs
changing from infinitive to participial to active forms, leading to the
italicized line "& dark here −." At this point it is difficult to know what
"here" Snyder means: the spring where they are drinking, the internal
organs cramped by the cold water, or some other place suddenly intuited
in this "rocked in pool." It is precisely the ambiguity of antecedent that
assists Snyder's intent. He has focused all of our attention up to this point
on a very literal "here," which the brief moment at the spring transforms. The epiphanic quality of the moment at the spring releases him,
for a moment, from the temporal activity to participate in a larger experience. But just as quickly, Snyder turns away from this brief epiphany:
"let's get back to the truck / get back on the job," as though such
moments are to be savored suddenly and without fanfare.

"The Spring," as a title, defines both the literal place where water
wells up from under the earth (a "dark" place) and the fertile potential of
change, transformation, and natural solace. Rather than identify the
spring as a symbol of such fertility, Snyder shows the processes by which

such significance is achieved. The italicized line, pointing beneath the surface of Snyder's concrete language, gains resonance not because it is rhetorically coded as metaphor but because it builds upon and sustains other concrete images in the poem. Like the drink of water, the line is "earned."

This is Snyder at his most rigorous – and most interesting. He attempts to return words to the condition of stone and to keep his eyes focused on the sensual surface of things. But he constantly finds patterns etched in the stone that point to redemptive ways of living and thinking. How, then, is one to relinquish claims of discursive and rhetorical authority while still illustrating the underlying design of things? His answer is to adopt a version of Pound's ideogrammatic method, juxtaposing one cultural tradition on top of another with a minimum of critical commentary – as he does in "Milton by Firelight":

> "O hell, what do mine eyes
>   with grief behold?"
> Working with an old
> Singlejack miner, who can sense
> The vein and cleavage
> In the very guts of rock, can
> Blast granite, build
> Switchbacks that last for years
> Under the beat of snow, thaw, mule-hooves,
> What use, Milton, a silly story
> Of our lost general parents,
>   eaters of fruit?
>
> The Indian, the chainsaw boy,
> And a string of six mules
> Came riding down to camp
> Hungry for tomatoes and green apples.
> Sleeping in saddle-blankets
> Under a bright night-sky
> Han River slantwise by morning.
> Jays squall
> Coffee boils
>
> In ten thousand years the Sierras
> Will be dry and dead, home of the scorpion.
> Ice-scratched slabs and bent trees.
> No paradise, no fall.
> Only the weathering land
> The wheeling sky,
> Man, with his Satan
> Scouring the chaos of the mind.
> Oh Hell!

Fire down
Too dark to read, miles from a road
The bell-mare clangs in the meadow
That packed dirt for a fill-in
Scrambling through loose rocks
On an old trail
All of a summer's day.

(R, 13–14)

Here, Milton's vision of a paradise lost through original sin is qualified by Snyder's vision of a paradise perpetually rediscovered in the permanence of mountains and rock. The "silly story" of Eden becomes a tale of "our lost general parents / eaters of fruit." As if to give form to this demythologizing tendency, Snyder introduces an actual eater of apples in the form of an Indian chainsaw boy. And against what he elsewhere calls "the ancient, meaningless / Abstractions of the educated mind" (MT, 7) Snyder juxtaposes "an old / Singlejack miner," who can build "Switchbacks that last for years." Miner and Indian boy are untouched by Christian eschatology; for them, like the mountains themselves, there is "No paradise, no fall / Only the weathering land / The wheeling sky." Milton's abstract hell of the opening stanza is turned into an expletive, "Oh Hell," in the penultimate stanza as Snyder expresses dissatisfaction with the limitations of Christian doctrine in the face of geological time.

The final stanza focuses the exact frame by which what has gone before may be seen. Milton's allegory may no longer be read when the dark is literal: "Fire down / Too dark to read. . . ." In the physical darkness all that can be heard is the "bell-mare," clanging in the meadow. The trailwork in which horse and man have participated is completely mundane, "All of a summer's day," uninvested with any vertical significance. At this point words like "old" and "day" take on new significance since they have been juxtaposed to the salvific temporality of Christianity. Time is given value by the work done in it, the creation of vital contact between humans, animals, and rock.

In "Milton by Firelight," Snyder employs a version of Pound's ideogrammatic method in order to sustain his two primary frames: Christian eschatology and natural temporality. Details like apples, rocks, and even darkness draw attention to the natural object, while providing another frame for viewing the same details within a scriptural context. Snyder's naturalistic use of details belies a much more conscious attempt to subvert poems like *Paradise Lost* that subordinate gardens, snakes, and fruit to allegorical ends. But despite its economical presentation, "Milton by Firelight" lacks some awareness of the complicity between the hierarchical religion being attacked and the implicit hierarchical position of Snyder's voice. Snyder is more successful when he allows several voices or perspectives to speak, thus diffusing his own tendency to orchestrate the ethical frames in which his fragments fall. The best examples of this multiple voicing occur in works like *Mountains and Rivers Without End* or *Myths and Texts,* where documentary materials provide the poet with a variety of textures and modes of presentation.

Myths and Texts is based on Snyder's logging, trail-making, and forest lookout work during the early 1950s. Much of its subject matter is drawn from Northwest Indian stories that Snyder found in Bureau of Ethnology reports and various collections of Indian tales in Boas, Kroeber, and others. The book's three sections, "Logging," "Hunting," and "Burning," represent a three-tiered spiritual journey from the historical destruction of the wilderness by entrepreneurial interests (and the ideologies of church and state that support such destruction) through the shamanistic animal magic of Indian hunting to the purifying fire and "inner heat" of Tantric Buddhism. By "journey," I do not mean to imply that *Myths and Texts* employs the usual diachronic narrative pattern of heroic epics; rather, it uses the contrastive possibilities of literal, historical events (what Snyder calls "texts") juxtaposed to their "mythical" implications.

We can see the workings of Snyder's method most vividly in the book's last section, which is divided into two parts: "the text," or literal occasion, and "the myth," the timeless, vertical dimension that extends from the occasion:

the text

Sourdough mountain called a fire in:
Up Thunder Creek, high on a ridge.
Hiked eighteen hours, finally found
A snag and a hundred feet around on fire:
All afternoon and into night
Digging the fire line
Falling the burning snag
It fanned sparks down like shooting stars
Over the dry woods starting spot-fires
Flaring in wind up Skagit valley
From the Sound
Toward morning it rained.
We slept in mud and ashes,
Woke at dawn, the fire was out,
The sky was clear, we saw
The last glimmer of the morning star.

the myth

Fire up Thunder Creek and the mountain –
    troy's burning!

The cloud mutters
The mountains are your mind.
The woods bristle there,
Dogs barking and children shrieking
Rise from below.
Rain falls for centuries
Soaking the loose rocks in space
Sweet rain, the fire's out
The black snag glistens in the rain
& the last wisp of smoke floats up
Into the absolute cold
Into the spiral whorls of fire
The storms of the Milky Way
"Buddha incense in an empty world"
Black pit cold and light-year
Flame tongue of the dragon
Licks the sun

The sun is but a morning star
                    (MT, 54)

These two sections do not, as it might appear, emphasize the mythic proportions of the forest fire, but indicate the interdependence of text and myth. Quiet homage is paid to Thoreau, whose final sentence of *Walden,* "The sun is but a morning star," becomes the last line of Snyder's poem. Thoreau, like Snyder, devotes most of his major work to plotting the correspondences between local circumstances – the depth of a pond, the contents of his shack, the clothing that he wears – and their participation in a larger economy. Thus, for Snyder, the "last glimmer of the morning star" is linked to the sparks of the forest fire as well as to the sun, each light reflecting the cleansing heat of "Buddha incense in an empty world."

Myths and Texts is "spoken" by no single narrator but by the collective voices of various cultures (American Indian, Buddhist, American frontiersmen) who respect the wilderness and who embody the potential wildness in every individual. By relinquishing his own voice to his native informants, Snyder is able to speak from what he calls the "vast interrelated network" of other cultures, creatures, and inanimate objects. The point of view shifts constantly from first to third person, individual to collective voice, to illustrate at the level of address the dialectical interplay between nature and culture.

This interplay of cultural sources can be seen in the poem's second section, "Hunting," which utilizes the voices of hunters and their prey as represented in various Northwest songs. The hunter, in silent pursuit of the prey, must project himself into the animal and take on its soul. It is an act not of violence but of empathy:

To hunt means to use your body and senses to the fullest: to strain your
consciousness to feel what the deer are thinking today, this moment; to
sit still and let your self go into the birds and wind while waiting by a
game trail. Hunting magic is designed to bring the game to you – the
creature who has heard your song, witnessed your sincerity, and out of
compassion comes within your range. (EHH, 120)

When this empathy fails, hunting becomes an act of wanton violence. In
"this poem is for deer," Snyder situates just such an act of violence
within the frame of two shaman songs, the first of which personifies the
deer's essential humanity:

> I dance on all the mountains
> On five mountains, I have a dancing place
> When they shoot at me I run
> To my five mountains
>
> (MT, 26)

Snyder then changes his persona to that of the hunter, who casually
describes killing animals from a car:

> Home by night
>   drunken eye
> Still picks out Taurus
> Low, and growing high:
>   four-point buck
> Dancing in the headlights
>   on the lonely road
> A mile past the mill-pond
> With the car stopped, shot
> That wild silly blinded creature down.
>
> Pull out the hot guts
>   with bare hands
> While night-frost chills the tongue
>   and eye
> The cold horn-bones.
> The hunter's belt
>   just below the sky
> Warm blood in the car trunk.
> Deer-smell
>   the limp tongue.
>
> (MT, 27)

Hunting in this passage is an endistanced and detached act. Blinded by
the car's headlights, the deer is shot from the relative safety of the car
itself. The unnamed hunter treats the animal as a "wild silly creature," its
dancing movements, celebrated in the Cowlitz deer song, turned into the
movements of fright and surprise as it is caught in the headlights. The

hunter's "drunken eye" is still able to pick out constellations above him (one of which is Orion, the hunter), but he remains blind to the larger implications of his act. While the stellar hunt goes on in the heavens, this hunter kills for sport or distraction. By contrast, the Indian hunter treats his prey with respect:

> Deer don't want to die for me.
>   I'll drink sea-water
> Sleep on beach pebbles in the rain
> Until the deer come down to die
>   in pity for my pain
>   (MT, 28)

The close relationship between hunter and animal is acknowledged in this song, in which the Indian takes on the voice of the deer. By appropriating the song for his own poem, Snyder signals his intertextual affinities with this tradition.

Such passages indicate important parallels with other forms of spiritual practice. The silence of the hunter, waiting for the animal to "come down to die," is a meditative silence in which the boundaries between self and world are gradually effaced. Snyder comments on this quality of empathy in his *East–West* interview:

> You learn animal behavior becoming an acute observer – by entering the mind – of animals. That's why in rituals and ceremonies that are found throughout the world from ancient times, the key component of the ceremony is animal *miming*. The miming is a spontaneous expression of the capacity of becoming physically and psychically one with the animal. (TRW, 107)

Animal miming is one of numerous models for achieving the egoless state advocated in Buddhist thought. Snyder wants poetry to aid in developing a consciousness that is not dependent on the material world, one that, through meditation, trance vision, or concentration, rejoins a primordial, ecological mind. *Myths and Texts* succeeds as well as any of Snyder's books in showing concrete instances of such consciousness, setting it dialectically in opposition to rationalistic, dualistic systems without introducing the author's stern voice of warning.

"[This] poem is for deer," like all of *Myths and Texts*, is based on an ethical world view that goes considerably beyond aesthetic considerations. What I have been describing as a matter of "voice" is an extension of the poet's sociocultural views, in which the oral tradition plays a unifying role. In his talk "Poetry and the Primitive," given at the Berkeley Poetry Conference in July 1965, Snyder states that the poet shares with the primitive a frame of values extending back to the upper Paleolithic. This frame includes "the fertility of the soil, the magic of animals, the power of vision in solitude, the terrifying initiation and rebirth, the love and ecstasy of the dance, the common work of the tribe."[19] The poems I have just discussed illustrate, at least thematically, several of these qualities. But Snyder feels that poetry is the ground as well as the expression of these values. To this end, he invokes the voice as the agency through which those spiritual and epistemological orders speak. Poetry is "the skilled and inspired use of the voice and language to embody rare and powerful states of mind that are in immediate origin personal to the singer, but at deep levels common to all who listen."[20] It is not simply that poetry speaks *of* such "rare and powerful states of mind" but that it "must sing or speak from authentic experience."

The problem with many of Snyder's remarks like those in "Poetry and the Primitive" is that in the interest of historicizing poetry by linking it to ancient traditions and cultural sources, he often uses firstness as a self-evident sign of authenticity. The term "primitive" quickly loses its descriptive or historical function and becomes a metaphysical category, an ideal of immediacy that has been lost to modern society. As I have stated elsewhere, these attitudes betray a logocentrism that pits oral cultural against literary and that identifies voice with some deeper source of value.[21] Snyder's view of orality (one that he shares with many other contemporary poets) fails to account for the degree to which "voice" is also a product – as well as a vehicle – of specific Western traditions based on the need for a self-sufficient, unitary ego.

When this unitary voice is fully aware of its pedagogical role – as it often is in his more recent poetry – the result can be a shrill, hectoring tone that seems intolerant of the reader. Instead of his haiku-like spareness, Snyder permits himself a degree of discursiveness that limits playfulness in language and diminishes acoustic richness, as in "Tomorrow's Song":

> The USA slowly lost its mandate
> in the middle and later twentieth century
> it never gave the mountains and rivers,
>   trees and animals,
>   a vote.
> all the people turned away from it
>   myths die; even continents are impermanent
>
>   Turtle Island returned.
>   my friend broke open a dried coyote-scat
>   removed a ground squirrel tooth
>   pierced it, hung it
>   from the gold ring
>   in his ear.
> We look to the future with pleasure

we need no fossil fuel
get power within
grow strong on less.
                    (TI, 77)

It is not that we disagree with any of the ecological or political issues raised here but that they are treated exactly as that: issues. The squirrel tooth discovered in a coyote dropping quickly becomes an icon or symbol when it is used by the countercultural friend for an earring – and, by extension, by the countercultural poet as a sign of the "power within." The reader, while enjoined to "grow strong on less," is given too much in the way of interpretive clues. The reader becomes a passive recipient *of* rather than participant *in* the critical forum that the poem encourages. In his early poetry, Snyder allowed the materiality of language its own role in embodying the contradictions between exploitation and ecological survival. The sheer force of his spare style and nominalized language gave added weight to his Buddhist naturalism. In his more recent poetry, however, he often treats language as a rhetorical lever for convincing an ignorant populace.

I have, perhaps inadvertently, made an evaluative distinction between two kinds of "voice" in Snyder's poetry: that of his haiku-like early lyrics, in which authorial presence is projected onto the landscape, and that of his polemical later poems like "Tomorrow's Song," in which the poet speaks from an authoritative position about how that landscape is to be read.[22] Rather than see them as two different kinds of voice, as some critics have, I would prefer to see them as two tendencies that inhabit all of his poetry. Snyder's most effective poems are those in which the dialectical structure of the haiku – the way it sets in motion conflicting movements – is maintained throughout and is not resolved by authorial intervention. When that impulse toward growth and expansion is qualified, what had been presentation becomes mimesis.[23]

Part of the problem with Snyder's lyrics lies in his handling of closure. What I have called the dialectical structure of Snyder's lyrics often depends on the final line's or stanza's capacity to set an entirely new dimension in motion, one that grows out of oppositional patterns within the poem. Consider the poem titled "Running Water Music":

under the trees
under the clouds
by the river
on the beach,

"sea roads."
whales   great sea-path beasts –

```
salt;   cold
    water;   smoky fire
steam, cereal,
    stone, wood boards.
bone awl, pelts,
    bamboo pins and spoons.
unglazed bowl.
a band around the hair.

    beyond wounds.
sat on a rock in the sun,
watched the old pine
wave
over blinding fine white
    river sand
```

(RW, 44)

The four prepositional phrases that begin the poem establish the various places where the individual interacts with water. But there is no agent in this poem; he or she is represented instead by representations, artifacts, and food. It is the individual who creates phrases like "sea roads" to describe the watery routes of migrating whales; it is the individual who creates cooking implements and tools with the help of that water in order to cook; it is the individual who creates poetry and meditates out of the sound of that water. The poem focuses on these "traces" left by running water on culture itself.

The final stanza continues the movement initiated by the rest of the poem but adds an important new dimension: an image of a specific, observing individual who watches "the old pine / wave / over blinding fine white / river sand." The isolation of "wave" on a separate line mixes verb and noun, suggesting that water is present, even where it is absent – in a pine that makes a "wave"-like motion and by the sand created by river water. Thus the "music" of the title is both embodied in the deft handling of vowels and consonants (particularly the assonance of "i's" in the final lines) and figured in the various traces of water on dry land. The closure of the poem draws elements together not by summary but by reopening the terms of the poem in a new direction.

In a companion poem, "Running Water Music II," something very different happens:

```
Clear running stream
    clear running stream

Your water is light
    to my mouth
And a light to my dry body
```

> your flowing
> Music,
>   in my ears.   free,
>
> Flowing free!
> With you
>   in me.
>
> (RW, 64)

Here the celebration of water is explicit; the connections between elements are spelled out, specifically through the rhetorical device of personification. And the final lines, rather than revitalizing the idea of movement and change implied by terms like "music," "running," "light," and "flowing," abstract the poem even further. The rather heavy-handed rhymes with which the poem concludes seem the antithesis of that "music" developed in the first poem.

"Running Water Music II" represents a contemporary version of the autotelic poem, freer than its modernist predecessors to assert connections, celebrate openly, declare connections between self and world, but bound by semantic and imagistic frames that derive from a single source. Closure occurs at the beginning as well as at the end of the poem since each line is subordinated to a unitary idea. Other poems in this volume (*Regarding Wave*) exhibit a similar tendency to close off or spatialize organic movement by the imposition of some unified rhetorical frame.

Although these two versions of "Running Water Music" were presumably written around the same time, their differences illustrate a tension throughout Snyder's work between the poet who regards his lyric skills as a dimension of an ecological, natural order and the poet who places those skills in the service of an ethical system beyond those orders. Snyder, like Pound, wants to write Paradise on earth and wants his poem to be a simulacrum of the values and aspirations he holds for building the "new society in the shell of the old." The success of Snyder's endeavor has been due largely to his ability to realize Buddhist values of attention, observation, and sympathy without resorting to Western forms of mediation. But the attendant danger is that the poet will move from seer to prophet and begin to instruct where he might present.

"A WALKING GROVE OF TREES": PHILIP WHALEN

Gary Snyder's name is usually linked with two other poets, Philip Whalen and Lew Welch, whom he met while an undergraduate at Reed College during the early 1950s. They became lifelong friends, sharing common interests in Eastern religion and philosophy, the poetry of William Carlos Williams and Kenneth Rexroth, and the mountains of the Pacific Northwest. One of the distinguishing marks of this triad is their rather elegant calligraphic script, modeled on a distinctive sixteenth-century hand called "Arrighi." Their instruction in calligraphy came to them by a teacher of graphic arts and English literature at Reed, Lloyd Reynolds, who exerted a profound influence on most students who came into contact with him – especially Philip Whalen.[24] In addition to his courses in calligraphy, Reynolds taught courses in eighteenth-century literature, and it was in these classes that Whalen first read the work of Pope, Swift, and Dr. Johnson, the last of whom became a kind of literary model:

> (Not that Johnson was right – nor that I am trying to inherit his mantle as literary dictator but only the title *Doctor, i.e., teacher* – who is constantly studying). I do not put down the academy but have assumed its function in my own person, and in the strictest sense of the word – *academy:* a walking grove of trees.[25]

Philip Whalen's poetry can be best approached through the two disciplines taught in Lloyd Reynolds's classes: writing as inscription performed by the hand and writing as a kind of peripatetic walking. What began with calligraphic exercises in Lloyd Reynolds's classes has become an important dimension of Whalen's poetry. He fills notebooks with lettering exercises, doodles, lists, drawings, quotations, and short poems that together produce a handsome and often witty verbal collage. Poetry, he has said, is a "graph of the mind's movements" (OBH, 93), and these notebooks are a vivid instance of this graphic intention.[26] Whalen loves the sensuous properties of letters, and he embellishes them on the page, turning words into elaborate designs. He loves the sensuous properties of thought as well, and many of his poems seem to be a desultory record of his mind at play just as his notebook page is a congeries of verbal doodles:

> I look through the notebooks I've been doing and sometimes, . . . it seems like it's all completed but then other times there are just stray lines and if I look through it and see that some stray line connects it reminds me of some lines that are in another notebook and I look at that and it may all go together or it may not and the very longest poems that are in *Memoirs of an Interglacial Age* or the real long poems that are in *On Bear's Head* were done that way. (OW, 14)

This description is like the poems themselves, full of qualifications, second thoughts, and reversals, all held together with conjunctions.

Whalen's discursiveness seems the very opposite of Gary Snyder's hard, impersonal lyrics with their emphasis on economy and precision of statement. The poems feel leisurely, as though written during a long walk. And, indeed, many of them were written if not *on* then *about* a walk. Take, for example, "America inside & outside Bill Brown's House in Bolinas":

> Some kind of early waking take about bread (should be
> whole-grain flour &c.) cheese, wine, vegetables & fruits.
> I can leave the meat for whoever must have *that* responsibility
>   (a fit of enthusiastic praise here to all the horses,
>   cows, chickens, ducks, turkeys, geese, pheasants &c.
>   whose (bear, deer, elk, rabbit) generosity & benevolence
>   I have (whales, oysters, eels and sea urchins) so much
>   enjoyed; I guess I can leave them alone, now.)
>
> Shall I go past John Armstrong's house & wake him up
> with bells, but it might disturb Lynne and the baby so
> I write now good morning joy and beauty to John and Lynne
> and Angelina
>
> I do have to move around outside the house. The sun wasn't
> quite up – a great roaring pink and salmon commotion in the
> east flashes and glitters among eucalyptus trees – here are
> no fields where food is growing, no smell of night-soil,
> here's all this free and open country, a real luxury that
> we can afford this emptiness and the color of dawn
> radiating right out of the ground
>
> Flowers thick & various, fuchsias all over everything
> Houses all scattered, all different, unrelated to the ground
> or to each other except by road and waterpipe
> Each person isolated, carefully watching for some guy
> to make some funny move & then let him have it POW
> Right on the beezer
>
> Monday Indian eye in the roofbeams
> Drumhead flyrod curtain-ring cloud
> This is Tony's room. Sound of whistle-buoy as at Newport
> Roaring water for the suicide's bath.
>
>   Dumb dirty dog
>   Dirty dumb dog
>   Dumb dirty dog
>
> Dumb dirty dog, dirty dumb dog, dumb dirty dog.
> Black spayed Labrador bitch. Molly Brown.
>   4:XII:67
>   (HB, 11–12)

The date that closes the poem emphasizes the fact that this poem is very much *about* a particular day, its diversity and distractions. In the opening lines the poet tries to remember food he is to buy that day, but in the midst of his shopping list he delivers a parenthetical ode to the various animals he has "so much / enjoyed." Then he speculates on where he will walk, a meditation that leads him to "John Armstrong's house," where he (at least hypothetically) leaves a message of greeting. He then reflects on the openness and freshness of the landscape of Bolinas at sunrise, the "luxury" of such "emptiness." But in the midst of this passage of celebration, he reflects on the houses of the neighborhood, "all scattered, all different, unrelated to the ground / or to each other except by road and waterpipe." The people who live in them are "isolated, carefully watching for some guy / to make some funny move & then let him have it POW / Right on the beezer." This observation is a casual aside like all the others, but it introduces a note of threat and uncertainty that qualifies the celebratory mood of the moment.

Soon, however, Whalen returns to his lists, noting the interior of "Tony's room" and the sound of water roaring into – and then out of – the "suicide's bath." Despite this ominous note, Whalen's reference to suicide is simply a form of self-mockery, as excessive in one direction as his celebration of animals is excessive in another. He ends his poem as he ends his bath with the sound of water rushing out the drain, rendered by the repeated phrase, "Dumb dirty dog." And even this phrase, chosen presumably for its onomatopoeia, leads to a final image: the literal "dirty dog" who lives at Bill Brown's house, Molly Brown.

In this poem we become so taken up with the welter of details and texture of sounds that we miss the title: This is a poem about "America," both inside and outside a specific house in a specific place. At another level it is about the America that lives inside and outside one citizen, a fact stressed by the poem's oscillation between descriptive and reflective passages. Whalen sees the glory and wonder of a landscape as well as the distrust and paranoia that lie behind the walls of "separate houses." He does not propose some panacea for joining the two landscapes but *shows* them as being part of the same world. And he does more: He walks, both physically and mentally among the houses, linking them together by praising, identifying, and noticing them. And he leaves notes to link persons by bonds of affection and care. Ultimately, he creates a poem that is its own kind of personal note to the world – as fragile as a notebook page or grocery list, but in its own way an enduring "fit of praise" for that which might be forgotten.

Whalen's poetry in general could be seen as providing such links between things; he sees an octopus as a "yummy and noble beast" or a spider web as "polygonal vacancies," but he notices himself noticing as well. It is in this quality of self-reflexiveness that he differs most radically from Gary Snyder. Whalen fully inhabits his poems, often relying on the ironic or melodramatic quality of his voice. Both poets reach toward the historic occasion, but for Whalen the occasion is always framed by an experiencing subject and a specific voice.

That voice is multiple in the range of its registers and personae, constantly shifting to accommodate a mood or heighten drama. Whalen can be alternately cranky, reflective, or pompous in the same poem. One of his characteristic voices is that of the philosopher manqué who ponders life's mysteries from a slightly pompous and ironic perspective. The titles of his poems read like chapter titles taken from treatises on art and aesthetics: "The Art of Literature," "Philippic, Against Whitehead and a Friend," "20:vii:58, On Which I Renounce the Notion of Social Responsibility," "All About Art and Life," "Theophany," "Technicalities for Jack Spicer," "Homage to Lucretius." These poems often interrogate a proposition by subjecting it to the author's immediate circumstances. Whalen at times resembles Wallace Stevens in his attempt to provide reflective variations on a single perspective. Consider "Absolute Realty Co.: Two Views":

1.
THE GREAT GLOBE ITSELF

I keep hearing the airplanes tell me
The world is tinier every minute
I begin believing them, getting scared.
I forget how the country looks when I'm flying:
Very small brown or green spots of cities on the edges
                    of great oceans, forests, deserts

There's enough room. I can afford to be pleasant & cordial to you
                    . . . at least for a while . . .
Remembering the Matto Grosso, Idaho, Montana, British Columbia,
New Hampshire, other waste places,
All the plains and mountains where I can get away from you
To remember you all the more fondly,
All your nobler virtues.

                                                            7:v:64

2.
Vulture Peak

            Although my room is very small
            The ceiling is high.

            Space enough for me and the 500 books I need most
            The great pipe organ and Sebastian Bach in 46 volumes
                    (I really NEED the Bachgesellschaft Edition)
                    will arrive soon, if I have any luck at all.

            Plenty room for everybody:
            Manjusri and 4700 bodhisattvas, arhats, pratyekabuddhas,
                    disciples, hearers, Devas, Gandharvas, Apsaras, kinnaras,
                    gnomes, giants, nauch girls, great serpents, garudas,

> demons, men, and beings not human, flower ladies,
> water babies, beach boys, poets, angels, policemen, taxi
> drivers, gondoliers, fry cooks and the Five Marx
> Brothers
>
> All of us happy, drinking tea, eating *Linsertorte,*
> Admiring my soft plum-colored rug
> The view of Mt. Diablo.
>
> 11:v:64
(OBH, 276–7)

The "absolute" real is relative, a matter of perspective and point of view. From the air, the world seems large enough to dispel any worries about overpopulation. From the perspective of Whalen's room, the world is no less capacious. The title of the second section, "Vulture Peak," invokes the famous story of Śakyamuni, the historical Buddha who in a sermon to his disciples at the Mount of the Holy Vulture held up a bouquet of flowers without saying a word. No one in the congregation understood the significance of this gesture except Mahakasyapa, who simply smiled at his teacher. Śakyamuni responded, "I have the most precious treasure, spiritual and transcendental, which this moment I hand over to you, O venerable Mahakasyapa!" To some extent, Whalen is playing Śakyamuni by refusing to make reality "absolute" and offering, instead, a vision of infinite potentiality. Vulture Peak, the site of the sermon, is replaced in the poem by Mt. Diablo as Whalen focuses his final line on a specific place in the distance – a nice retrieval of that aerial view of the world initiated in the poem's first section. Whalen's cheerful, open-armed embrace of both "views" of reality dispenses with formal analysis and puts the burden of proof squarely on the shoulders of the perceiving individual.

This emphasis on the situational frame resembles the "personism" of New York poets like Frank O'Hara and Ted Berrigan, whose poetry insists on the temporary and contingent in art. Consider Whalen's "Hymnus ad Patrem Sinensis":

> I praise those ancient Chinamen
> Who left me a few words,
> Usually a pointless joke or a silly question
> A line of poetry drunkenly scrawled on the margin of a quick
>   splashed picture – bug, leaf,
>   caricature of Teacher
>   on paper held together now by little more than ink
>   & their own strength brushed momentarily over it
> Their world & several others since
> Gone to hell in a handbasket, they knew it –
> Cheered as it whizzed by –

> & conked out among the busted spring rain cherryblossom winejars
> Happy to have saved us all.
>
> (OBH, 61–2)

As in many of O'Hara's "I do this I do that" poems, Whalen's rhetoric here performs and demonstrates the very immediacy he admires in "those ancient Chinamen." Phrases like "Gone to hell in a handbasket" or words like "whizzed," "conked," and "busted" have the same particularity and contingency of the Zen art described in the opening stanza. The ponderous Latin title is gradually debunked as his hymn of praise illustrates the endurance of the absolutely temporary.

Whalen has acknowledged the influence of William Carlos Williams on his development of these qualities of brevity and immediacy. One can see this influence in the short, single-image poems like "A Couple Blocks South of the Heian Shrine":

> She builds a fire of small clean square sticks
> balanced on top of a small white clay hibachi
> which stands on a sewing-machine set between her
> house wall and the street where my taxi honks past
> (HB, 10)

The four, evenly balanced lines steadily "build" the image of the woman until the last few words, when the camera swings around to reveal the observer driving by in his taxi. Whalen's other lyric mode comes from Japanese haiku, which, in his hands, becomes a considerably more self-conscious genre:

> 25:I:68
>
> Sadly unroll sleepingbag
> The missing lid for teapot!
> (HB, 12)

> Saturday 15:ix:62
>
> No help for it. I'm so funny –
>   looking that I can't see the trees.
> (OBH, 175)

Such sudden, often whimsical observations form the basis for his longer poems – and Whalen is a writer of long, occasionally *very* long, poems. Works like "My Songs Induce Prophetic Dreams," "Minor Moralia," "Homage to Rodin," "The Best of It," "The Education Continues Along," and the book-length *Scenes of Life at the Capital* allow Whalen a broad canvas on which to trace the movements of his ruminative, speculative imagination. *Scenes of Life at the Capital* is a case in point. It was written while Whalen lived in Kyoto, Japan, during the years 1969–71. It was the period of the late expansionist stages of the Vietnam War, and in a sense the poem is about the war seen from the standpoint of Asia. The "capital" in the title is both Kyoto and Washington, although the latter makes an appearance only through its effects on the rest of the world. The many references to Western food, clothing, television, and literature suggest the enormous influence of American life on the East. But lest the reader expect a polemical jeremiad on the order of Robert Duncan's "Up-Rising" or Robert Bly's "The Teeth Mother, Naked at Last," *Scenes of Life* remains quietly meditative. The poem seems more a journal than an antiwar poem, but this is part of its strength: that it focuses its global theme on one Western individual trying to make sense of his cultural origins in an Eastern setting.

There is not enough space here to do justice to *Scenes of Life at the Capital,* but one can see how Whalen focuses global issues on the particular in a shorter poem like "Homage to Rodin." Like so many others, it is a "walking" poem, a sort of docent tour of three pieces of sculpture in San Francisco: Rodin's *The Thinker* located at the Palace of the Legion of Honor, *The Shades* adjacent to the palace, and finally Rodin's small statue *Iris* at the De Young Museum.[27] These three pieces of sculpture serve as foci for Whalen's reflections on various subjects, the general theme of which is an ideal of muscular beauty embodied in the work of Rodin. The poem's three sections describe the poet lost in a series of gloomy reflections on the state of the world until he is able to relieve his depression by recognizing the possibility of human intercourse made palpable through art.

Whalen begins by interrogating Rodin's heroic nude, *The Thinker:*

> Rodin says: "ANIMAL WHO SITS DOWN
>   which is one difference, apparently doing
>   nothing
>   TO CALCULATE, CEREBRATE"
>   & that's of the first significance:
>   Meat thinking and got hands to build you what he
>   Means or throttle you if you get in the way, either action
>   without too many qualms
>   (OBH, 225)

Whalen answers those who dismiss Rodin's perpetuation of the heroic tradition:

> Old stuff, we say, "Oh, Ro-*dan.* . . .
> Rilke's employer . . . oh yes, Rodin, but after all –
> Archipenko, Arp, Brancusi, Henry Moore –
> Sculpture for our time . . ."
>   (they appear in Harpo's Bazzooo, modern, chic,

> seriously discussed in *Vogue* –
> Epstein and Lipchitz are OUT, the heroic
> tedious as Rodin)
>
> (OBH, 226)

Rodin's *Thinker* reinforces the outmoded idea that thinking is done by a physical being, "BODY: with head containing brains, / hands to grab with, build. . . ." The art of Rodin, unlike the more streamlined work of Brancusi or Arp, is Whitmanian, "Hulking Beefy Nude." The male figure, subject of "old *New Yorker* cartoons," is valued all the more for its solidity and mass.

In the second section, Whalen frames his celebration of the heroic mode against the backdrop of contemporary dehumanization. He describes himself walking along the cliffs overlooking the Golden Gate straits, beginning at Playland at the Beach and ending at the Palace of the Legion of Honor. At Playland, he pauses to admire the merry-go-round and "2 old men" who watch it:

> No amount of sympathetic observation will do any good
> Why not get older, fatter, poorer
> Fall apart in creaky amusement park and let the world holler
> Softly shining pewter ocean
> Or let it quit, who cares?
>
> (OBH, 227)

What appears to be a fairly casual question, "who cares?", becomes the central issue of the poem: Who cares enough about the physical world to see it as a dimension of the human universe? Who cares enough about other humans to sympathize truly? Some answer would seem to be provided by the Palace of the Legion of Honor, which is dedicated to the war dead. But the monument seems as empty as the concrete bunkers left over from World War II that molder on the cliffs overlooking the straits. The "Formal building pillared propylon and stoa" devoted to the principles of "HONNEUR ET PATRIE" strikes a hollow note, even if it houses the work of Rodin.

Presiding over the entire vista is another Rodin statue, *The Shades,* three figures who stand "heads bent down, three arms pointing toward / The ground that covers them." But instead of honoring "the noble prospectless dead," they are "blanked, puzzled-looking." Their legacy seems only to be a quality of "loose hatefulness" that Whalen finds embodied in a conversation between a hysterical young kid and his equally hysterical father:

> Fat kid wants expensive camera Daddy to put two-bits into Cliff House
> binoculars his father screams in reply, furious insane, "Whaddaya wan-
> na looka them rocks whaddaya gonna see in this fog?" "Come on!" the

fat kid hollers, "Gimme twenny-five cents, put the twenny-fi'cents in, gimme ten-ficens I wanna see them !R O C K S! out there is COME ON! Gimme twenty-five cents!" and his father screaming back at him like he might tear the kid limb from limb but actually looking in another direction, quite relaxed. (OBH, 228)

Whalen juxtaposes to this incident a woman playing in the surf who, "Oblivious to her girlfriend hollering at her from the sand . . . plunges, laughing, through a wave." Her gesture stands in vivid contrast to the hysteria of the father and son and introduces, for the first time, an idea of independence and solitude that is an alternative to the personal malaise the poet observes everywhere.

In the poem's third section, dedicated to the waterlilies growing in the reflection pool in front of the De Young Museum, Whalen becomes less gloomy and begins to contemplate forces of growth and life that exist near to hand. He finds solace in the sexual appearance of waterlilies, "No mystery, genes in every cell manifest themselves / Bulb of the earth showing itself here as lilies / The summer flowers, underwater globes of winter all the same." The flowers remind him of a former lover, whose memory is invoked by the manifest sexuality of the flowers:

> Since you'd gone I hadn't thought of other women, only you
> Alive inside my head the rest of me
>   ghosted up and down the town alone
> Thinking how we were together
> You bright as I am dark, hidden
>
> Inside the Museum I see Rodin's IRIS
> Torso of a woman, some sort of dancer's exercise
> Left foot down, toes grasping the ground
> Right hand clutches right instep
> Right elbow dislocating
> Reveals the flower entirely open, purely itself
> Unconscious (all concentration's on the pose;
>   she has no head)
>
> Its light blasts all my foggy notions
> Snaps me back into the general flesh, an order
> Greater than my personal gloom
> Frees me, I let you go at last
> I can reach and touch again, summer flesh & winter bronze
> Opposite seasons of a single earth.
>
>   (OBH, 229–30)

In these concluding lines, all of the previous descriptions and images are refocused. Whalen is "hidden" inside the museum and inside himself until he encounters a female counterpart to *The Thinker*, who "blasts" all of his "foggy notions" and provides a "light" to match his darkness. Rodin's sculpture is not Keats's Grecian urn, freezing time in mythic stillness. It is a sensual object that returns the observer to the "general flesh, an order / Greater than my personal gloom." The poet has reconciled a series of dichotomies, "summer flesh & winter bronze," life and art, immediacy and reflection, by releasing his focus from himself and looking outward. Rodin's *Thinker* had already proposed an ideal of solitude, but as the second section of the poem evidences, the ideal has not become identified with Whalen's own condition. It is only when Whalen is able to relate Rodin's sculpture to another person that he is able to get outside his "foggy notions" and "touch again."

Despite Whalen's numerous disparaging remarks about the "mothball smell" (HB, 60) emanating from English romantic poetry, "Homage to Rodin" resembles poems like "This Lime Tree Bower My Prison" or "Fears in Solitude," in which Coleridge broods on "Carnage and groans beneath this blessed sun" only to discover at the end of the poem "a livelier impulse and a dance of thought" inspired by his ability to project himself beyond his own self-consciousness. Whalen, like Coleridge, comes to a similar understanding by first dramatizing the conflicting postures – righteous anger, self-mortification, reverence, self-delusion – that the ego provides as temporary hedges against solitude. Only after projecting these voices of self-identity can he see the world without grasping it:

> One of the most wonderful and magical actions
> We can perform: Let something alone.
>
> (HB, 85)

Philip Whalen's poetry is firmly rooted in the romantic anxiety that Geoffrey Hartman has characterized as "anti-self-consciousness."[28] The poet, seeking one kind of dissolution of the ego, despairs over his tendency toward extreme self-analysis, thereby raising self-concern to an even higher level. Whalen often wants to "Let something alone" but must account, at the same time, for cognitive and ethical frames in which "something" exists at all. His great advantage, unlike that of most other poets of the San Francisco Renaissance, lies in being able to manipulate a wide range of registers and voices. He is also arguably the wittiest poet of the group, able to debunk the more transcendental claims of his peers without sacrificing Buddhist beliefs in numinous reality.

"THE INCARNATE NOW"

The title of this chapter is taken from a poem by Gary Snyder, "Vapor Trails":

Twin streaks twice higher than cumulus,
Precise plane icetracks in the vertical blue
Cloud-flaked light-shot shadow-arcing
Field of all future war, edging off to space.

Young expert U.S. pilots waiting
The day of criss-cross rockets
And white blossoming smoke of bomb,
The air world torn and staggered for these
Specks of brushy land and ant-hill towns –

    I stumble on the cobble rockpath,
Passing through temples,
Watching for two-leaf pine
     – spotting that design.

                  (BC, 37)

The final stanza could speak for both Snyder and Whalen in their attempt to identify connections between natural, social, and spiritual orders. In the case of "Vapor Trails," the design exists at two levels: those features that distinguish one plant from another and those that indicate American global adventurism. Both levels are readable by the poet as a "design," implying both structure and intent, and it is ever Snyder's purpose to articulate those correspondences in his capacities as ecological activist and as poet. Writing is a kind of hermeneutics in which, like his transcendentalist forebears, Snyder reads the signature of the divine etched in the great book of nature. These patterns do not translate into nonhuman, transmundane terms, but reflect, like the whorls of the redwood, the larger life of the planet.

Like Snyder, Whalen sees himself as a reader of larger designs in things, but in his case the man, Philip Whalen, is always part of the design – a large, sensual, often cranky, sometimes rhapsodic, and always curious historical individual who not only spots the design but suffers its effects. To adapt a remark by Frank O'Hara, he is "needed by things,"[29] not because things are valuable in themselves but because they provide him with occasions for reflection and observation. He is more willing than Snyder to find the design in the artifacts and intellectual traditions of western Europe or in the distinctly material world of the city. He admits to liking such decadent pleasures as linzertorte, Rodin, Edward Gibbon, Charles Baudelaire, ice cream, and Gabriel Fauré. He has a "taste for marble in a wooden age / a weakness for the epic that betrays / a twiddy mind." Whalen's openness to the multitude of things, natural and cultural, creates a certain vulnerability that allows him a wide variety of what I have called "voices." These voices allow him to dramatize the specific contours of the mind as it reads the world.

In my introduction to this chapter I spoke of the sacramental impulse among San Francisco poets – their attempt to participate with a numinous or spiritual presence found in nature and realized through a process of self-expiation. It may seem that, at least in speaking of Whalen, I have moved rather far from my topic. Whalen thrusts his ego directly in front of the reader and seems far more concerned with listing the attributes of birds and plants than he does with enlightenment. Such acts of naming and annotating are very much a part of Zen practice. As Whalen observes, there is

> the problem of right now: what are you doing right this minute and how do you get through that and how can you make it alive, vivid, solid? In Zen there is a great deal to understand – the long historical tradition, the connections with the various sutras and so forth – but the Zen experience cannot be explained, you have to be it, you have to practice it. (OW, 60)

Poetry, like Zen practice, involves participating with the "right now," whether presented objectively in photographic images or filtered through the mind's eye. New Critical versions of sacramentalism tended to emphasize the parallel between metaphor and incarnation and the ability of the creative imagination to synthesize a concrete universal. For Snyder and Whalen there is no hierarchical relation between flesh and spirit, word and logos. Snyder holds that "the universe and all creatures in it are intrinsically in a state of complete wisdom, love and compassion; acting in natural response and mutual interdependence" (EEH, 90). The poet's task is to respond in kind, provide constant testimony to the "mutual interdependence" of all things. "I keep trying to live as if this world were heaven," Philip Whalen says (OBH, 346), and he and Gary Snyder have devoted their poetic careers to erasing the "as if."

4

"Cave of Resemblances, Cave of Rimes"

Tradition and Repetition in Robert Duncan

TRADITION AND THE HERETICAL TALENT

Robert Duncan always insisted that the renaissance of San Francisco writing had its basis not in the North Beach milieu of the mid-1950s but in the group of writers who met around him in Berkeley during the late 1940s.[1] The "Berkeley Renaissance" represented, for young poets like Duncan, Jack Spicer, and Robin Blaser, the first flowering of a Bay Area literary community based less on region than on coterie spirit. Writing to Blaser in 1957 following the publication of the "San Francisco Scene" issue of *Evergreen,* Duncan makes this distinction clear: "It's just that by some damnd incident of geography I am so solidly placed in region, and not in coterie. And I'm a coterie poet not a regional one."[2] The acknowledgment of such a coterie spirit would seem to reinforce Charles Olson's accusation that the San Francisco scene had become an "école des Sages ou Mages" like the theosophical community in Ojai, California.[3] Duncan did not share Olson's localist ethos, preferring instead an almost cultic sense of group identity. His enabling myth of poetic community was based less on the accidents of proximity or the lures of region than on the revival of heretical traditions within a brotherhood of loyal believers. That this brotherhood was often homosexual was no small feature of Duncan's projection.

The paradox of Duncan's antiregionalist remarks is that of the writers considered in this book, he is the only one native to the area. He grew up in Alameda and the Central Valley and, with the exception of brief stays on the East Coast and Mallorca, Duncan has made San Francisco his home. What he distrusts about the designation "regionalist" is the separation of place from culture, the divorce of locale from the poetics of locale. "Place" is not a geographical or demographic entity so much as a conceptual field in which propositions of place are generated. His most famous lines on this subject suggest that it is not the person who makes the place but the place that permits the person to enter it:

> Often I am Permitted to Return to a Meadow
>
> as if it were a scene made-up by the mind,
> that is not mine, but is a made place,
>
> that is mine, it is so near to the heart,
> an eternal pasture folded in all thought
> so that there is a hall therein
>
> that is a made place, created by light
> wherefrom the shadows that are forms fall.[4]

Clearly "place," like the poem itself, is an imaginative construct, the boundaries of which are constantly under revision. Such notions derive, in part, from Duncan's adopted parents, whose theosophical teachings portrayed the West as Atlantis, a spiritual plentitude waiting to be revived. And it was this same sense of spiritual renewal within specific cultural and theological traditions that he felt should define any literary movement with which he was involved.[5] In this sense, then, Duncan's literary renaissance was "traditional."

Among the poets who met with Duncan in the late 1940s in Berkeley, the issue of tradition loomed large. They were less worried about Eliot's then-dominant version – an organic totality in which the values among the canon are altered by the noncanonical – than by the prescriptive application of certain aspects of Eliot's criticism to delimit "a" tradition, presumably one circumscribed by Western, Judeo-Christian cultural values. Certainly the ethical imperative behind an aesthetics of "impersonality" was anathema to the kind of testimentary and elegiac poetry appearing in the Bay Area during that period. Looking back to this period from the vantage of the later 1950s, Duncan remembered "powers of love" in

> the Berkeley we believed
> grove of Arcady –
>
> that there might be
> potencies in common things,
> "princely manipulations of the real."
>   (OF,14)

The spirit of romance that such lines memorialize is an obvious contrast to New Critical versions of Eliot's tradition. It is not that Duncan and his peers substituted the romantic tradition for some Augustan fashion of the times – a replacement of one canon with another – but that he so radically transformed the notion of tradition altogether. And this transformation was made possible through the more insurgent terms of romanticism itself.

For Duncan, the romantic tradition represents more than a historical period or canonical body of texts. It represents an ancient quest for knowledge that, for a variety of reasons, has been suppressed or marginalized. In cultural terms, this quest is most vital when informed by heterodox theories and religious practices of the sort that animated the Hellenistic period or the early Renaissance. Duncan often refers to theological and philosophical writings from these periods as being a fruitful admixture of Eastern and Western, classical and modern, pagan and Christian influences.[6] In literary terms, this quest is reflected through those works in which a mythopoeic strain is dominant. Myth occurs in two forms, "the lordly and humble, . . . mythological vision and folklorish phantasy" (FC,27). The spirit of romance can be found alike in *The Odyssey* and in "The Owl and the Pussycat" or "Wynken, Blinken and Nod." For Duncan, romanticism involves "powers of love" that are primordial, locked in the forms of biological and psychological life but intuited in the narratives and images of certain intellectual traditions. Because of their potency, these ideas are deemed spiritually dangerous in times of religious orthodoxy or artistically inferior in times of cultural orthodoxy. They cannot appear except in veiled or occult forms, or else they manifest themselves in despised "naive" or sentimental genres like children's stories or fables. What Duncan calls "permission" refers to the poet's ability to participate (not control) these "potencies in common things" and release them, beyond all reference to literature, to a swirling, changing universe.

This participatory stance toward the "lordly and humble" aspects of tradition has little to do with what we usually designate as "originality," the creation of new or unique artistic artifacts. In a paradox central to his poetics, Duncan speaks of his originality as an ability to resuscitate origins:

> I am concerned with forms and not with convention, with an art and not with a literature, I may be a modernist. But I do not care particularly about the brand-newness of a form, I am not a futurist, I work toward immediacy; and I do not aim at originality. The meanings in language are not original, any more than the sounds; they accrue from all the generations of human use from the mists of the *schwa* and first objects to the many vowels and common universe of things of today; they are radical, sending roots back along our own roots. I am a traditionalist, a seeker after origins, not an original.[7]

The poet's individual talent is expressed not in originality – the transformation of tradition as Eliot has defined it – but in an ability to respond to the demands of immediacy. Implicit in this idea is the notion of repetition or what Duncan prefers to call "rime," by which original moments, events, and ideas are interrelated into a dense weave. The structure of rime or repetition refers to the poem's ability to resonate with the world without either representing or destroying it. Where "tradition," to the New Critical aesthetic, implied artisanal mastery within a specifically literary history, for Duncan and others of his generation it meant cooperation with and response to the largest field of creative life.

Duncan's radical traditionalism marks him as one of the most contradictory of contemporary poets. He enjoys claiming as his orthodoxy the rejection of all orthodoxies. He gleefully professes to be "unbaptized, uninitiated, ungraduated, unanalyzed,"[8] a parody of Eliot's description of himself as Anglican, royalist, and monarchist. Duncan resolutely refuses to accept the designation "modernist" or (more vehemently) "postmodernist." As he says in an interview, "I'm not a Modernist. . . . I read Modernism as Romanticism; and I finally begin to feel myself pretty much a 19th century mind."[9] This idiosyncratic stance is accompanied by a series of seeming contradictions: He is a poet of "open" forms who continues to write, as well, in classical modes like the sonnet and ballad; he is a firm believer in verbal immediacy and testimony who, nevertheless, uses a heightened rhetoric more appropriate to the Victorian age; he is an avowedly romantic poet who has written masques and satires in the Augustan manner; he is a political poet who, while attacking American imperialism in Southeast Asia, is still capable of celebrating war. The litany of artists whom he is ambitious to "emulate, imitate, reconstrue, approximate, duplicate" would confuse even the most subtle literary genealogist. It includes

> Ezra Pound, Gertrude Stein, Joyce, Virginia Woolf, Dorothy Richardson, Wallace Stevens, D. H. Lawrence, Edith Sitwell, Cocteau, Mallarmé, Marlowe, St. John of the Cross, Yeats, Jonathan Swift, Jack Spicer, Céline, Charles Henri Ford, Rilke, Lorca, Kafka, Arp, Max Ernst, St.-John Perse, Prévert, Laura Riding, Apollinaire, Brecht, Shakespeare, Ibsen, Strindberg, Joyce Cary, Mary Butts, Freud, Dali, Spenser, Stravinsky, William Carlos Williams and John Gay.
> Higglety-pigglety: Euripides and Gilbert. The Strawhat reviewers, Goethe (of the *Autobiography* – I have never read *Faust*) and H. D.[10]

Such eclecticism was found to earn Duncan some detractors, but his most important negative assessment came not from a conservative critic but from his peer and mentor, Charles Olson. In "Against Wisdom as Such," Olson admonishes Duncan for aestheticizing knowledge, removing it from its sources and processes. Wisdom, Olson feels, "like style, is the man." It is not

> Extricable in any sort of a statement of itself; even though – and here is the catch – there be "wisdom," that it must be sought, and that "truths" can be come on (they are so overwhelming and so simple there does exist the temptation to see them as "universal"). But they are, in

no wise, or at the gravest loss, verbally separated. They stay the man.
As his skin is. As his life. And to be parted with only as that is.[11]

Reading between the lines of Olson's cryptic prose we may see a certain
Coleridgean faith in the organic synthesis of ideas and form, an assertion
of the creative will over a world of fluctuating ideas. Duncan is accused
of trafficking in knowledge for its own sake without reference to its
immediate applicability to the individual's life and projects. Wisdom, for
the creator of *The Maximus Poems,* is the product of the self-reliant individual, wresting time out of a continuum in order to create rhythm
rather than suffer its effects:

> . . . I compell
> backwards I compell Gloucester
> to yield, to change
>   Polis
> is this[12]

Duncan's response to "Against Wisdom as Such" exhibits a Freudian
bias in favor of surfaces; wisdom is regarded as variable fiction rather
than as symbol:

> In a sense [Olson] is so keen upon the *virtu* of reality that he rejects my
> "wisdom" not as it might seem at first glance because "wisdom" is a
> vice; but because my wisdom is not real wisdom. He suspects, and
> rightly, that I indulge myself in pretentious fictions. I, however, at this
> point take enuf delight in the available glamor that I do not stop to
> trouble the cheapness of such stuff. I like rigor and even clarity as a
> quality of a work – that is, as I like muddle and floaty vagaries. It is the
> intensity of conception that moves me. (FC, 65)

The argument between the two men (an enormously generative one, as
Don Byrd points out)[13] is an argument over two notions of tradition:
one as the archaeological (and archetypal) structure of certain dynamic
ideas realized throughout history by a few capable imaginations, the
other as the open-ended series of variations on a corrupt and corruptible
text. Olson's theory of tradition is recuperative; Duncan's is interpretive.
For Olson, a writer like Melville transforms not only literature but physical space as well; he exists as a nodal point in the nineteenth-century
imagination along with Keats, Rimbaud, the geometers, Bolyai and
Lobatschewsky, and the mathematician Riemann, within which constellation an entirely new conception of space was developed.[14] For Duncan, by contrast, previous authors represent spirit guides in the contemporary poet's attempt to reanimate a core myth of creation. They help
lead the poet back to a "cave of resemblances" in which everything
rhymes.[15]

As Michael Bernstein says, this treatment of past masters involves a reciprocal recognition on the part of both master and ephebe:

> But if . . . a poet's "permission" to enter into his poethood depends upon a reciprocal selection – his being "called" by a certain constellation of "masters" requires, of course, that he himself also be ready to heed just those voices, be ready, that is, to constitute himself as their successor – then one of the surest indices of a potentially new voice is the enrichment/subversion he can bring to the established heritage of his own mentors, his capacity significantly to add to the horizon of "pre-texts" already marked out as canonic by the prior selection of his teachers.[16]

As verification of Bernstein's remarks, one has only to look into Duncan's encyclopedic meditation on modernism, *The H.D. Book*, in which the poet's personal history is fused with a reading of certain modernists so that, ultimately, the distance between private and literary life is broken down. The poet H. D. is the subject of the book, but not simply as an influence on Duncan's work. Rather, she projects and anticipates Duncan's life and art just as in her work she sees herself as the reincarnation of certain prophetic and visionary women from the past. By reading through her works (and the works of her generation) Duncan is permitted to reenter the world of his personal identity in which fictions, stories, poems, and tales are formative influences. In fact, a substantial portion of the early chapters of *The H.D. Book* are devoted to the very earliest hearings of certain poems (H. D.'s "Heat," Basho's frog-pond-plash poem, Joyce's "I Hear an Army Charging Upon the Land") and to the circumstances of their initial appearances in his life. He wants to record the luminous aura surrounding his own entry into story so that he may suggest how this moment "rhymes" with his later vocation as a poet. The great reading of modernism (and ultimately of tradition in general) becomes a reading of origins.[17]

Although Duncan's appropriation of modernism in *The H.D. Book* is phrased in aesthetic terms, it has its own oppositional force in the way that it conflicts with a dominant tradition of high art. Where Pound and Eliot established their ties to Italian Renaissance poets or the English metaphysicals, Duncan willfully includes sources well beyond the specifically literary masters. And more important for our concern with artistic communities, Duncan's literary genealogy conflicts with that of peers like Olson or Creeley (but not with Spicer or Blaser) in its feminization of tradition. Duncan's alliances to modernist forebears like Gertrude Stein, H. D., Marianne Moore, Dame Edith Sitwell, Dorothy Richardson, Virginia Woolf, and others conflict with Olson and Creeley's predominantly male line, with its valorization of Lawrentian sexuality and Poundian phallocentric historicism. One of the major agendas of *The*

H.D. Book is Duncan's creation of ties not only to a great woman modernist but to the women teachers and friends who brought H. D. to the young poet:

> Writing these opening pages of a book "On H. D." or "For H. D." a tribute and a study, I came at this point to see this first part of or movement of the book as relating how I had found my life in poetry through the agency of certain women and how I had then perhaps a special estimation not only of the masters of that art but of its mistresses, so that certain women writers instructed as well as inspired me.[18]

These lines suggest that Duncan's willful eclecticism is a matter not only of textuality but of sexuality as well. When Duncan refers to his entry into a "life in poetry," he means the coincidence of his own sexual preference, as a homosexual, with a tradition of women writers and teachers. Without denying Duncan's own considerable debt to figures like Lawrence and Pound, I would add that this reading must be tempered by an examination of the way his version of modernism is shaped within a narrative of personal and sexual identity. Hence his reading of other traditions becomes a way of establishing a canon of which he is the author as well as the representation.

READING, WRITING, AND REPETITION

What I have described as Duncan's reading of modernism as the revival of a certain (heretical) tradition within the context of a coterie spirit involves more than adopting a critical stance toward certain authors; it implies specific hermeneutic acts within individual poems. For Duncan, writing is always a form of reading, the use of poetry as an occasion for interpretive acts that lead outward to a larger realm of story. He often figures the interplay between reading and writing in terms of Jacob wrestling with the Angel, an allegory as much about interpretation as about salvation.[19] Instead of recovering the text in an act that leaves it essentially unchanged, the poet actively translates its terms into a new text:

> Our work is to arouse in a contemporary consciousness reverberations of old myth, to prepare the ground so that when we return to read we will see our modern texts charged with a plot that had already begun before the first signs and signatures we have found worked upon the walls of Altamira or Pech-Merle.[20]

It is not simply that the poet represents old stories and myths thematically but that the poem itself, by actively interrogating those texts in the present act of writing, reenacts a story that has been lost to cultural memory.

This charged, participatory act of reading gains definition through contemporary theories of "open field verse," to be sure, but for Duncan its origins can be found in the theosophical tradition that he inherited from his adopted family.[21] For his parents, "the truth of things was esoteric (locked inside) or occult (masked by) the apparent, and one needed a 'lost' key in order to piece out the cryptogram of who wrote Shakespeare or who created the universe and what his real message was" (FC, 3). Within this environment every event was significant as an element in a larger, cosmological scheme. Although Duncan has never practiced within any theosophical religion, he has easily translated its terms into works like Freud's *Interpretation of Dreams,* which proposes an analogous form of interpretation. Within both theosophical and Freudian hermeneutics, story is not simply a diversion or fiction but an "everlasting omen of what is" (OF, 7). The dream becomes a model for the way that omen is received as a cryptic condensation and displacement of an imperative or sentence:

> I ask the unyielding Sentence that shows Itself forth in the
> language as I make it,
>   Speak! For I name myself your master, who come to serve.
>   Writing is first a search in obedience.
>
> (OF, 12)

These lines from the first of the "Structure of Rime" series reflect the basic double bind in Duncan's version of romanticism: The poet "makes" sentences only as he is made by them; he obeys a law of writing that he may write himself. The sentence is both an imperative (an "unyielding Sentence") and a grammatical construct, just as the dream text is *beyond* yet *of* the dreamer:

> It is in the dream itself that we seem entirely creatures, without imagination, as if moved by a plot or myth told by a story-teller who is not ourselves. Wandering and wondering in a foreign land or struggling in the meshes of a nightmare, we cannot escape the compelling terms of the dream unless we wake, anymore than we can escape the terms of our living reality unless we die.[22]

The consequences of this collapsing of subject and object is a poetry deeply conscious of its textuality. Many of Duncan's finest poems are readings of other texts, his own poem serving as meditation and transformation: *Medieval Scenes* (1947) originated around a series of epigraphs that inspired the individual poems; "A Poem Beginning with a Line by Pindar" reads the story of Eros and Psyche into a line by the Greek poet: *Passages* begins with two texts from the Emperor Julian's "Hymn to the Mother of the Gods" and includes many other texts within its individual poems; *A Seventeenth Century Suite* consists of variations on poems by

Raleigh, Southwell, Herbert, and others; *Dante Etudes* similarly involves poetic reflections on passages from Dante's prose; and poems often begin in the margins or blank pages of the poet's own books *(Poems from the Margins of Thom Gunn's Moly, The Five Songs)*. In such long series, other texts appear within Duncan's poems not as privileged signs of cultural order (as they often do in Pound or Eliot) but as generative elements in the composing process.

Duncan's mythopoeic hermeneutics derives, as I have said, from his family's theosophy as well as from Freudian dream analysis and romanticism. Such models propose a search for origins, but for Duncan this search is not merely a constitutive recollection of lost innocence. Returning to a "place of first permission" is to see it for the first time since, to take a phrase from Williams, "the spaces it opens are new places / inhabited by hordes / heretofore unrealized."[23] That is, the poetic descent into origins occurs in time, the present thus contributing to and charging those early stories with new significance. A naive reading of Duncan's poetic statements on the subject of origins might see him yearning toward some totalizing or archetypal scheme of correspondences whereby time, in a Proustian or Joycean epiphany, is at last stilled or transcended. Although Duncan's moments of "first permission" serve to link him to the past, they do so only to engage the present more fully. On the one hand, he desires a kind of participation with the world; on the other, he recognizes that the temporal apprehension of the world structures the way that involvement might occur:

> But this putting together and rendering anew operates in our apprehension of emerging articulations of time. Every particular is an immediate happening of meaning at large; every present activity in the poem redistributes future as well as past events. This is a presence extended in a time we create as we keep words in mind. (BB, ix)

A suggestive model for Duncan's structure of repetition is that described by Kierkegaard, who distinguishes between "recollection," the attempt to reconstitute the past, and "repetition," the adumbration on what has been. Recollection, Kierkegaard says, is what the Greeks called knowledge, the realization of eternal forms. Repetition, however, continually generates life out of that which was once partially glimpsed but never fully realized. "The dialectic of repetition is easy, for that which is repeated has been – otherwise it could not be repeated – but the very fact that it has been makes the repetition into something new."[24] For Duncan, poetry is also a structure of repetition, a return to "roots of first feeling" and yet a projection based on the terms discovered in that return:

> The morphology of forms, in evolving, does not destroy their historicity but reveals that each event has its origin in the origins of all events;

> yes, but in turn, we are but the more aware that the first version is
> revised in our very turning to it, seeing it with new eyes. (FC, 37)

A useful place to explore Duncan's ideas on repetition as well as his
relationship to the romantic tradition is his open-ended series "The
Structure of Rime." Originally conceived as imitations (readings) of
Rimbaud's prose poems in *Les Illuminations,* "Structure of Rime" has
become the poet's ongoing study of the role of rhyme, measure, and
language. Duncan treats these categories as dramatic voices or, as he
prefers to call them, "persons of the poem":

> I started a series without end called *Structures of Rime* in which the poem
> could talk to me, a poetic seance, and, invoked so, persons of the poem
> appeared as I wrote to speak. I had only to keep the music of the
> invocation going and to take down what actually came to me happening
> in the course of the poem.[25]

In Duncan's theory of dictation, structures of poetic language appear as
mythic figures – Black King Glélé, The Woman who Resembles the
Sentence, the Master of Rime, The Beloved – who serve as voices in a
drama played out on the stage of language.[26] They are archetypal presences, in that they return throughout the poet's life, but they appear only
in language and thus are subject to the local vicissitudes of human speech.

Presiding over the series is the Master of Rime, a Zarathustrian muse,
who makes his first appearance in "Structure of Rime IV":

> The Master of Rime, time after time, came down the arranged ladders
> of vision or ascended the smoke and flame towers of the opposite of
> vision, into or out of the language of daily life, husband to one word,
> wife to the other, breath that leaps forward upon the edge of dying.
> (OF, 17)

The Master of Rime represents poetry's ability to defamiliarize the language of everyday life into rhymes and repetitions. He urges the poet to
"lose heart" and encounter severe deprivations in order to experience the
"opposite of vision." He warns the poet to search within absence for the
*"rimes among the feathers of birds that exist only in sight. The songs you hear
fall from their flight light like shadows stars cast among you"* (BB, 170). The
individual "Structure of Rime," as the passage above illustrates, does not
replicate daily language but provides a rhetorical arena in which the
process of visionary translation occurs.

As the theory and practice of rime, it is perhaps all the more appropriate that the series is, for the most part, written in prose. "The Structure
of Rime" is not a versified discussion of poetics on the order of Pope's
"Essay on Criticism" or Karl Shapiro's "Essay on Rime." Rather, it is a

dramatization of poetics, acted out by Duncan's heightened rhetoric and convoluted syntax:

> You too are a flame then and my soul quickening in your gaze a draft upward carrying the flame of you. From this bed of a language in compression, life now is fuel, anthracite from whose hardness the years springs. In flame
>
> beings strive in the Sun's chemistry as we strive in our meat to realize images of manhood immanent we have not reacht, but leave, as if they fell from us, bright fell and fane momentary attendants. (BB, 37)

In this passage, Duncan addresses another "person" of the poem, the figure of the "first Beloved" derived from Plato's erotic demon in *The Symposium*.[27] The Beloved's power to transform and transfix is embodied in the poet's characteristically subordinated and suspended syntax. Just as erotic boundaries are destroyed in the lover's gaze, so linguistic boundaries dissolve in Duncan's prose. To adapt the imagery of the passage, the language has taken fire from a "language in compression" in which terms are collapsed and boundaries blurred. Qualifying phrases and subordinate clauses suspend the syntactic period while predicates are further and further separated from their subjects. The fullest use of acoustic values (assonance, alliteration, rhyme, and near rhyme) are exploited to give the passage the same sense of excitement and wonder that the lover inspires. Language here does not simply describe the erotic; words, by their sensual interplay, are eroticized.

Another muse of the series is the "woman who resembles the sentence": "She has a place in memory that moves language. Her voice comes across the waters from a shore I don't know to a shore I know, and is translated into words belonging to the poem" (OF, 12). On one level this figure represents Duncan's mother, who died shortly after his birth. She speaks to him through a kind of biological memory from beyond the grave. On another level, she is syntax itself, a scale upon which the poet plays his individual variations. Biological life (genetic coding) and literary life are thus fused under a common law:

> *Have heart*, the text reads,
> *you that were heartless.*
> *Suffering joy or despair*
> *you will suffer the sentence*
> *a law of words moving*
> *seeking their right period.*

I saw a snake-like beauty in the living changes of syntax.
Wake up, she cried

> *Jacob wrestled with Sleep – you fall into Nothingness*
> *and dread sleep.*
> *He wrestled with Sleep like a man reading a strong*
> *sentence.*

(OF, 12)

Here Duncan translates the imperatives of syntax into a parable of creation itself. He seeks to return to some prelapsarian state in which words and things, poetry and discourse, son and mother are reunited. But he may only return via the language as he has inherited it, original speech having been lost through the temptations of a "snake-like beauty" of syntax. His punishment, to continue the Edenic analogy, is to "suffer the sentence" of that first mother of language, to struggle like Jacob with a received language rather than attempt to master language and gain authority. Thus the poet will remain an adept in the service of words creating "sentence after sentence" in her image: "In the feet that measure the dance of my pages I hear cosmic intoxications of the man I will be" (OF, 12).

As a dramatization of poetics, "Structure of Rime" is informed by a doctrine of linguistic and mythological correspondences whose implications are ultimately social. Poetics is defined as an interactive process by which individual speech is claimed out of a swirling heteroglossia of other voices. The history of language, from its inception in childhood to its most complex manifestations in poetry, is also the history of fictions by which the human race coheres. To differentiate among phonemes or recognize similar sounds as a rhyme is to enter the realm of story and the cultural matrix in which story is enmeshed. Duncan attempts, in "The Structure of Rime," to describe the process by which we become "written," inscribed in a text larger than ourselves that we must yet translate into our own terms. But at the same time, it is in the immediacy of the moment, in its specific and time-bound nature, that our sense of commonality is discovered. In such charged moments of attention and apprehension we join "the company of the living."

"THE TROUBLE OF AN EROS"

But what does that "company" look like? Duncan's romantic rhetoric obscures the degree to which his Blakean or Whitmanian desire for a redeemed *polis* is expressed as a problematic of gender difference. In the preface to *Bending the Bow*, from which the statement about "company of the living" is taken, Duncan also warns that "where you are *he* or I am *he,* the trouble of an Eros shakes the household in which we work to contain our feeling. . . .A girlish possibility embarrasses the masculinity of the reader" (BB, vi). This erotic confusion of sexual identities is less a matter of pronouns in Duncan's poetry than it is, for instance, in someone like John Ashbery, where the boundaries between grammatical positions are constantly being destroyed. Duncan's caution comes more from the particular register of his speech, a tone and rhetoric that he identifies as "girlish" but that others might see as "sentimental" or "fey." This rhetoric is the vehicle within which Duncan's single voice may encounter a plurality of other voices and thus claim commonality. Rhetoric is figured as a seance table around which other voices may enter the poem:

> In the poem this very lighted room is dark, and the dark alight with love's intentions. *It* is striving to come into existence in these things, or, all striving to come into existence is It – in this realm of men's languages a poetry of all poetries, *grand collage,* I name It, having only the immediate event of words to speak for It. (BB, vii)

We can see the drama of this rhetorical "seance" in Duncan's long poems, where the poet directly interacts with other texts and sources, but it is no less available in his shorter lyrics. Far from being a vehicle for solitary reflections, Duncan's lyrics are invariably dialogues with other poets, living and dead. A poem like "Forced Lines," to take one example, incorporates Jack Spicer's criticism of an early draft of the poem, which at that point was called "Forced Images." Spicer wrote Duncan, complaining that "forced Images isn't as you say, finished, but it's so nearly finished that it scares me that you do anything with it. Only allow yourself one line (one forced line) and then write a new poem."[28] Duncan did just that, incorporating not only Spicer's epistolary remarks as his penultimate stanza but "allowing himself" another line:

> At the moon's teat
> having exceeded the excess
> an image forced.
>
> (RB, 119)

Duncan then changed the title of the poem from "Forced Images" to "Forced Lines" and wrote "A New Poem (for Jack Spicer)," which continues the dialogue:

> You are right. What we call Poetry is the boat.
> The first boat, the body – but it was a bed.
> > The bed, but it was a car.
> And the driver or sandman, the boatman,
> > the familiar stranger, first lover,
> is not with me.
>
> (RB, 120)

Such deliberate interplay of private and public voices is a common feature of Duncan's as well as Spicer's serial aesthetic whereby the lyric sequence provides a kind of extended conversation.[29] And in many of these sequences, the lyric tradition itself is implicated in the conversation. This is particularly the case with Duncan's sonnets in *Roots and Branches*, where the contemporary poet reaches into Dante's rime for an alternative vision of Love.[30] In "Sonnet I" Duncan translates that portion of *Inferno XV* in which Dante and Virgil encounter the sodomites who burn in an eternal flame:

> Now there is a Love of which Dante does not speak unkindly,
> Tho it grieves his heart to think upon men
>   who lust after men and run
>   – his beloved Master, Brunetto Latini, among them –
> Where the roaring waters of hell's rivers
> Come heard as if muted in the distance,
>   like the hum of bees in the hot sun.
>
>   (RB, 122)

Dante's vision of his master, Brunetto Latini, among the sodomites becomes, in Duncan's hands, a testimony of faith within the homosexual world: "Love has appointed there / For a joining that is not easy." Duncan extends Dante's metaphor of the needle ("and they knit their brows at us as the old tailor does at the eye of the needle")[31] beyond its sexual connotations to refer to the homosexual household and its domestic activities:

> For it is as if the thread of my life
> had been wedded to the eye of its needle.
>
> In the sunlight his head
> bends over his sewing,
>
> Intent upon joining color to color
> working the bedclothes of many cloths.
>
> This patch of Dante's vision in like art
> he keeps in Love's name and unites
>
> to the treasured remnant of some velvet shirt.
>
>   (RB, 123)

Here, in the second sonnet, Duncan creates a vision of the cult of Eros, identified as both homosexual and heterosexual, domestic as well as erotic. The lover is shown sewing a quilt just as the poet creates his poem out of patches of Dante's poetry. The making of a household and the making of art are united in a common work of love, which, though "not the angel Amor of Dante's song," is nevertheless "a worker among men / who has taken our lives as one thread." What Duncan claims as a common spirit of romance between himself and his Renaissance master is not simply a literary inheritance but a sense of communal identity and shared experience that finds its presence in a new definition of household and social relations.

This new dispensation among men becomes the explicit theme of the third sonnet of the series. Duncan continues the weaving metaphor by invoking his own contemporary brotherhood of poets, Robin Blaser and Jack Spicer:

> Robin, it would be a great thing if you, me, and Jack Spicer
> Were taken up in a sorcery with our mortal heads so turnd
> That life dimmd in the light of that fairy ship
> *The Golden Vanity* or *The Revolving Lure,*
>
> Whose sails ride before music as if it were our will,
> Having no memory of ourselves but the poets we were
> In certain verses that had such a semblance or charm
> Our lusts and loves confused in one
>
> Lord or Magician of Amor's likeness.
> And that we might have ever at our call
> Those youths we have celebrated to play Eros
> And erased to lament in the passing of things.
>
> And to weave themes ever of Love.
> And that each might be glad
> To be so far abroad from what he was.
>
> (RB, 124)

Duncan here provides a free translation of Dante's sixth sonnet[32] ("Guido, i'vorrei che tu e Lapo ed io"), which celebrates the friendship of companions under the magic of Amor. In Duncan's version, the brotherhood of love transports the three poets away from the contemporary world into the realm of spirit. The word "fairy ship" means both fantastic and "gay," in our current usage, implying that the sorcery in which they participate involves sexual as well as philosophical mysteries. And this playful language combines with a somewhat archaic diction as if to imitate Victorian translations of Dante like those of Tennyson or Rossetti, thus establishing another intertextual layer to Duncan's literary patchwork. He is claiming a heritage that predates literary history (a Neoplatonic or Orphic cult of Eros) by inscribing himself into a textual tradition within history. Just as Dante's poem or Rossetti's rhetoric transports Duncan "abroad from what he was" into the spirit of romance, so the homosexual community invoked in "Sonnet 3" will take him outside a dominant heterosexual world. Duncan uses the lyric tradition represented by the *dolce stil nuovo*, as well as the Neoplatonic thematics of Dante, Guido Cavalcanti, and other Renaissance poets, to weave a new Eros for his own time. Within this context, we read the conditional "would" of the poem's opening line as more than a faint desire for oblivion in a fin de siècle aestheticism and more of a utopian hope for sexual tolerance and acceptance, one glimpsed in the structures of Dante's rime.

"THE UNDERSIDE TURNING"

Duncan's Dante sonnets are but one example among many of his poems in which the poet reaches toward "kindred men" who pass on essential lore from generation to generation. Dante is revered not only for having written *The Divine Comedy* but because he provides the means by which later poets can transform their local, secular community into a vision of humanity. Dante so inhabits the Christian universe of the thirteenth century that he may "enter it in a poem as primary vision and explore even its mysteries in the structure of his rimes" (BB, viii). In a similar vein, Whitman is able to transform the conflicts and tensions of antebellum America into a visionary statement of democracy. The idea that poetry permits one to enter life as a fiction is hardly new, but for Duncan it is the central bequest of the romantic tradition. It is what enables him to read a contemporary event like the Vietnam War as a repetition of "America's unacknowledged, unrepented crimes" (BB, 83) or to create out of Dante's heterosexual Christian view a paradigm for homoerotic love. In each case, "entry" means re-vision and transformation.

Of course, in order to "enter" the text of his life, the poet must engage more than the surface of a prior text. Dante's rime becomes only the first stage of a rereading that takes the poet "far abroad" from the original. It is a process that Duncan describes as his version of a "field" poetics: the ability to encounter novelty and naturalize it in the poem. "Opening" the field of the poem is always a genealogical matter, since it involves participation within a "Grand Collage" of previous creative works. Harold Bloom has defined this genealogical process as an anxious oedipology in which the ephebe unconsciously struggles to dethrone paternal authority, a process that in order to be successful must occur in an unreflective state.[33] For Duncan, however, the process is a conscious, critical activity of reading, imitating, and revising. It may begin in innocence, but it quickly establishes its own evaluative terms:

> Working in words I am an escapist; as if I could step out of my clothes and move naked as the wind in a world of words. But I want every part of the actual world involved in my escape. I bring the laws that bound me into an aerial structure in which they are unbound as outlines of a prison unfolding. (BB, v)

The interplay of "bound" and "unbound," prisons and escape embodies the way Duncan's poetry oscillates between closed and open forms, between law as limit and law as proposition. He often invokes legal jurisprudence to exploit the paradox whereby "the Law / constantly destroys the Law." Each informing particular is a law that establishes the terms of its violation.

We have seen this revisionism at work in lyric series like the Dante sonnets, but it is in long poems like "Apprehensions," "The Propositions," and many of the "Passages" that Duncan most dramatically reads a tradition in order to inhabit it. In such poems, Duncan works with informing details (other poems, newspaper stories, scientific articles) as passages in a text under formation. A passage, as the series by that name makes abundantly clear, is both a thing and a process, a text to read and a process of reading, and Duncan often exploits the duplicity of such terms to suggest how a static object may become a temporal field. In this, Duncan continues a long tradition in American poetry – from the Puritans through Emerson and Whitman – whereby the poet reads a hieroglyphic representation of God's mysterious intention, transforming textual or natural objects into personal, salvific acts.[34]

From his very earliest writing, Duncan desired a form flexible enough to handle both the wide range of his readings and his characteristically paratactic, nonlinear thought. In an early work like "The Venice Poem," as we have seen, Pound's Cantos provided an important precedent. But despite certain thematic similarities (Venice as a city of art, the interplay between secular city and *civitas dei*), the poem's ornamental rhetoric and personal address resemble the Pound of the pre-*Cantos* era. Duncan's more characteristic method for handling a diverse body of materials during this period was to write in a serial mode. "Medieval Scenes" and "Domestic Scenes," for example, consist of separate lyrics, written during a relatively short period and linked, one to the next, by common procedural or thematic elements. This "serial" or book-length poem was to become a dominant compositional mode for Duncan's colleagues Jack Spicer and Robin Blaser throughout their careers.

During the early 1950s Duncan temporarily dropped his more baroque style for an experimental mode in imitation of Gertrude Stein. In "Writing Writing," for example, Duncan uses repetition and variation of phrases to create a continuum of movement without imposing any particular narrative or overall form. Rather than reclaim a previous tradition for the present, he creates the present out of participial constructions, repetitions, and modulations of syntactic units. As in Stein's portraits, everything exists in a perpetual present: "Beginning to write. Continuing finally to write. Writing finally to continue beginning."[35] And although this represents an important stage in Duncan's development, it could not accommodate the poet's larger historical and intellectual concerns. Whereas Duncan's Blakean rhetoric seems entirely appropriate to later antiwar jeremiads like "Up-Rising" or "The Multiversity," his Steinian mode diminishes his criticism of the Kōrean War:

> Now if we are in the evening of the world we are at home writing
> home. Now if a history is beginning, we are not beginning in history.

> Now if in Korea as we hear there is continual killing, now if we rightly
> have no longer faith in our nations, now if we tire of futile decisions, we
> are at home among stranger relations.[36]

The fault here is not with repetition per se but with the attempt to make
it serve certain mimetic and narrative ends.

With the gradual discovery of Louis Zukofsky, Charles Olson, Denise
Levertov, Robert Creeley, and others during the 1950s, Duncan found a
variety of new formal models that enabled him to combine his interest in
an intellectual, historical poetics with an open-ended, processual style.
His best-known version of field poetics can be found in "Poem Beginning with a Line by Pindar," a work in which our Kierkegaardian definition of repetition can be fully explored. It is a poetic meditation on "first
things" that return or repeat but do so in terms modified by the poem as
it is being written. The line by Pindar that inaugurates the poem leads
Duncan into a long speculation on the origins of love and on the historical forces that diminish its power. In terms already developed in this
chapter, it is a poem about the transformation of spirit into history or the
reification of time into causality. And like the Dante sonnets, it attempts
to revive the spirit of romance in distinctly personal terms.

The "Pindar" poem is a multileveled reading of a primary text
through its appearance in various other versions. The story of Eros and
Psyche, as found in Apuleius's *The Golden Ass,* serves as the core text,
versions of which Duncan finds in Pindar's first Pythian ode, a painting
by Goya, Whitman's elegy for Lincoln, Pound's *Pisan Cantos,* the story
of Jason and Medea, a novel by Charles Williams, and, most important,
Duncan's own dreams. Each of these texts, in some way or another,
redefines the nature of Eros as a desire for articulation and speech. Duncan is acutely aware that his selection of materials (or, as he might prefer,
their selection of him) is governed by the very principle he explores in
the poem. Hence, his poem participates directly in the labor of Psyche's
search.[37]

The story of Psyche and Eros is the story of the soul's union with love,
the discovery of desire through loss and restitution. "Soul and Eros are
primordial members of the cast," Duncan says in *The H. D. Book,*
"personae of a drama or dream that determines, beyond individual consciousness, the configurative image of a species."[38] In Apuleius's account, Psyche is told by the oracle at Miletus that she will wed a monster
or serpent. She does not know that this prophecy has been orchestrated
by jealous Venus, whose own beauty has been eclipsed by this most
beautiful of mortal women. Psyche gives herself to her monster husband, but she is prevented from seeing him since he visits her only at
night and leaves the marriage bed before it is light. Psyche is well treated
by her mysterious companion, and whatever hideous physical qualities

he may manifest are more than compensated by his kindness toward her. One night, provoked by her jealous sisters and driven by curiosity, Psyche lights a lamp, only to discover that her husband is not a terrifying serpent but the most beautiful of all the gods, Eros. Seeing that he is discovered, Eros flees, leaving Psyche, now fully in love with Love, to search for him. She appeals to his spiteful mother, Venus, who creates tasks that she must perform in order to regain her husband. These tasks – sorting grain, retrieving golden wool from cannibal sheep, obtaining water from the River Styx, descending to Hades to capture a portion of Persephone's beauty – are quite impossible, but aided by certain of the gods, Psyche is able to accomplish all of them. Thus through her love and labor, Psyche is reunited with Eros, and the soul is incarnated in bodily form.

Duncan sees the story as, among other things, an allegory of the modern artist: The poet is an alienated Psyche, unaware of love's power and thus tempted by "Scientia" to reify beauty in an image. Having lost the true spirit of romance to *scientia,* the artist must search for vestiges of that primary force among other poets – Rilke, Emerson, Williams, Pindar, Whitman – who, like Psyche, sort the seeds of an alternative tradition. He must go against the grain, like Jason, "widdershins" to recover a living tradition. The poet becomes the primary player in his own poem, beginning his tale in innocence, "reading late at night the third line of the first Pythian ode in the translation by Wade-Gery and Bowra" (FC, 17), unaware of potencies in the line "The light foot hears you and the brightness begins." These words become "powers in a theogony, having resonances in Hesiodic and Orphic cosmogonies where the foot in the dance of the poem appears as the pulse of measures in first things" (FC, 17). Pindar's line leads Duncan's into his own poem:

> god-step at the margins of thought,
>   quick adulterous tread at the heart.
> Who is it that goes there?
>   Where I see your quick face
> notes of an old music pace the air,
> torso-reverberations of a Grecian lyre.
>   (OF, 62)

These "Hesiodic and Orphic" resonances, encountered in a translation of Pindar, begin a chain of associations or rhymes that constellate around the idea of an occult tradition. The bacchic dance inspired by Apollo's lyre becomes the poet's own verbal dance in the poem, allowing him to play his own variations in light-footed meters, alliterations, and puns.

These thoughts "of an old music" remind Duncan of Goya's painting of Eros and Psyche in the de Cambo collection in Barcelona, which depicts the moment in which Psyche first sees Eros, thus precipitating her fall from innocence. The "light" that has illuminated Pindar's page as well as the "light foot" of his meters now illuminates a canvas. In Goya's version, the two figures "have a hurt voluptuous grace / bruised by redemption"; they exist not in a physical landscape but "in an obscurity" in which all forces – including Goya's manipulation of chiaroscuro – conspire to "serve them" in the working out of their story. It is this atmospheric quality in Apuleius that Ezra Pound remarks on most forcefully: "The mood, the play is everything; the facts are nothing."[39] Pound contrasts the Hellenistic author with the more literal-minded Ovid, who "raises the dead and dissects their mental processes." For Pound, as for Duncan, the confusion of tale teller with its hero, of story and dream, is an essential component of the romance tradition. Hence Goya's painting is admired not because it renders figures in virtual space but because it establishes "A bronze of yearning" and "Waves of visual pleasure" that facilitate a mood.

This first part of the poem is an homage to the romance tradition in distinctly modernist terms. It inaugurates a mythic search for lost innocence within the folds of specific aesthetic artifacts. Part II investigates the historical consequences of the same search as Duncan invokes the failure of America to heed the advice of its poets. Instead of youthful, erotic potential as depicted in Goya's canvas, "it is age / that is beautiful":

> It is toward the old poets
> we go, to their faltering,
> their unaltering wrongness that has style,
> their variable truth,
> the old faces,
> words shed like tears from
> a plenitude of powers time stores.
>
> (OF, 63)

Duncan invokes this "faltering" and "unaltering wrongness" in the person of Whitman, whose elegy for Lincoln provides a measure of the affection that a poet might feel for a national leader. Compared with Whitman's love for Lincoln, the contemporary poet's relation to the president is sadly diminished. Now the "faltering . . . unaltering wrongness" can be viewed only in the aphasic speech of Eisenhower following his stroke:

> damerging a nuv. A nerb.
> The present dented of the U
> nighted stayd.   States.   The heavy clod?
> Cloud.   Invades the brain.   What
> if lilacs last in *this* dooryard bloomd?
>
> (OF, 63)

Duncan seems to be referring to Williams's "Asphodel, That Greeny Flower," another great poem of a displaced Eros, in which the atomic bomb ("The heavy clod? / Cloud") is invoked:

> All suppressions,
> from the witchcraft trials at Salem
> to the latest
> bookburnings
> are confessions
> that the bomb
> has entered our lives
> to destroy us.[40]

How different, Duncan suggests, was America during Whitman's time, when a poet could express his love for a president in a great funeral elegy. Now, in Eisenhower's Cold War era, there is only the shadow of nuclear annihilation: "What / if lilacs in *this* dooryard bloomd?"

The "dooryard" of American History that Duncan next invokes is one in which the power of Eros is displaced into the mechanical redundancy of institutional and bureaucratic labor. Whitman's celebration of Lincoln is displaced by a litany of little-remembered presidents of the industrial era:

> Hoover, Coolidge, Harding Wilson
> hear the factories of human misery turning out commodities.
> For whom are the holy matins of the heart ringing?
> Noble men in the quiet of morning hear
> Indians singing the continent's violent requiem.
> Harding, Wilson, Taft, Roosevelt,
> idiots fumbling at the bride's door,
> hear the cries of men in meaningless debt and war.
>
> (OF, 64)

The rhythm of this section recalls Emerson's "Hamatraya," a poem that contrasts the bounty of the earth with the attempt to master it through entrepreneurial ownership:

> Bulkeley, Hunt, Willard, Hosmer, Meriam, Flint,
> Possessed the land which rendered to their toil
> Hay, corn, roots, hemp, flax, apples, wool and wood.
> Each of these landlords walked amidst his farm,
> Saying, "'Tis mine, my children's and my name's.
> How sweet the west wind sounds in my own trees! . . ."[41]

Where Emerson mocks the claims of landlords against the earth's song of mutability ("Mine and yours; / Mine, not yours. / Earth endures"), Duncan stridently measures the failure of vision in mercantile presidents. They appear like Psyche's suitors, "idiots fumbling at the bride's door."

Emerson, acknowledged obliquely through his rhythmic cadence, joins
other poets invoked for their vitality and sense of possibility, poets for
whom "power" is measured by vision, not by accumulated capital.
Duncan turns toward them and "strikes again"

> . . . the naked string
> old Whitman sang from. Glorious mistake!
>   that cried:

> "The theme is creative and has vista."
> "He is the president of regulation."
>
> (OF, 64)

Whitman's vision of a democratic ensemble is a "Glorious mistake"
perhaps, but it is one the contemporary poet relies on in his search for a
lost potential. As Roy Harvey Pearce has said of these lines, "Whitman
as poet succeeded not as he portrayed failure, but rather as he gave us the
means to measure success, thus to know that our forebears' failures, and
our leaders', may well be our own."[42] This is a reading very much in
concert with Duncan's pervasive dialectic of error whereby certain excesses and mistakes testify to rigorous challenges.

If alienated labor is the theme of section II, productive labor becomes
the theme of section III. Where in Emerson's "Hamatraya" the fruits of
the earth ("Hay, corn, roots, hemp, flax, apples, wool and wood") are
envisaged as the products of landowners, in section III the same bounty
("wheat barley oats poppy coriander") becomes part of Psyche's
labor in rediscovering her lost husband. In Apuleius's story, Psyche is
aided by insects, which help her sort seeds according to Venus's instructions. In the same context, Duncan remembers Ezra Pound, who listens
to the counsels of an "insect instructor" while imprisoned at Pisa. Quoting a line from "Canto 76," Duncan sees Pound *as a lone ant from a
broken ant-hill*" of postwar Europe. Psyche's solitude resembles Pound's
at Pisa, where he wrote some of his most lyrically powerful work.

Another fellow laborer in this section is Jason, who returns to Thessaly
after winning the golden fleece by sailing counterclockwise around the
Black Sea. He struggles "widdershins to free the dawn," a contrary
motion that thematically links him with other "first riders" who "ad-
vance into legend" as well as with the children's circle dance at the end of
the poem. Jason's westward journey also links him, in Duncan's mind,
with the West itself, a landscape that has been lost to legend:

> It was the West. Its vistas painters saw
>   in diffuse light, in melancholy,
> in abysses left by glaciers as if they had been the sun
>   primordial carving empty enormities
>   out of the rock.
>
> (OF, 66)

Here the romantic vistas of western painters like Bierstadt and Remington rhyme with Goya's painting of Eros and Psyche; it is less a landscape
that they paint than an idea, molded by the "light that is Love."

In the poem's final movement, Duncan makes his own poem and its
inception a coparticipant in all of the mythological and historical parallels
discussed thus far. In a long parenthesis, he returns to Pindar and to the
physical book in which it first appeared to him:

> (An ode? Pindar's art, the editors tell us, was not a statue but a mosaic,
> an accumulation of metaphor. But if he was archaic, not classic, a
> survival of obsolete mode, there may have been old voices in the sur-
> vival that directed the heart.
>
> . . . .
>   the information flows
>   that is yearning. A line of Pindar
>   moves from the area of my lamp
>   toward morning.
>
> In the dawn that is nowhere
>   I have seen the willful children
> clockwise and counter-clockwise turning.
>   (OF, 69)

Duncan's use of editorial commentary opens the possibility that Pindar
was indeed "archaic, not classic" and may very well have included within his poem works that survived from earlier traditions. Duncan's poem,
too, is a "mosaic" of other texts, quotations, and cultural references,
much as Pindar's ode may have been. The mosaic evolves not according
to a set of thematic centers – a spatial grid of discontinuous but equivalent icons – but by "yearning," the associative pattern through time
inaugurated by Pindar's opening line. "The information flows / that is
yearning" contains a double entendre: The intertextuality that informs
Duncan's poem is information *about* yearning (the story of Eros and
Psyche) that proceeds *by means of* yearning. This information, if elusive,
is "no more than a nearness to the mind / of a single image."

The children's circle dance that closes the poem is just such a nearness,
in this case an image taken from a recurrent childhood dream. Duncan
describes it as his "Atlantis" dream:

> . . . there was a circle of children . . . dancing in the field. They choose
> or have chosen someone who is "IT" in the center of the ring, but I see
> no one there. The Dreamer is in the Center, the "I" or Eye of the
> Dream. And just here, I realize that this "I" is my self and second that I
> have been "chosen," but also that in dreaming I am the Chosen One, I
> have been caught in the wrong – a "King" or victim of the children's
> round dance. Ring a round of roses. Pocket full of posies. Or is it poses?
> for I had been proposed or I had posed as King, posed myself there.
> Ashes, ashes. All fall down![43]

What children enact in their "innocent" dance is a cosmic ritual of creation and destruction, of discovery, loss, and recovery. They mimic creation itself in the strophe and antistrophe of their movements, rhyming with the bacchic dance invoked in Pindar's opening line. But for Duncan it is also a dance of self-discovery in which the "I" seeks to identify itself among the dancers, a task that for the homosexual poet becomes another complication in his rereading of the dream. For to be "caught in the wrong," to engage in "poses" that are also "posies," is to be the victim, not the subject, of the children's dance. Granted, these are meanings that the adult imposes upon his early dream; but they suggest that intimations of otherness were present from an early age.[44] And although the Pindar poem does not make specific reference to homosexuality, it does situate the "song of kindred men" within a tradition of heresies, whether literary or sexual.

As I said earlier, Duncan often refers to himself as a "derivative poet," and the Pindar poem illustrates exactly what he means. It is a poem "of" derivations even while it creates its own "mosaic" or field of conjecture. Michael Bernstein sees this paradoxical mode as central to modernist intertextuality, as compared with earlier forms of quotation and allusion. A modernist reliance on prior texts

> does not so much draw upon a canonic tradition as seek to establish one; how in the absence of a relatively homogeneous and stable hierarchy of values, a communally acknowledged nexus of aesthetic, spiritual, and political models, each writer is not only free to select his own *exempla*, but also has the responsibility, implicitly or explicitly, to justify the terms of his selection.[45]

In the light of Duncan's "Atlantis" dream we could see the desire to establish a tradition as paralleling a desire to identify oneself as an individual. Throughout his work, Duncan repeatedly refers to childhood as a privileged moment of awakening when a conflict of sensations announces or projects the adult who is yet to be born. Duncan's long poems like the "Pindar" poem and the later *Passages* represent attempts to return to inaugural moments of discovery, both in childhood and in adult life, and see them as being "informed / by the weight of all things." That these moments of self-discovery are invariably textual as well as sexual means that the poems are interpretive, even as they exploit the lyric voice.

Where Duncan differs from his modernist masters is less in the manipulation of derivations, allusions, and quotations as Bernstein has outlined them than in the uses to which they are put. Where Pound and Eliot attempted to isolate themselves within a particular cultural edifice, informed by dynastic cultural values, Duncan strives to reenter a "Commune of poetry" that is necessarily pluralist and eclectic. The Pindar poem, as I have said, is a "reading" of a text along certain associative and textual lines in an attempt to regather a certain heretical tradition immanent in a variety of sources. We recognize at least the outer surface of this impulse as a continuation of certain modernist collage strategies, allowing for important variations as outlined earlier. Although issues of gender are not foregrounded in that poem, I see Duncan's thematics of dispersion and sexual plurality as being defined not only by means of a Neoplatonic Orphism but in terms of the homosexual writer attempting to enter modernism on his own terms.

This same re-visioning of modernism along gender and sexual lines also informs Duncan's alliances and oppositions with the San Francisco Renaissance, a movement that sought to provide an alternative society for the rest of the 1950s, but within the more egalitarian terms of a Whitmanian or Emersonian democratic ensemble. Duncan's "Berkeley Renaissance" was conceived around aesthetic circle and homosexual coterie, an attitude seemingly at odds with the participatory poetics it encouraged. This sectarian position, as we shall see in the case of Jack Spicer, generated a sense of opposition and conflict that was important for a poetic movement but that was also felt as a distinct legacy from earlier literary traditions. It is within this forum that we must go back, as Duncan goes to Pindar, and reread the "light foot" of an Orphic lyre.

5

"The City Redefined"

Community and Dialogue in Jack Spicer

"BOTH OF US WERE OBJECT"

One of the outrageous events of North Beach life during the 1950s was Blabbermouth Night, a weekly feature at one of Grant Avenue's best-known literary bars, The Place. Using a kind of spontaneous and unrehearsed glossolalia, poets would babble into the mike, the best babbler winning a free drink. One function of Blabbermouth Night was to "bug the squares" pouring into North Beach in search of Beatniks, but another, more important function was to reinforce the sense of community that had arisen within the North Beach bar scene. For this community, poetry was a public event, something performed on stage in front of an audience. Blabbermouth Night extended this public dimension, introducing an element of competition – complete with hecklers, claques, and door prizes. Jack Spicer was one of the event's strongest supporters, helping to organize the participants and sometimes presenting the victor's prize. To some extent Blabbermouth Night was the perfect embodiment of Spicer's poetics: a public gospel in which the Logos speaks through the spontaneous jabberwocky of poets.[1]

Jack Spicer's position in the North Beach poetry scene was central, and at the same time, eccentric. His table at The Place was the focus of a circle of poets who remained fiercely loyal to him and to the spirit of play and competition that he encouraged through events like Blabbermouth Night. The Spicer circle maintained an uneasy truce with the more recognizable North Beach bohemians and used them as foils for a good deal of barbed wit and occasional grumbling. Spicer certainly shared with the Beats their sense of linguistic freedom and iconoclasm, and he approved of their public mode of address, but he deeply distrusted the hipster persona, its projection of cool detachment and mindlessness. He satirizes these qualities in "Ferlinghetti," a short poem from *Heads of the Town, Up to the Aether*:

Be bop de beep
They are asleep
There where were they like us
It goes
From nose to nose
From stop to stop
Violations are rare
And the air is fair
It is spring
On the thing
We sing.
Beep bop de beep
They are all asleep
They're all asleep.[2]

Spicer's leaden endrhymes, his use of passive verbal forms, and his repetitious phrasing suggest that the "bebop" poem induces a kind of torpor in which "Violations are rare." In the "explanatory note" attached to this poem, he indicates that "Ferlinghetti is a nonsense syllable invented by the Poet."

Behind Spicer's resentment of the Beats as a social phenomenon lies a more complicated rejection of their visionary, expressivist poetics. He regards the poem not as originating within the individual but as a foreign agent that invades the poet's language and expresses what "it" wants to say. The poet must clear away the intrusive authorial will and allow entrance to an alien and ghostlike language. Nor does poetry find its source in the natural landscape, where acts of sympathetic identification connect the poet to numinous qualities latent in all living things. For Spicer, the poet is a medium through whom a disinterested message must penetrate, often at some cost to the receiver. As he says in the Vancouver Lectures, "I don't think the messages are for the poet . . . anymore than a radio program is for the radio set."[3]

If we were to concentrate solely on the act of writing, Spicer's theory of diction would not seem so different from Ginsberg's ideas of spontaneity or Kerouac's sketching. What is different about Spicer is what might be called his negative theology, his rejection of immanent or essentialist ideologies in favor of an utter dualism of subject and object, word and thing, human and God. This view, radically Protestant in impulse, emphasizes learning through opposition and confrontation. James Herndon tells how Spicer "refuted child psychology" by encouraging Herndon's young son Jay to say "Chicken-ship" in his nursery school: "Jack figured that if Jay said Chicken-ship enough times to the nursery-school teacher, she would in the end get mad and forbid Chicken-ship and betray herself as a tyrant, and then Jay would learn Where It

Was At."[4] According to Spicer's somewhat perverse pedagogy, the truth value of any act cannot be tested by reference to qualities inherent in the act itself; it must be subjected to the world, and the world is not a friendly place. For the poet as well as for the three-year-old Jay Herndon, words "Turn mysteriously against those who use them." That is, words often subvert the purposes to which they are put:

> Dante would have blamed Beatrice
> If she turned up alive in a local bordello
> Or Newton gravity
> If apples fell upward
> What I mean is words
> Turn mysteriously against those who use them
> Hello says the apple
> Both of us were object.[5]

Spicer adapted this Protestant poetics to his personal relations as well. I have already spoken of the insularity of Spicer's North Beach bar scene, and this quality was formalized in his "Poetry as Magic" workshop at the San Francisco Public Library in 1957. Participants included many of the most active poets on the scene – Ebbe Borregaard, Jack Gilbert, George Stanley, Helen Adam, Joe Dunn, Robert Duncan – and, as Robin Blaser points out, the curriculum was hardly that of the conventional creative writing workshop: "For all the magical interest of the workshop, magic, it became clear, was a matter of disturbance, entrance and passion, rather than abracadabra. Jack once commented that there was no good source from which to learn magic; it was something we did among ourselves" (CB, 353). Spicer heightened the "secret society" quality of the workshop by seating everyone at a round table with himself facing west. Assignments involved tasks like writing blasphemies, impersonating characters from the Oz books, and creating a universe. Participation in the workshop was restricted to poets willing to fill out a questionnaire that asked, "What political group, slogan, or idea in the world today has the most to do with Magic," "What card of the ordinary playing-card deck . . . represents the absolute of your desires?" and "What animal do you most resemble?" These rituals were designed less for the purpose of evaluating students than for reinforcing bonds among members already within the magic circle. Each test was designed to place the student in a state of vulnerability and risk, conditions Spicer felt were essential to poetry.

Though Spicer's effect on poets within his own circle was substantial, he was relatively unknown outside the Bay Area. One of the reasons for this is that he refused to participate in any traditional sort of literary self-promotion. He did not publish through established literary channels (if, in fact, his work would have been accepted by them in the first place), and he avoided copyrighting his books. When Duncan published *The Opening of the Field* with Grove Press, Spicer admonished him publically by reprinting the copyright page of that book, including its list of publication acknowledgments, as the frontispiece to his own *Lament for the Makers*. In Duncan's version of the incident, publication of his book "had been sold to the papists or the heathen or it had been sold out to the grownups world."[6]

Spicer's output was limited to a series of twelve small poetic sequences, or "serial poems" as he called them. All of these were published by small presses in limited editions. Spicer made access to his work difficult by demanding a geographical limit to its distribution, not to extend beyond the San Francisco Bay Area – a deliberate (or half-playful) attempt to ignore the East Coast literary scene. And, as if this were not enough, Spicer and his friends often wrote fake poems of other local poets, aping the styles of those currently held in disrepute. These poems were then published in local magazines under the name of the poet being imitated.

This oppositional stance was more than a series of schoolboy pranks. It reflected Spicer's view that poetry is a world, and in it are warring camps, traitors, loyal subjects, secret codes, and internecine conflicts. The enemy is the academic establishment, presided over by the New Critical ideology and supported by a hegemonic publishing network. On the other side was the small group of poets who met with Spicer in various North Beach bars for whom he served as teacher, critic, and goad. Spicer's almost medieval sense of poetic trothes and fealties emerged early in his career, during the Berkeley period that I have described in earlier chapters. And throughout Spicer's life such circles became increasingly important as a public forum in which poetry could be debated and argued into existence. The Magic Workshop, Sunday poetry readings, favorite bars like The Place and Gino Carlos, group magazines like *J* and *Open Space* were the major venues for the Spicer group, each held together by pledges of loyalty and claims of territoriality. However insular such a community might have been, it created an audience that could set itself against a heathen world that had failed to listen.[7]

"THE CITY THAT WE CREATE IN OUR BARTALK"

For Spicer, listening is everything. In a 1949 symposium sponsored by the University of California literary magazine *Occident*, he introduces a theme that will preoccupy him throughout his career:

> Here we are, holding a ghostly symposium – five poets holding forth on their peculiar problems. One will say magic: one will say God: one will say form. When my turn comes I can only ask an embarrassing question – "Why is nobody here? Who is listening to us?"[8]

This question was to reappear many years later in the first poem of *Language*:

> This ocean, humiliating in its disguises
> Tougher than anything.
> No one listens to poetry. The ocean
> Does not mean to be listened to.
>   (CB 217)

We could regard such remarks as typical of any poet's worries about audience, but in the case of Spicer the question of who is listening implies something quite different. The fact that no one listens to poetry means two things: No one listens to the poetry that "we" write but, also, poets consistently fail to listen to the poetry that reaches their ears all the time. The first proposition pertains to the creation of community – those persons joined by a common willingness to listen to one another; the second pertains to the particular dispensation such a community makes toward communication. The two areas are inextricably linked. Spicer's poetics is based on the premise that the audience for poetry will, of necessity, be limited, and therein lies its virtue.

In the *Occident* symposium of 1949, Spicer complains that the New Critics have "taken poetry (already removed from its main source of interest – the human voice) and have completed the job of denuding it of any remaining connection with person, place and time."[9] What Spicer wanted returned to poetry was a kind of vaudeville Orphism in which theatrical gestures, props, and pratfalls could defuse any expectations of high seriousness. When he said, as he did in the *Occident* symposium, that poets "must become singers, become entertainers,"[10] he was reacting against the more reflective and meditative tone of the then–popular metaphysical lyric and was, at the same time, anticipating the poetry-reading revolution of the 1950s. But unlike Charles Olson or Allen Ginsberg, for whom the voice is the outward sign of a unitary, emotive subject, voice for Spicer is a dimension of public, interactive experiences. Poetry is created in dialogue and argumentation, whether it takes place between poet and friend or between poet and God. If that dialogue is contentious (and it almost always is in Spicer's world) so much the better, since it means that language is being tested (to adapt a line from Frank O'Hara) between persons instead of between pages.[11]

The role of community and dialogue in Spicer's poetics is important to stress, since much of what little commentary on him exists has tended to see his work in service to a metaphysical ideal of the "outside."[12] Spicer contributed to this view by using certain theological and metaphysical models to explain his poetics. As I said earlier, Spicer regards poetry as something dictated from an endistanced "Other" through the poet, who, through a process of self-emptying, serves as a medium. His primary image of the poem is that of the radio in Cocteau's *Orphée*, which is tuned by the receptive poet to receive cryptic messages from Hell. The idea of poetic dictation coming from the outside is set against what Spicer called the "big lie of the personal," in which objects are subsumed by intention, in which lemons, oceans, and seagulls "become things to be traded for a smile or the sound of conversation" (CB, 48). Spicer, in going beyond an expressivist poetics, reaches in the other direction – to surrealism, fantasy, nonsense rhymes, games, and cartoons – to find discursive models that circumvent lyrical subjectivity. In so doing he appears to privilege another kind of aestheticism, based on a disinterested poetic source outside or beyond. In other words, he creates a metaphysics. I would like to qualify this metaphysical view of his poetics in order to see Spicer's dictation as being more dialogical and social. That is, I would like to propose that the "outside" has its base in human intercourse within a community and that its reception takes the form of a conversation or, in Spicer's words, "an argument between the dead and the living" (CB, 171).

Cocteau's radio metaphor has tended to obscure the degree to which Spicer's outside is a world of voices, contending and arguing like those in the bar world of North Beach or in the linguistic playfulness of the Magic Workshop. The voices that intrude into poems like "The Imaginary Elegies" or "Homage to Creeley" may be ghosts, but they speak a very human rhetoric. "It is as if we conjure the dead and they speak only / Through our own damned trumpets, through our damned medium" (CB, 333). Spicer himself seems to have become dissatisfied with his radio motif toward the end of his life and in *Language* qualifies the metaphor: "The trouble with comparing a poet with a radio is that radios don't develope scar-tissue" (CB, 218). He then goes on to amend Cocteau's formulation: "The poet is a radio. The poet is a liar. The poet is a counterpunching radio." The metaphor has become too static, leaving little room for the possibility of response.

It is out of this spirit of verbal sparring and contention that Spicer's poetics merges with his politics. That politics is based on anarchist principles of private refusal and mutual aid.[13] Spicer believed that power relations are acted out in language, and language is subject to contextual transformations with each new utterance. Things like electoral politics, bureaucracies, and social programs only sediment power in intransigent discursive modes like contracts and legal briefs. For Spicer, real power is created in dialogue:[14]

> The city redefined becomes a church. A movement of poetry. Not merely a system of belief but their beliefs and their hearts living together.

> But the city that we create in our bartalk or in our fuss and fury about
> each other is in an utterly mixed and mirrored way an image of the city.
> A return from exile. (CB, 176)

Spicer's model here is Dante, who, exiled from Florence, creates a divine
comedy out of historical contingency and in the process turns his local
city into a system of belief. In Spicer's imagination, San Francisco could
be such a city, "redefined" through its poetry movement and acted out
in its "bartalk."[15] It is little wonder that Spicer placed such faith in the
poetry wars of North Beach since they became, in his imagination,
latter-day versions of the Albigensian Crusade.

An interesting portrait of the dynamics of Spicer's bar community can
be seen in a chapter from his unpublished detective novel. In this chapter,
an East Coast college professor named J. J. Ralston comes into a Grant
Avenue Bar called the Birdcage (modeled on The Place) to "dig the San
Francisco Renaissance." He has published his poems in the *Partisan Review* and *Hudson Review*, and his book has been reviewed by no less than
Randall Jarrell in the *New York Times Book Review*. For the group of
scraggly poets who patronize the bar he is a perfect foil. He represents
the "outside" in every sense: East Coast academic, liberal humanist,
established writer, literary critic. Ralston's strategy for dealing with the
strange characters he encounters is to pigeonhole them as various bohemian types, all the while pigeonholing himself as an uptight square (at
one point, in a gesture of self-mockery, he begins calling himself W. H.
Auden). After some uncomfortable banter, one of the young poets does
the unspeakable thing: he rips Ralston's copy of the *Paritsan Review* in
half. Infuriated, Ralston leaves the table to drink his ale in solitude, but
the offending poet brings him an odd peace token: a live fish in whose
mouth is a folded piece of paper:

> Ralston unfolded the wedge of paper. It was, he could see, two pages of
> poetry written in large childish handwriting. Without allowing himself
> to read so much as a word of what was written, he folded over the pages
> once and then methodically began to tear the paper to shreds.
> "See," Ralston said, "I can tear paper too." The boy watched the
> pieces of paper flutter down to the floor. He looked as if he were going
> to cry. "It was a poem," he said softly. "You bastard. Oh, you bas-
> tard." Almost as a single movement he grabbed the fish in his hand and
> ran out of the door. Ralston waited for a moment then stumbled out of
> the bar himself, in what he hoped was the other direction. (CAT, 161)

We recognize Spicer in the "large childish handwriting" sending, through
a young Orpheus, a cryptic message to a poet who will not recognize the
gesture and in a vehicle very much the opposite of the *Partisan Review*. The
poem does not exist solely on the piece of paper but in the complicated
social interaction between alien and denizen.

These dramas of "inside" and "outside," of private language and public gesture are social versions of the same arguments that occur in Spicer's poems themselves. From *After Lorca* on, the poetry develops more and more strategies for engaging dialogue, whether it is between living poet and dead poet (*After Lorca*), between poet and friends (*Admonitions*), between text and commentary ("Homage to Creeley"), or between pronouns (*Language*). Comments from conversations are embedded in the poems, often without address and in many cases without quotation marks. And the serial poem itself, as described in *Admonitions*, offers its own kind of dialogue, each poem within the book engaged in a dialogue with others: "Poems should echo and reecho against each other. They should create resonances. They cannot live alone any more than we can" (CB, 61).

Nowhere are the full implications of this dialogism more prevalent than in *Language*, where the outside is given a linguistic frame. In its original edition, the book's cover reproduces the July–September 1952 cover of *Language: The Journal of the Linguistic Society of America*, in which Spicer's first and only professional publication appeared.[16] The essay, "Correlation Methods of Comparing Idiolects in a Transition Area," was coauthored with David Reed and represents a summary of research the two linguists were doing on California dialects, research that was to take the form of a comprehensive linguistic atlas. The essay is worth considering in relation to Spicer's poetry, if only because it indicates that as a linguist and as a poet, Spicer was concerned with language as a body of objective data, whose meanings were directly affected by specific geographical locales and small communities. In terms of the linguistic atlas that Spicer helped to compile, this language was dictated from a native informant to a participant-observer and then to Spicer, who, in turn, translated it into phonetic equivalents.

Although Spicer's daily professional work was largely empirical, he endorsed the theoretical position of American structural linguistics as formulated by Sapir and Whorf, who, in a series of articles, speculated on the close relationship between social behavior and language. Their well-known thesis is that what we call knowledge is the direct result of inherited linguistic structures. What we know and how we act are a function of acceptable ways of stating such knowledge. Though Spicer's *Language* is by no means a systematic working-out of the Sapir–Whorf thesis, it does speculate on the linguistic basis of cognition and the social structures that accrue thereby. Consider "Transformations II":

> "In Scarlet Town where I was born
> There was a fair maid dwelling."
> We make up a different language for poetry
> And for the heart – ungrammatical.

It is not that the name of the town changes
(Scarlet becomes Charlotte or even in Gold City I once heard a
    good Western singer make it Tonapah. We don't have
    towns here)
(That sort of thing would please the Jungian astronauts)
But that the syntax changes. This is older than towns.
Troy was a baby when Greek sentence structure emerged. This
    was the real Trojan Horse.
The order changes. The Trojans
Having no idea of true or false syntax and having no
    recorded language
Never knew what hit them.

                                        (CB, 233)

Spicer suggests that at the source of culture is the structure of its syntax. In a tone half playful and half serious, he implies that the fall of Troy owes less to any relative weakness of its arms or troops than to its weak sentence structure. The fact that we have only the Greek side's version of this war reinforces Spicer's point: that what we call "history" is, to a large extent, the function of what narratives survive. The endurance of culture depends upon the ability of any individual to translate the "ungrammatical" language of the heart into the "language of poetry." The fact that a folk tradition may change the names of proper nouns to accommodate a specific locale is less significant than the fact that "syntax changes" and, with it, the development of culture. Hence Spicer moves from the local tradition with its specific folk songs to the larger oral epics, mocking the Jungian tendency to universalize and emphasizing instead the power of local variants.

The Trojan War, in this sense, is no different than the minor internecine conflicts within poetry communities. In the "Transformation" that precedes this poem, Spicer takes on the warfare within his own poetry circle:

They say "he need (present) enemy (plural)"
I am not them. This is the first transformation.
They say "we need (present) no enemy (singular)" No enemy in the
    universe is theirs worth having. We is an intimate pronoun
    which shifts its context almost as the I blinks at it.
    Those
Swans we saw in the garden coming out of the water we hated
    them. "Out of place," you said in passing. Those swans and I
    (a blink in context), all out of place we hated you.
He need (present) enemy (plural) and now it is the swans and
    me against you
Everything out of place

(And now another blink of moment) the last swan back in place. We
Hated them.

(CB 232)

Spicer had been accused by Robert Duncan and George Stanley of need-
ing enemies in order to create poetry.[17] Using the descriptive procedures
of transformational linguistics as formulated by Chomsky, Spicer takes
the basic kernel, "he needs enemies," and subjects it to various permuta-
tions. The shifting of pronouns throughout the passage undercuts the
thrust of the attack, turning it upon itself until "he" and "they" switch
places. In so doing he denudes the phrase of its ontological status by
establishing its deixis, its relation to an audience. All claims to truth in
the phrase "he needs enemies" are called into question by the framing
phrase "They say." Once "they" becomes the governing basis for an
accusation, "they" too must be seen as contributing to the creation of
enemies.

These examples indicate that, for Spicer, the outside is language – not
a symbolist language purified of all contingency, but a social language
used by individuals to celebrate their local villages in song or to argue
with others. It is dialogic in the sense that it is always addressed to an
other, one presumably with whom one cares to argue. And this dialogism occurs within a closed community. For a homosexual poet,
living in Cold War America during the 1950s and 1960s, such community was especially vital. Spicer's cultivation of insularity (what Duncan
calls Tom Sawyer's gang) may have been a necessary strategy in gaining
speech at all. The McCarthy trials, HUAC hearings, and civil rights
clashes were providing plenty of models of the "outside" (Communists,
blacks, eggheads, ethnics, and queers) against which average white citizens should defend themselves. Spicer, rather than rejecting such exclusionary rhetoric, inverted it to his own uses.

Unfortunately, Spicer's cultivation of group affiliations and cult loyalties tended to exacerbate the poet's own xenophobia, misogyny, and
anti-Semitism.[18] Rather than opt for "safe" political positions (the Democratic Party, the Sierra Club, Marxism–Leninism), Spicer chose the
considerably more dangerous route of cadre and cell with their attendant
restrictions and prejudices. It would be wrong to justify Spicer's problematic attitudes toward women or even toward homosexuals by seeing
them strictly in aesthetic terms, but it is important to note how cultural
conditions of the country at large were being acted out at the local level.
"The enemy," Spicer says in *The Holy Grail*, "is in your own country"
and not in some far-distant jungle or State Department office. And if the
audience for poetry is limited, at least you know everyone in the audience by name.

FROM LOGOS TO LOWGHOST

One of Spicer's preferred methods of engaging the personal and local is to address his poems to specific individuals. Whether in the form of dedications or epistles, these gestures give to the poems a directness and specificity usually reserved for private communications: "Each [poem] is a mirror, dedicated to the person that I particularly want to look into it. But mirrors can be arranged. The frightening hall of mirrors in a fun house is universal beyond each particular collection" (CB, 55). Many of Spicer's books contain letters addressed to friends, and his personal correspondence with people like Graham MacIntosh and Jim Alexander has been published in separate poetic series.[19] Spicer also wrote "fake" letters to dead persons (García Lorca, Rimbaud, Billy the Kid), addressing them in much the same manner as he addressed his living friends. In so doing, he blurred the distinction between the dead and the living, letter and poem, private address and public communication. As Lori Chamberlain points out, such strategies draw reality into his work in a decidedly nonmimetic fashion.[20] A letter, after all, is an actual piece of communication with a private reference, but when it appears in a book like "Admonitions" (which contains letters to Robin Blaser), it gains a public role as well. The letter is real in the way a "newspaper in a collage is a real newspaper" (CB, 34) or, ultimately, the way that an image in a poem by García Lorca may become a new object in Spicer's translation. By addressing García Lorca in a letter, Spicer may "correspond" with him in both senses of the term: in a personal letter and in a new work created from Lorca's poems.

Spicer's best-known remark on poetics makes a felicitous use of both interpretations of the term: "Things do not connect; they correspond. That is what makes it possible for a poet to translate real objects, to bring them across language as easily as he can bring them across time" (CB, 34). The distinction here is between images that connect by shared features (metonymy, synecdoche) and images that correspond by parallel but discontinuous features (metaphor). Spicer puns on the etymology of metaphor – "to bear across" – by suggesting that the basis of poetic correspondence is the incarnation of the Logos in the form of Christ: one who bears a cross. The poet as correspondent or translator is one who defines one object by means of another and in this sense participates in the theological idea of incarnation.

The relationship between poetic and theological incarnation is a central feature of Spicer's poetics and derives from his own, highly idiosyncratic Protestantism. He resembles his Puritan forebears in conceiving of God as absolutely alien, "blind as a gigantic bat" (ONS, 49), and is fascinated by the thorny logic of Calvinist thought with its emphasis on God's unknowable nature, its scriptural hermeneutics, its dualism. And he was well read in American nineteenth-century writers like Hawthorne, Melville, and Dickinson, who wrote the history of that Protestant spirit as it came into conflict with modern, capitalist society. The Puritan's impossible dialogue with God becomes, for Spicer, the poet's impossible dialogue with the outside.

In terms of Spicer's poetics this dialogic quality manifests itself as an attempt to undermine poetic logocentrism. The Logos must become "lowghost," brought down to words and given form as discourse. For Spicer the linguist, Christ's humanity is less important than his role as speaker: "To proclaim his humanity is to lie – to pretend that he was not a Word, that he was not created to Explain. The language where we are born across (temporarily and witlessly) in our prayers" (CB, 169). The language that "we are born across," the discursive structure that we inherit in order to explain our existence or that we use in prayer, is beyond or outside us. Hence when we speak we use the words of the dead, and paradoxically this is what gives us life. In the language of poststructuralism, we do not *speak* but are *spoken* by means of structures and systems that precede us. It is for this reason that Spicer often asserts that poetry is written by the dead since it is only by giving up one's control over words – one's life in language – that one may actively receive the "Word" from outside.

As I indicated earlier, theological terms in Spicer's poetics have distinctly nonmetaphysical origins in his concern for the creation of community. These terms come together most fully in *Heads of the Town up to the Aether*, a work whose three sections are based roughly on Dante's tripartite division in the *Comedia*. Like Dante, Spicer is interested in the hierarchical relationship between God and individual, relationships that are replicated in secular history.

The book's title is derived from Jean Doresse's *The Secret Books of the Egyptian Gnostics*,[21] in which the Peratae sect is discussed. One of the sect's books is called *Heads of the Town up to the Aether*, which contains "a description and enumeration of the powers of the lower heavens."[22] In a letter to Jim Alexander, Spicer uses similar language to describe the "powers of the lower heavens" within the poetry community in San Francisco:

> How is it then our business to talk of revolution – we heads of poets one named Jack and one named James, three in the distance named Ebbe, Charles and Robert? It is because we as their victims, as their mouthpiece must learn to become complete victims, complete pieces of their mouth. We must learn that our lips are not our own. A revolution is a savage education. (CAT, 166).

The "lower heavens" include the poet's North Beach milieu every bit as much as it includes the angels and demons of the Gnostic text, a fact given additional weight by the inaugural reading of *Heads of the Town*, which occurred in a bar. Wearing a baseball cap, Spicer read the poems of the book's first section while from the chair behind him Robin Blaser read the "Explanatory Notes."[23]

Spicer's theme, as he acknowledges in his Vancouver Lectures, is incarnation, both as a central metaphor in Christian thought and as a process of representation (dictation) in poetry.[24] We have encountered this theme elsewhere in poets like William Everson and Robert Duncan, for whom incarnation implies the manifestation of God in nature as energy or numinous presence. For Spicer, such immanence is impossible. The nature of deity is incomprehensible and must be discovered by a kind of poetic legerdemain. "*Credo quia absurdum,*" Spicer quotes from Tertullian, and if belief in God is absurd, no attempt to imagine him in language will be adequate. The only adequate form of belief is astonishment:

> Esstoneish me," the words say that hide behind my alarm clock or my dresser drawer or my pillow. "Etonnez moi," even the Word says.
>
> It is up to us to astonish them and Him. To draw forth answers deep from the caverns of objects or from the Word himself. Whatever that is.
>
> Whatever That is is not a play on words but a play between words, meaning come down to hang on a little cross for a while. In play.
>
> And the stony words that are left down with us greet him mutely almost rudely casting their own shadows. For example, the shadow the cross cast.
>
> No, now he is the Lowghost when He is pinned down to words.
>
> (CB, 178)

Spicer's pattern of reiteration and reformulation here suggests how difficult the discovery of God's nature can be. The supplicant must "draw forth answers," not from scriptural authority but from "a play between words." Only by being faithful to duplicity and polysemy can any authentic answer be obtained. The drama of Christ's passion is transformed (but not reduced) to a childhood skit: "meaning come down to hang on a little cross for a while. In play."

In order to accomplish this incarnation, Spicer employs a variety of literary and nonliterary genres. He draws from popular sources (jokes, puns, popular songs) as well as more literary ones (Dante, Rimbaud, Cocteau, surrealism) in order to find alternative discursive modes to traditional theological argument. Literary practices like surrealism or Rimbaudian poetics circumvent mimesis and "play leapfrog with the unknown." Jokes and puns perform a similar function since they engage a public world in which issues of literariness are not at issue. At the same time that these modes debunk literariness, they deconstruct linguistic presence by multiplying meanings and resisting interpretive closure.

Heads of the Town begins with a rather cryptic homage to the poet Robert Creeley, acknowledged perhaps for his development of a short, highly compressed lyric imitated in this section.[25] Within Spicer's Dantean schema, this first section represents Hell, but as Robin Blaser says, it is a "hell of meanings" in which the hierarchical relationship between text and commentary is subverted. The two parts of this section are printed one on top of the other, text and "Explanatory Notes," in the manner of Williams's *Kora in Hell*. Like Williams, Spicer mocks the idea of explication by providing interpretations every bit as opaque as the texts. But the vertical relation of each pair emphasizes the Heaven–Hell dichotomy of the rest of the book; the text stands above as an obscure message translated below by a ghostly interpreter. This mock hermeneutics is extended by the section's reference to Cocteau's *Orphée*, in which messages sent from the afterlife are received (interpreted) by the Orphic poet. Such complicated mythical and figural structures create a dialectical interplay between poem and context. The text lives in a troubled Hades of mirror games, double entendres, and shifting pronouns.

Cocteau's Hell (like that of Creeley and Spicer) is one of confused identities: "In hell it is difficult to tell people from other people" (CB, 123), Spicer says. The line that separates text and commentary can be compared to Cocteau's mirror, which, to the human world, offers the illusion of identity but which, with the proper props (linguistic play and puns), allows passage into the underworld. Consider, for example, "Wrong Turn":

> What I knew
> Wasn't true
> Or oh no
> Your face
> Was made of fleece
> Stepping up to poetry
> Demands
> Hands.

Jacob's coat was made of virgin wool. Virgin wool is defined as wool made from the coat of any sheep that can run faster than the sheepherder.

There are steps on the stairs too, which are awfully steep.

(CB, 121)

The meaning of this poem must be sought in the larger thematics of the book, but we can see that at one level the explanatory note functions to adumbrate associations that are partially developed in the poem. Thus "fleece" becomes the material of Jacob's (actually Joseph's) coat of many colors, which, in turn, leads to a joke concerning the nature of "virgin wool"; "Stepping up to poetry" leads to "steps on the stairs," a phrase that literalizes the remark about poetry. Whatever is going on here cannot be rendered in ordinary terms of exegesis unless we are willing to accept the poem's title in the most literal sense: a series of wrong turns (tropes? turns of phrase? twists of logic?) that become poetry.

Those wrong turns (including the major one that traverses the line separating poem from explanatory note) extend patterns and movements that one can find throughout *Heads of the Town*. The sheep resemble the rabbits and other creatures that appear elsewhere in the book; Jacob is a man thrown into a pit, another visitor to the underworld like Dante or Orpheus; the steps to poetry are "awfully" steep, emphasizing the awe that one experiences in the face of the unknown. The alliterations of "step," "stairs," "sheep," and "steep" parallel the gradual modulation of images, each term of which begins to accumulate semantic and phonemic resonances. As in many of Spicer's poems, the individual word or phrase ("What I knew," for example) has no referent outside its surrounding semantic environment. The relationship between "knew" and "true" is complicated by a series of negations, jokes, non sequiturs, false commentaries, and puns. When we return to the lines "Stepping up to poetry / Demands / Hands," we understand Spicer to mean something like the following: Take poetry as truth only at the risk of your life; you may have to use your hands to hold on, it's that perilous.

Upon the chaos of confused identities and contending voices in "Homage to Creeley" Spicer in his next section builds a purgatory out of the biography of Rimbaud.[26] As its title implies, "A Fake Novel about the Life of Rimbaud" is neither a novel nor a biography but a narrative based upon the world of meanings that Rimbaud helped to invent. Spicer creates this hybrid work by miswriting Rimbaud's biography and by mistranslating several poems from *Les Illuminations*, but if readers go to these works to find sources, they will be disappointed. Rather than translate Rimbaud, Spicer imitates the poet's style in a work like "Une Saison en Enfer" by writing an imaginary biography based on incidents in the poet's life. Spicer seems to be saying that what we know about Rimbaud is not the events that comprise his outward life but rather the poems made of those experiences. Rimbaud becomes a dimension of his own incarnation in language.

Spicer's fake biography produces bizarre variations on the French poet's life. Rimbaud's birthplace, Charleville, becomes "Charlieville"; the Franco-Prussian War becomes "The Frank Terrors"; Rimbaud's first poetic mentor, George Izambard, becomes "Izzard, Cixambert and David the Pig"; the river Meuse, which ran beside the Rimbaud family home, becomes "a piece of water that looked twisted." Rimbaud's birth-place is turned into a post office (appropriately for the author of "Voy-elles"). Each of these transformations of biography into poetry is man-dated by Rimbaud's inaugural attempt to make a new language, one that Spicer sees originating at birth: "After he had been born in the postoffice he began to practice his mouth with a new language" (CB, 151).

As this passage indicates, Rimbaud's youth is a central concern of the book. Spicer is obsessed with the poet's entry into poetry at age fifteen and his equally youthful rejection of it at age twenty – the two poles within his poetic life. Spicer's version of Rimbaud's earliest poem, "Les Étrennes des Orphelins," recognizes the importance of that youthful entry into language:

> *The Poem Rimbaud Wrote on October 29, 1869*
>
> I do not proclaim a new age,
> That I am fifteen God only knows.
> I keep the numbers in my head
> When I am dead
> I will fall into a rage
> And bite off all my toes.
>
> (CB, 153)

Spicer's translation bears no resemblance to the original (which depicts a sad New Year's morning at an orphanage). What intrigues Spicer more is the image of Rimbaud as a perpetual baby – as someone who refuses to grow up. When Rimbaud begins to write at age fifteen, he joins that larger community of poets that Spicer calls "The Word." At this point, Rimbaud ceases to be a historical individual and incarnates himself: "The Word puts on flesh when he becomes sixteen, seventeen, eighteen. The Word before Whom all of us are witless" (CB, 161). Or is it "witness"? By witnessing (reading) that Word we make up a life somewhere in between Rimbaud's and ours. We are "witless" in the face of the word that Rimbaud transforms.

Just as the life and poetics of Rimbaud provide a basis for "A Fake Novel," surrealism provides a similar basis for the third, paradisaical section, "A Textbook of Poetry." As a historical extension of Rimbau-dian poetics, surrealism provides its own doctrine of correspondence, transcription, and dictation, and is linked to Spicer's ongoing concern with incarnation:

> Surrealism is the business of poets who cannot benefit by surrealism. It was the first appearance of the Logos that said, "The public be damned," by which he did not mean that they did not matter or he wanted to be crucified by them, but that really he did not have a word to say to them. This was surrealism. (CB, 169)

Spicer, in his cranky way, also says "the public be damned" at least insofar as the idea of a public directs the writing of the poem. The generalized audience becomes a barrier to transcription, whether the message comes from Calvin's God or from the Freudian unconscious. Like the surrealists, Spicer wants to surrender himself to language: "To be lost in a crowd. Of images, of metaphors . . . of words" (CB, 169).

As a "textbook of poetry," this third section mocks the traditional college anthology like Brooks and Warren's *Understanding Poetry* with its selection of approved exhibits and attached "questions for further study." What the student will find in Jack Spicer's textbook is a series of prose pieces, most of which deal with poetics. Thus poem and theory, prose and poetry are fused into a single work. Spicer wants, by his title, to emphasize that poetry is also a methodology, a practice of reading. He wants to erase the distinction between text and interpretation (as he had done in the Creeley section), and to eliminate the hierarchy of student and teacher that the textbook institutionalizes.

Spicer's alternative to traditional academic theories of interpretation and reading is what he calls the "Indian rope trick":

> The Indian rope trick. And a little Indian boy climbs up it. And the Jungians and the Freudians and the Social Reformers all leave satisfied. Knowing how the trick was played.
>
> There is nothing to stop the top of the rope though. There is nothing to argue. People in the audience have seen the boy dancing and it is not hypnosis.
>
> It is the definition of the rope that ought to interest everyone who wants to climb the rope. The rope-dance. Reading the poem.
>
> Reading the poem that does not appear when the magician starts or when the magician finishes. A climbing in-between. Real. (CB, 173)

Reading becomes a "climbing in-between" multiple meanings just as the Indian boy climbs between earth and an unknowable heaven. The Jungians, Freudians, and Social Reformers may create rational explanations for the way the trick is performed, but the "astonishment" remains. Incarnation is just such an astonishment, never stable but always in process among multiple propositions of God's nature. Or in the language of "A Textbook of Poetry," God "descends to the real. By a rope ladder. The soul also goes there. Solely – not love, beyond the thought of God" (CB, 172). And although the metaphor here is vertical, a descent from upper to lower, Spicer also intends his "in-between" to be horizontal and temporal as well, a debate between those multiple propositions as expressed by persons in history: "I mean the thought of thinking about God. Naturally I mean the real God."

THE CITY AS DIAMOND

Where one is is in a temple that sometimes makes us forget that we are
in it. Where we are is in a sentence. (CB, 175)

I began this chapter by speaking of a "city redefined" into a
church through the "fuss and fury" of private conversation. The city
remained for Spicer a place of personal challenges and public competi-
tions, and its transformation into a *civitas dei* would exact a certain toll
from those who believed in it. For Spicer, as for William Everson, such
extremity was the essence of the West Coast:

> "The dog wagged his tail and looked wonderfly sad" Poets in
>   America with nothing to believe in except maybe the ships in
>   Glouchester Harbor or the snow fall.
> "Don't you remember Sweet Betsy from Pike,
> She crossed the big mountains with her lover Ike."
> No sense
> In crossing a mountain with nobody living in it. No sense
> In fighting their fires.
> West Coast is something nobody with sense would understand.
>
> (CB, 263)[27]

Spicer contrasts a more sentimental belief in localism (Olson's Gloucester) to his own West Coast, a place "nobody with sense would understand." The West is the stuff of legend and folk song, woven out of tall
tales and barroom ballads. And it is precisely this lack of "sense" that
provides an alternative form of faith for Spicer and his circle. "Wit is the
only barrier between ourselves and them" (CB, 261), he says, and if wit
is a barrier, it is also a tool with which to undermine idealisms of various
sorts, whether national or literary.

Although Spicer thought of the ideal city as something created out of a
community and a conversation, he made at least one attempt to formu-
late an image that would embody all of his desires for secular and spiritual perfection.[28] Appropriately, the image Spicer chose was that of a
baseball diamond:

> We shall build our city backwards from each baseline extending like
>   a square ray from each distance – you from the first-base line,
>   you from behind the second baseman, you from behind the
>   short stop, you from the third-baseline.
> We shall clear the trees back, the lumber of our pasts and futures
>   back, because we are on a diamond, because it is our diamond
> Pushed forward from.
> And our city shall stand as the lumber rots and Runcible mountain
>   crumbles, and the ocean, eating all of islands, comes to meet
>   us.
>
> (CB, 259)

Spicer, who followed the San Francisco Giants with fanatic loyalty, saw baseball as the perfect spiritual model. At the center is God who figures as "a big white baseball that has nothing to do but go in a curve or straight line" (CB, 258). There is no intention within the baseball, or God; the ball's movements are determined by actors on the field who pitch, hit, and field according to the rules. The sacraments are shared by a pitcher and a catcher, who figure, in Spicer's scheme, as the two parts of poetic dictation: outside and poet. The catcher sends signals to the pitcher, who then translates them into a curveball, fastball, or whatever. The batter as reader attempts to play "between" these sacraments in order to anticipate the pitch. The endurance of the game is based on faith: The players must have enough belief in the game to play by the rules. The big variable, of course, is the movement of the ball, and it is this variability, the uniqueness of each play, that makes the game diverting. The baseball diamond itself offers an image of the "utter logic of form and color" within which the illogic – the non-sense – of the game takes place.

Spicer had arrived at this felicitous model while visiting Vancouver, British Columbia, where a new and vital poetry community was evolving – a scene in which he was a central figure. No doubt the fact that he located his ideal city "high / In the Runcible Mountain wilderness" attests to his feeling that the Vancouver was offering a new hope for community that his own lacked. Spicer had become increasingly skeptical about the literary situation in San Francisco during his last years, no doubt a result of his alcoholism. The local North Beach bar scene had been coopted by entrepreneurs of bohemia and, worse, by the topless nightclubs that began to appear in the early 1960s. Spicer felt, whether accurately or not, that his fellow poets – the true "heads of the town" – had sold out to what he called the big "fix" of corporate/academic America. Some, like the Beats, had become media celebrities, others had started publishing with large commercial houses and had taken jobs in universities. Poets had "nothing to believe in except maybe the ships in Glouchester Harbor or the snow fall." The defection from a belief in nonsense and magic signaled a more generalized American malaise:

> I can't stand to see them shimmering in the impossible music of the
>   Star Spangled Banner. No
> One accepts this system better than poets. Their hurts healed for a
>   few dollars.
> Hunt
> The right animals. I can't. The poetry
> Of the absurd comes through San Francisco televisions.
>   Directly connected with moon-rockets.

If this is dictation, it is driving
Me Wild

(CB, 265)

The "Star Spangled Banner," seen and heard (according to Robin Blaser) through the shimmering television images of the first unmanned moon landing, is perhaps the most extreme generalization of community possible; the music invades the television just as the signal through which it is transmitted invades space. If this is dictation, it is driving Spicer wild.

If Spicer was troubled about global politics, he was equally skeptical about the possibilities of political action within his own community. In his final public appearance at the Berkeley Poetry Conference on July 14, 1965, one month before his death, his theme was the inadequacy of political poetry:

> There are bosses in poetry as well. . . . If you're poets you ought to figure out what the power system is within your own community. . . . Your enemy is simply something that is going to stop you from writing poetry. . . . A magazine is a society: I think *Open Space* proved that. . . . I don't believe in the society [*Poetry* Magazine] creates. . . . Of all the poems I've seen in the last ten years coming from this area I haven't seen one good political poem.[29]

As a discussion of the artist's role in society, especially at the beginning of the Vietnam War, these remarks are woefully inadequate. And no doubt to the Berkeley community that had recently gone through the free-speech movement, the idea that the enemy is "something that is going to stop you from writing poetry" seemed beside the point. Yet Spicer's remarks are consistent with his general feeling that community begins with one's local constituency and that there are "bosses" in poetry as well as in Washington.

This warning is especially strong in *A Book of Magazine Verse*, in the last poem of which Spicer addresses Allen Ginsberg:

> At least we both know how shitty the world is. You wearing a
> beard as a mask to disguise it. I wearing my tired smile. I
> don't see how you do it. One hundred thousand university
> students marching with you. Toward
> A necessity which is not love but is a name.
> King of the May. A title not chosen for dancing. The police
> Civil but obstinate. If they'd attacked
> The kind of love (not sex but love), you gave the one hundred
> thousand students
> I'd have been very glad. And loved the policemen Why
> Fight the combine of your heart and my heart or anybody's heart.
> People are starving.

(CB, 267)

The occasion for this poem was Ginsberg's 1965 trip to Czechoslovakia in which he had been crowned king of the May by students, causing a near riot in the streets of Prague and resulting in Ginsberg's expulsion from the country. Spicer, rather unfairly, attacks what he sees as Ginsberg's generalized humanism when, in fact, "People are starving." This last line is not so much Spicer's appeal for compassion for the underprivileged as it is his use of a cliché about the human condition to focus on the inadequacy of terms for love. Spicer implies that Ginsberg hides behind a rhetoric ("a beard as a mask") of transcendental identification to hide "how shitty the world is." People *are* starving, Spicer suggests, but they are hungry for more than platitudes.

The poem to which Spicer's is addressed is "Kral Majales," in which Ginsberg cries:

> And I am the King of May, which is the power of sexual youth,
> and I am the King of May, which is industry in eloquence and action
>   in amour,
> and I am the King of May, which is long hair of Adam and the
>   Beard of my own body
> and I am the King of May, which is Kral Majales in the
>   Czechoslovakian tongue,
> and I am the King of May, which is old Human poesy, and 100,000
>   people chose my name . . .[30]

By comparing these lines with those of Spicer, we can see the extreme poles of poetry within the San Francisco Renaissance in the mid-1960s. On the one hand, we see Spicer addressing a specific other, using the poem to argue, cajole, and criticize. Its personal address and highly specific reference focus the argument on a particular occasion. On the other hand, we see Ginsberg presenting himself as a microcosmic source of utopian unity. His voice becomes a direct agent in that transformation through his identification with "old Human poesy" marshaled from its visionary past to serve the modern era. Where Spicer presents himself as a single interlocutor and confidant, Ginsberg is a representative man, capable of taking upon himself the combined desires and aspirations of millions.

We can see in Spicer and Ginsberg the difference between an operational poetics that produces meanings and an immanent poetics that discovers them. Spicer's struggle to avoid the interference of the ego or of public reputation forces him back upon a kind of objectivism in which form articulates the disparity between language and the world. The poem does not "connect" with the world; it "corresponds" to it by discontinuous means. For Ginsberg, form is a conduit into a larger world of transcendent truths whose source is the body and whose end is the cosmos. These differences parallel those within American poetry in general. The same antinomian spirit that drove Poe to a rigid determinism of style and poetic language also drove Emerson toward a no less determinist natural supernaturalism. The question, as Roy Harvey Pearce states it, is, "How to say no with Ahab, so to say yes with Ishmael?"[31] Spicer never formulated his "Poetic Principle" or "Philosophy of Composition," preferring to let the poems provide their own adequate poetics, but like Poe he staked everything on the radical sufficiency of poetic language to create a world – or, in terms germane to this chapter, to create a city. The poem "does not have to fit together," he says. "Not as a gesture of contempt for the scattered nature of reality. Not because the pieces would not fit in time. But because this would be the only way to cause an alliance between the dead and the living" (CB, 176). Unlike Ginsberg, who often speaks for the nation, Spicer absented himself from it, forming his own singular community that, once he died, seemed to evaporate with him. "It does not have to fit together," then, refers as much to the community as to the poem. The spirit of that community in San Francisco, under Spicer's tutelage, was crazy and in this, perhaps, it was most like the nation.

6

Appropriations
Women and the San Francisco Renaissance

In 1957, Denise Levertov visited the San Francisco Bay Area for the first time. In order to introduce her to local poets Robert Duncan arranged a party that included, among others, Jack Spicer.[1] On that occasion Spicer read from a new series called *Admonitions*, one poem of which seemed directed at the guest of honor, although its message was anything but honorific:

> People who don't like the smell of faggot vomit
> Will never understand why men don't like women
> Won't see why those never to be forgotten thighs
> of Helen (say) will move us into screams of laughter,
> Parody (what we don't want) is the whole thing.
> Don't deliver us any mail today, mailman.
> Send us no letters. The female genital organ is hideous, We
> Do not want to be moved.
> Forgive us. Give us
> A single example of the fact that nature is imperfect.
> Men ought to love men
> (And do)
> As the man said
> It's
> Rosemary for remembrance.[2]

Levertov's response to this hostile poem was to write "Hypocrite Women," which takes Spicer's remark about female genitalia and turns it into an assertion of female power:

> And if at Mill Valley perched in the trees
> the sweet rain drifting through western air
> a white sweating bull of a poet told us

172

> our cunts are ugly—why didn't we
> admit we have thought so too? (And
> what shame? They are not for the eye!)
>
> No, they are dark and wrinkled and hairy,
> caves of the Moon . . .[3]

Spicer's unqualified misogyny becomes a vehicle by which Levertov asserts an authority repressed by women. She chastises "hypocrite women" who "Whorishly" accommodate the male in his condescension, who repress their own dreams and fears, paring them "like toenails, [clipping] them like ends of / split hair." In a letter attached to *Admonitions*, Spicer likened his poems to mirrors "dedicated to the person that I particularly want to look into it" (CB, 55). Levertov looked into that mirror – and turned it back on the one holding it.

However hostile to women, Spicer's poem is hardly a celebration of homosexuality. His misogyny is linked to a profound sexual ambivalence, expressed in its most violent form in the poem's opening lines. Nor does the poem address heterosexuality in ways that might moderate or qualify his attitude about women. Rather, he offers the most extreme version of sexual preference: either "faggot vomit" or the "hideous" vagina. Spicer implies that acknowledging one's homosexuality involves adopting several corollary attitudes about women as well as about fellow gays. It is an absurd logic, of course, one that Spicer both parodies and entertains at the same time. Rather than make discriminations about sexual preference, he uses language to provoke and challenge. Self-disgust mixes with spleen to create a poem that, to adapt Levertov's lines, "is not for the eye."

Another frame for reading Spicer's poem is Levertov's visit itself, an event that occasioned much interest among local San Francisco writers and that Spicer used to test group loyalty against an outsider. This group loyalty applied to at least three contiguous communities: the largely male, homosexual milieu in which Spicer lived, the poetic circle in which he wrote (and which included women artists like Helen Adam, Fran Herndon, Joanne Kyger, and others), and the San Francisco writing community in general, which stood, in Spicer's view, in opposition to Levertov's East Coast, Black Mountain affiliations. The fact that Robert Duncan, who organized the event, maintained his own ties to Black Mountain was another frame. A thorough reading of Spicer's poem must take into account these communities and the ways in which they created their own dramas of inside and outside. For Spicer it was essential to use such conflicts to create a disturbance, however unpleasant, and thereby challenge complacency and tolerance. Such disturbances were a way of verifying the loyalty of community members and at the same time excluding those who would enter from without.

To some extent, Spicer's sectarian and oppositional spirit can be found in all bohemian enclaves, based as they were on elaborate pecking orders and cult loyalties. One has only to think of the complex class and sexual hierarchies of the Bloomsbury, Sitwell, and Stein circles of the 1920s to realize the important roles that boundaries played in the evolution of modernism. Literature written within such groups derives much of its impetus from specific personalities and occasions (like the Levertov visit), and to deny this exclusive and exclusionary quality is to ignore one of the central features of literary production. At the same time, bohemian enclaves seldom escape issues of gender and sexual preference that are given outward form in avant garde literary practice. As Shari Benstock illustrates in her work on women writers in Paris during the first half of the century, salons, circles, and sects became major forums for new aesthetic positions as well as supportive environments for women – both heterosexual and lesbian – within masculinist culture.[4] The "prison house of language" with which modernism struggled was also a patriarchal institution (a fact that Gertrude Stein parodies in "Patriarchal Poetry")[5] for which the women-centered salons of the period offered a salutary alternative.

If European bohemia of the teens and twenties had its share of important venues for women, American bohemia of the 1950s lacked all but the most perfunctory recognition of women as artists. Without the supportive environment of either an underground salon network or a feminist movement, women writers of the 1950s and early 1960s defined themselves largely within the male "circles" that I have discussed in this book. Whatever their marginal position, however, women poets did exert an important effect on the San Francisco scene and in many respects set the stage for a powerful revolution in women's writing that continues to this day.

Central to any consideration of the San Francisco Renaissance would be the names of Helen Adam, Madeline Gleason, Joanne Kyger, Diane DiPrima, Josephine Miles, and Lenore Kandel, all of whom participated actively in events that this book chronicles. Helen Adam served as a good witch and medium for the Duncan–Spicer circle, introducing Blake's ballads to workshops and sustaining an already strong romantic and mythopoeic spirit. Madeline Gleason was instrumental in starting a reading and performance series in the late 1940s that predated the more famous poetry reading movement of the 1950s, and her poems, with their strong emphasis on play and fairy tale, were widely read during the period. Both Joanne Kyger and Diane DiPrima were strongly identified with the Beats, and later with the Duncan–Spicer circle. Kyger's first poems were written in the context of Spicer's workshops, and Diane DiPrima, although she arrived in San Francisco after the period this book covers, was introduced to the local writers through early books like *This Kind of Bird Flies Backward* (1958) and *Dinners and Nightmares*[6] (1961) as well as through the publication of her magazine, *The Floating Bear,* which she edited with LeRoi Jones. Josephine Miles was one of the first tenured women faculty members at the University of California, Berkeley, and became a guiding influence for Jack Spicer and Robin Blaser, both of whom had been her students during their undergraduate days. Although there is little resemblance between her work and the action-oriented poetry of the Beats or the hermetic work of Duncan and Spicer, she was a supporter of the movement and offered a certain academic imprimatur to many of the more extravagant bohemian gestures of the post-"Howl" generation. Lenore Kandel's erotic poem *The Love Book* caused a storm of controversy when it was brought to trial for obscenity in 1966, drawing attention not only to the poem but to the fusion of eroticism and mysticism that was associated with both Beat and 1960s youth cultures. Other women poets (Sister Mary Norbert Korte, Eve Triem, Mary Fabilli, Joanna McClure, Eileen Kauffman) also contributed to the origins of women's poetry in San Francisco, so that younger writers like Kathleen Fraser, Alta, Judy Grahn, Pat Parker, Susan Griffin, Bev Dahlen, Carla Harryman, and Lyn Hejinian could gain the substantial audience they now enjoy. In order to understand the contributions of these and other women to the San Francisco Renaissance, it is necessary to understand their "absence" within it.

THE BOYS' CLUB

Eat me, drink me, love me;
Laura, make much of me;
For your sake I have braved the glen
And had to do with goblin merchant men
> (Christina Rossetti)

Among male writers of the 1950s the representation of women was sexist, to say the least. The Beat ethos relegated women to the role of sexual surrogate, muse, or mom; it did not raise them to a position of artistic equality. Literary friendships throughout the period were marked by a kind of boys' club mentality in which women were excluded – or if admitted, only on conditional grounds. Robert Duncan describes the Spicer circle in such terms:

> We were the champions of the boys' team in Poetry, and some day our fellow students would know that Poetry was the name of the game. . . . [Spicer] met now with his group of poets as once he had met with his Sunday School group. George Stanley, Harold Dull, Joe Dunn, Ebbe Borregaard, Jim Alexander, Lew Ellingham, Ron Loewin-

sohn, Stan Persky – there were star players, bench sitters, and water boys. Joanne Kyger could play on the team, but she was a girl. Helen Adam was team godmother. Fran Herndon would make the posters, pennants, and paint the portraits of the old guard – Spicer, Blaser, and Jess and me – and the gang would rally round.[7]

I have already described the medieval cultishness of this circle, and these remarks illustrate how thoroughly hierarchical gender roles could be. The same could be said of the Beats, for whom the comradeship of males was crucial: "The social organization which is most true to the artist is the boy gang," Allen Ginsberg recorded – and then added, "Not society's perfum'd marriage."[8]

To be fair, we must search for the roots of sexism among San Francisco poets in the society at large; to criticize their work on feminist grounds requires a look at 1950s attitudes toward women. This critique has already been undertaken by feminist scholars, and several recent studies have focused on the context of women in avant garde art circles. Barbara Ehrenreich, in *The Hearts of Men*, discusses the repressive quality of postwar social life, its subordination of women to housekeeping and childrearing roles, when, only a few years earlier, they had entered the marketplace in unprecedented numbers as part of the war effort. Ehrenreich acknowledges that many of the same misogynist attitudes could be found in bohemian culture as well as in suburban America, but that within the former one could discern a potentially liberating alternative to then-prevalent sexual roles: "In the Beat, the two strands of male protest – one directed against the white-collar work world and the other against the suburbanized family life that work was supposed to support – come together into the first all-out critique of American consumer culture."[9] The critique that Ehrenreich describes occurred in the context of male bonding that one finds in novels like *On the Road* and *The Dharma Bums*, where the companionship of men offers a healthy release from the obligations of suburban, heterosexual family life.

There is no question that the Beats stressed independence and isolation rather than commitment and responsibility: "In their own lives, the leading ideologues and personalities of the Beat generation were indeed often irresponsible to women and vulnerable to every psychiatric suspicion about the 'immature' male."[10] But the alternative, as Ehrenreich goes on to say, was the point of view promulgated by the *Life* magazine author who speculated that "the 'chicks' who are willing to support a whiskery male [must be] middle-aged and fat."[11] Worse, they might actually hold down a job (to support their out-of-work consort) and demand a sexually dominant position. The Beats offered a new complex set of possible roles for males that, even if they subordinated women, at least offered an alternative to the consumerist ideology of sexuality projected by the *Playboy* magazine stereotype of heterosexuality and to the *Saturday Evening Post* version of the nuclear family.

If a boys' club mentality pervaded literary associations, a patriarchal ideology pervaded the poems. The revival of a primitivist ethos carried with it a psychic division of labor in which the male was regarded as the maker and the female as the formless material of his art. To some extent this represented the heritage of a romantic masculine tradition based on a feminized natural landscape which, as Margaret Homans points out, was the "necessary complement to [the male poet's] imaginative project, the grounding of an imagination so powerful that it risks abstraction without her."[12] Gary Snyder's "Praise for Sick Women" epitomizes this view. From our perspective – and perhaps from Gary Snyder's today – this poem invokes the myths about women that have been used both to praise and to censure them:

> The female is fertile, and discipline
> (contra naturam) only
>   confuses her
> Who has, head held sideways
> Arm out softly, touching,
> A difficult dance to do, but not in mind.[13]

Granted, Snyder is invoking ancient prohibitions against menstruation ("Apples will sour at your sight. / Blossoms fail the bough, / Soil turn bone-white"), but in the name of the primitive imagination, he uncritically reinscribes those patriarchal and tribal values in the modern era. Women do a "difficult dance," he admits, "but not in mind."

Diane DiPrima, who shares many of Gary Snyder's ethnological and mythological interests, wrote a response to this poem. "The Practice of Magical Evocation" begins with a strong assertion of the poet's powers as a creative individual:

> i am a woman and my poems
> are women's: easy to say
> this. the female is ductile
> and
>   (stroke after stroke)
> built for masochistic
> calm.   The deadened nerve
> is part of it:
> awakened sex, dead retina
> fish eyes;   at hair's root
> minimal feeling
>
> and pelvic architecture functional
> assailed inside & out
> (bring forth) the cunt gets wide

and relatively sloppy
bring forth men children only
                        female
                        is
                        ductile
woman, a veil thru which the fingering Will
twice torn
twice torn
                inside & out
the flow
what rhythm add to stillness
what applause?[14]

DiPrima rehearses Snyder's characterization of woman, but situates it in
an ironic frame. She changes Snyder's word "fertile" to "ductile," implying that woman is, by her fertility, malleable, pliable, and without will;
she has no mind or nerve ("at hair's root / minimal feeling"); she is "built
for masochistic / calm"; her fertility leads only to the production of
children – and "men children only." Women are empty vessels through
which the male "fingering Will" penetrates and begets his progeny – an
echo of Yeats's "Leda and the Swan," in which the raped Leda is "So
mastered by the brute blood of the air" that she assumes Zeus's "knowledge with his power." And after the rape, after the childbirth ("twice
torn"), what does the woman receive from all this: "what rhythm add to
stillness / what applause?" The answer must be found in the poem's
opening lines – in DiPrima's assertion that she writes a woman's poetry,
that she does more than simply procreate. She brings forth another kind of
rhythm, one in language, capable of seizing the words of the male poet and
using them in a kind of "magical evocation," as her title suggests.

Irony in this poem is accretional. The more DiPrima asserts woman's
passivity, the less we believe her and thus recognize her ability to use
rhetoric to her own advantage. Adrienne Rich calls this rewriting of the
patriarchal text "revision," an act that is "more than a chapter in cultural
history; it is an act of survival."[15] DiPrima's poem is a good example of
such revision since it directly appropriates Snyder's naturalist rhetoric
and turns it to her own uses. This poem (like "Hypocrite Women") is
even more remarkable for having been written in the late 1950s before
the revisionist imperative was common in feminist discourse. We could
see her poem as an indication of what directions her peers have taken in
poetry, appropriating the coercive rhetoric of the masculine tradition and
using it against itself.

My epigraph for this section is taken from Christina Rossetti's
"Goblin Market," which describes just such an appropriation. Rossetti
rewrites Keats's "La Belle Dame Sans Merci," in which a young man is

placed under the spell of an enchantress, who, after luring him to her "elfin grot," abandons him to dark dreams and solitude. Rossetti retells the story from the standpoint of two sisters, one of whom, Laura, succumbs to the succulent "fruits" of the male goblin merchants and then suffers a strange and powerful lethargy that threatens to take her life. In order to save her, her sister Lizzie withstands the temptations of the goblin merchants who attempt to force her to eat the delicious but lethal fruit. They battle her, smearing the fruit pulp and juice over her body, but she stands fast and forces them to retreat. When she returns home, she attempts to save her dying sister by an act of feminist redemption and communion: "Eat me, drink me, love me; / Laura, make much of me; / For your sake I have braved the glen / And had to do with goblin merchant men."[16] When Laura kisses the fruit from Lizzie's face and lips, she is healed, and what had been fatal nectar from the goblin males becomes restorative balm from a sister's love. This act of sacrifice by sister for sister is achieved not only against male merchants but against a masculinist mythology in which women are treated – as in Keat's poem – as dangerous, possessed, or evil presences, "hysterical," in their links to uncontrollable nature. Rossetti's appropriation of Keats's ballad stands as a synecdoche for what women in a later postromantic age have done with a similar tradition, transforming the powerful mythopoeia of quest romance into dramas of female independence and authority.

This appropriative stance was, as I have already indicated, especially important within the San Francisco Renaissance, where the forum for poetic debate often involved questions of power and cult loyalty. We have seen how Levertov and DiPrima responded to two specific male poems, but we could see the same revisionism at work in the poetics of Helen Adam, Joanne Kyger, and Judy Grahn, who represent three different versions of this appropriative stance. For them, the act of rewriting the romantic tradition is always a matter of reinventing gynocentric authority, however conscious the intent may be. To some extent all three poets have been empowered to write by the feminist movement, but they were given specific permission within various San Francisco communities whose closeness – and even exclusivity – created a necessary oppositional spirit.

HELEN ADAM: "POSSESSED BY LOVE"

Mrs. Mackie Rhodus: "BE QUIET. A talking woman likes a silent man." (*San Francisco's Burning*)[17]

"Jack read the poem with extraordinary venom," Robert Duncan said of the Spicer–Levertov event in Mill Valley, and that evening Helen Adam, who had been present, had a vivid dream concerning the day's events. In Duncan's retelling of it, "she was delivering messages – she was [actually] a messenger in the financial district – and she'd go knock at each office door and they'd open it, and she'd hand them an envelope and she'd say, 'I'm sorry, but I'm a woman,' all night long at different offices."[18] Helen Adam's dream serves as a metaphor for the general condition of women writers at this time. She interprets Spicer's binarist (and genitalized) logic of sexual preference as a drama of exclusion. Anticipating the rejection she knows she will meet, the female poet-messenger apologizes at the doors of the male institutions she serves. The fact that Adam actually was, at that time, a messenger in the financial district serves our analogy: Working not *in* the centers of trade but moving *among* them, she may translate and transfer but never create herself. It was a role that Helen Adam played out in very different terms within the San Francisco Renaissance, where she served, quite literally, as a medium for her male colleagues. Her dream, like her legendary tarot readings, was an interpretation of tensions within a community that, as we have seen, often manifested the same exclusivity that Adam encountered in the financial district.

Helen Adam was born in Glasgow, Scotland, in 1909 and by the age of sixteen had already established herself as a gifted balladeer and songwriter. Under the name of "Pixy Pool" she published several books of songs, much indebted to the Scots and British ballad tradition.[19] She came to the United States with her sister Pat (a novelist, poet, and songwriter) in 1939 and eventually found her way to Robert Duncan's workshop in 1953. In that workshop, she brought the ballad tradition, especially in its romantic incarnation, to a literary culture already primed to receive it. Her themes were those of many early narrative poems – love-smitten knights, wicked witches, beautiful but treacherous women – and her meters played few variations on the traditional form. If she was an original in her revival of the English ballad tradition, she was the absolute incarnation of that spirit in her performances, singing or chanting her songs in a high, strong voice that had retained its Gaelic lilt. Her willingness to "sing" her songs provided the impetus for many local poets to try, with various degrees of success and voice, to do likewise.

Feminist scholarship has discussed the implications of romantic female stereotypes – the madwoman in the attic, the domestic muse, la belle dame sans merci – within the psychosocial realm of male power. The dying ladies of Poe's poems, the Pre-Raphaelite consumptives, the possessed sorceresses of Keats's and Coleridge's ballads all represent, according to one canonical version, a nineteenth-century male anxiety over paternity and authority in a secularized world. The female author may claim her identity only by killing what Virginia Woolf called the "angel in the house," or that passive domestic muse bequeathed to generations of women poets. At the same time, as Sandra Gilbert and Susan Gubar have shown, she must also kill the Medusan opposite of the domestic muse, the monster who represents woman's independence and creativity.[20] It is the latter figure – the woman as demon or monster – that Helen Adam exploits for her own purposes. Like Mary Shelley before her, Adam's Gothicism is a stylistic frame in which an allegory of creativity is figured and manipulated.

By reviving many stock topoi of romanticism, Adam might seem to be merely a latter-day version of that tradition. But her songs and ballads about werewolf brides and witches are really small dramas of female power set against the familiar landscape of quest romance and fairy tale.[21] The most common narrative in Helen Adam's poems is that in which an earnest but naive male asserts his right to "possess" love, discovering too late that he becomes possessed *by* it. The allegory is a Gnostic retelling of the Fall in which Eve, by eating the fruit of knowledge, is possessed of a divine wisdom about the unity of all nature. Man's attempts to suppress – or possess – that knowledge are futile since the more he binds nature to his will, the more nature replicates itself in new, unrecognizable forms.

Helen Adam's allegory of male desire and female power can be found throughout the poet's work but nowhere more brilliantly than in "I Love My Love." Like "Goblin Market," it owes a good deal to "La Belle Dame Sans Merci," but where Keats's pale knight suffers a bad dream at the hands of the fairy queen, Adam's young husband undergoes a physical and psychological mutilation of frightening proportions. As in all such tales, the events begin in innocence:

> There was a man who married a maid. She laughed as he led her
>   home.
> The living flesh of her long bright hair she combed with a golden
>   comb.
> He led her home through his barley fields where the saffron poppies
>   grew.
> She combed, and whispered, "I love my love." Her voice like a
>   plaintive coo.
> Ha! Ha!
> Her voice like a plaintive coo.
>
> (NAP, 114)

The bride's bright laughter and her repeated assertions of love ("To my love I give my All") soon turn ominous as she weaves a "secret web" with her long, golden hair – first trapping and then suffocating her husband.

The husband, furious at being caught in the bride's hair (and by extension smothered by love), strangles her and then buries her, using the hair as a funeral shroud. But the hair has a mind of its own and soon grows out of the grave, all the while singing its ghastly song:

> "I love my love with a capital T. My love is Tender and True.
> I'll love my love in the barley fields when the thunder cloud is blue.
> My body crumbles beneath the ground but the hairs of my head will grow.
> I'll love my love with the hairs of my head. I'll never, never let go.
> Ha! Ha!
> I'll never, never let go."
>
> (NAP, 115)

As the hair grows, the husband vainly attempts to cut it down, but like the broom in Walt Disney's *The Sorcerer's Apprentice*, each fragment grows into new and more ominous strands of the ever-expanding web. Finally, in the poem's powerful close, the hair billows over the husband's house, "Rolling, lashing o'er walls and roof, heavy, and soft, and warm. / It thumped on the roof, it hissed and glowed over every window pane." The hair rushes in, surrounds the husband in his bed, and in one moment reduces him to a child — and then to a corpse:

> The hair rushed in. He struggled and tore, but whenever he tore a tress,
> "I love my love with a capital Z," sang the hair of the sorceress.
> It swarmed upon him, it swaddled him fast, it muffled his every groan.
> Like a golden monster it seized his flesh, and then it sought the bone,
> Ha! Ha!
> And then it sought the bone.
>
> (NAP, 117)

The gradual elaboration of the hair motif is structurally replicated in the poem's variation on the refrain "I love my love," first with an "A" for "All," then with a "T" for "True" and "Tender," and finally with a "Z" for the "Zero" state of annihilation. In each strophe we see the increasing power of the sorceress-bride reflected in the gradually diminishing power of the husband until he is reduced, quite literally, to a child. The hair that represents love and youthful beauty gradually reveals its other face as the unceasing process of growth and decay of which love is only the prelude.

Many of Helen Adam's songs repeat this motif. In "The Fair Young Wife," the drama is enacted by a girl who marries a much older man.[22] A werewolf herself, the young bride lies awake listening to the howling of wolves in the forest and desires to run with them, "naked and unafraid." Finally she turns on her aged husband, killing him and then joining her comrades howling in the snow. Here the allegory is seasonal: The husband represents the old year that must be killed in order for Spring to pursue her sexual youth. However symbolic they may be, Adam's wicked women and vengeful wives often struggle out of a marriage net in order to have identity as individuals. They do not wither and die, like those in Poe and Keats, but gain strength and authority by their violation of the marital frame.

Although Adam revives a much earlier ballad tradition, she often transforms it to suit contemporary political and social reality. Her "Miss Laura," for example, is a variation on the English lyric "Black is the color of my true love's hair," only in Adam's version "hair" becomes "skin," and the poem becomes a protest against racial prejudice and a plea for understanding in mixed-race relationships. "Jericho Bar" is the plaint of a forlorn youth, corrupted by life in a wild bohemian hangout of drug addicts, rock and roll singers, beatniks, and oddballs. "Cheerless Junkie's Song" is a satiric look at life on the contemporary Lower East Side of New York. And perhaps her most wonderful transformation of a traditional motif is "Apartment on Twin Peaks," which depicts the bizarre goings-on of a coven of witches behind the blinds of a middle-class apartment.[23] All of these poems appropriate the narratives and forms of an earlier poetry and adapt them to the historical events of Adam's own period. In many of these refashioned versions, women occupy positions of power when all around them the male population is weak and ineffectual. Women's socially appointed roles as mothers, wives, and homemakers become the subject of Adam's savage humor so that the witch wife of "Apartment on Twin Peaks" can remark:

> I re-decorated every spring and fall.
> I hung [my husband's] guts in the entrance hall.
> My girl-friends called him a selfish beast.
> And we all wolfed him up at our full moon feast.
>
> Rich man, poor man, beggar man, thief,
> Any damn husband's sure to bring you grief.
> Keep him working for his very life
> To prove he's worthy of a virtuous wife.[24]

The world of Helen Adam's haunted ballads is dominated by powerful women ruled not by institutional authority (marriage, the nuclear family, traditional religions) but by nature. Unlike Snyder's "fertile" mother archetype – or, for that matter, Levertov's moon-ruled goddesses – Adam's witches and weirds have an impish sense of humor that delights in undermining the high resolve of their male victims. Not only do Adam's women triumph over weak-willed knights and autocratic husbands, they contrive a verbal magic for which masculine action is no match. Under their power, men become impetuous, bothersome little boys whose sexual authority is countered by the woman's fiendish irony:

> "Wife, are you ready to come to bed?"
> Her husband calls from the room overhead.
> "The lights are out in the distant town.
> And I can't sleep until you lie down."
>
> Softly panting, she climbs the stair.
> The moon lights the bed with a livid glare.
> "I'll draw the curtains, and hug you near.
> And we'll lie hid from the moon, my dear."[25]

The opéra bouffe of this gynocentric universe is *San Francisco's Burning*, a drama of cosmic fate set against the background of fin de siècle San Francisco.[26] Written in the late 1950s and presented at James Broughton's Playhouse in 1961, *San Francisco's Burning* represents the triumph of that "performative" tendency we have seen elsewhere in the San Francisco Renaissance. It combines music, drama, poetry, and theatrical staging in the manor of Victorian melodrama and includes a cast of vaudeville "types" drawn from British music hall farce as well as astrology and tarot. Like James Broughton's or Robert Duncan's masques of this period and anticipating Michael McClure's plays of the 1960s and 1970s, *San Francisco's Burning* represents a synthesis of popular and traditional theatrical genres in which large mythic themes are developed through broad farce and popular song. As with so much else in relation to the San Francisco Renaissance, *San Francisco's Burning* was also a source of personal conflicts within the poetry community itself, a conflict having less to do with the play and more to do with its production. In this sense, then, *San Francisco's Burning* is a play not only "about" the mythical city of San Francisco but about the historical community in which that myth was played out.[27]

This ballad opera is set in San Francisco before the great earthquake of 1906. It is the period of the riotous Barbary Coast in which the spoils of westward expansion, gold rush frenzy, and eastern mercantilism have made the city a center of wealth and corruption. Adam satirizes both the aristocracy of San Francisco's robber barons and the rough waterfront milieu of opium eaters, gamblers, and floozies. Both social worlds attempt to alleviate their limbo existence with material and sensual pleasures, but none can escape the power of death, given vivid form by the eerie Worm Queen, who dispenses judgment on aristocrat and ruffian alike. Wearing a gigantic black headdress with its Medusa-like branches hiding her blind worm head, she represents a sexuality of the grave from which no man may escape:[28]

My crown is crusted with carrion flies
And my head is bald and wet,
But the loveliest women of living flesh
With me you will quite forget.

I am the Fair Forgetfulness
Whom men seek only in pain.
Who sleeps in the bed of the Worm Queen
He never will weep again.

(SFB, 18)

The fact that Helen Adam played the Worm Queen in the original performance adds a wicked bit of irony to a play in which women rule the
fortunes (figuratively and literally) of the western estate.

The Worm Queen is countered by the Hanged Man, drawn from the
Tarot Deck, who serves as a Barbary Coast version of Hades. His house
– a waterfront dive that the Brechtian underclass frequents – is the center
for much of the action. The Drug Eater, the Hanged Man's Beauty,
Spangler Jack, various sailors, and the Murdered Babe all sing their songs
of woe while the Hanged Man brandishes bones over his head and promises dire ends to all of his guests. Some of the play's most hilarious songs
are sung by tarnished beauties like Loving Lily Babe, "a warm-hearted
hussy of the waterfront," whose only joy in life is searching for miserable men to love:

If a man's a success
I won't say Yes,
Not while he's winning every play.
But I've only to look at a miserable man,

A drooping, stooping, failed and fallen man,
A kicked out, knocked about, rags and tatters man,
To adore him right away.

(SFB, 81–2)

In contrast to the Hanged Man's disreputable crew is the Nob Hill
society world of the "dragon dowager," Mrs. Mackie Rhodus. Secure in
class and affluence, she is impervious to the Worm Queen's rhetoric of
fate – as, indeed, she is impervious to just about everything. Her solution
to the trials of daily existence is a trip to Grace Cathedral followed by tea
at Blum's:

A time comes
When one is only saved from absolute frenzy
By knowing one can count on Grace Cathedral
And afterwards crumpets
With plenty of cream at Blum's.

(SFB, 69)

Mrs. Mackie Rhodus is accompanied by an equally daft countess who affronts Nob Hill proprieties by roller skating around the Rhodus house and celebrating the odd May rituals of her native Barth Malone.

Although *San Francisco's Burning* is set in the frontier West, its actual drama is that of the astral realm. That eternal drama concerns Mrs. Mackie Rhodus's niece, Susan, and the Scotch Sailor, whose love is thwarted by the world's vanity and the Worm Queen's law. Susan has been engaged by her unfeeling aunt to marry the self-enamored Neil Narcissus, who seeks only to see himself reflected in others. His love songs to her are a lyric mockery:

> Look at me! Look at me!
> Your eyes must never close.
> In your eyes I'll gaze awhile.
> Myself, myself I'll see.
> Ah! do not weep,
> Your eyes must smile
> And mirror only me.
> (SFB, 104)

But in Susan's nocturnal sleepwalking trances, she meets with her true love, the Scotch Sailor, who has lost his life early in the play to the Worm Queen. The two lovers speak across a lethean barrier that is bridged only when Susan dies during the great earthquake at the end. Thus the burning of San Francisco becomes a cathartic transformation, permitting a reunification of spirit even as it represents a destruction of material reality.

Adam has drawn the characters of her astral dramas from the two-dimensional world of melodrama and popular fiction. Neil Narcissus, the cliché-quoting Mr. McCann, the sponging Well Kept Man, and the wealthy bachelor and reformer Barty Malone are all taken from popular histories of the Barbary Coast and the West. Even the play's chorus, a couple of mechanical automatons representing Puss 'n Boots and Anubis, are drawn directly from the mechanical marvels that Adam had seen at San Francisco's Playland-at-the-Beach Amusement Park.[29] Hence as much as Adam has resuscitated a certain romantic tradition based on the dualism of spiritual and temporal worlds – the natural super-naturalism of Keats or Wordsworth – so she has revived the luddic dimension of theater itself by emphasizing its relation to popular culture and children's play.

The subplots and love dramas of various figures in the play have their apotheosis in the final scene when the great earthquake occurs. The automatons' dire warnings finally become a reality as fire and earthquake level both the lowlife world of the waterfront and the aristocratic houses of Nob Hill. Adam's conclusion is an Atlantean transformation of all dualities as the Worm Queen holds her death card, the ace of spades, over the stage at the end. But Mrs. Mackie Rhodus offers a comic apotheosis of her own, pushing the Worm Queen aside:

> Out of my way, Trollop!
>
> Troublesome fire, and earthquake,
> But we know that whatever comes . . .
> We'll still have Grace Cathedral,
> And crumpets and cream at Blum's.
>
> (SFB, 163)

It may seem a sacrilege to subject Helen Adam's plays and songs to any deeper analysis; they are, after all, "entertainment" in the best sense. Their esoteric origins owe as much to the world of table rapping and the medicine show as they do to Egyptian papyrus writings and Madame Blavatsky. But as entertainment they participate directly in that intimate relationship with an audience other poets, as different as Jack Spicer and Allen Ginsberg, wanted. The enchantment that the audience experiences is not only that of revival – the reappearance of familiar stories told by a slightly wicked grandmother – but of revision – the transformation of romantic ballad conventions to adumbrate gender-specific themes.

Within the San Francisco Renaissance, Helen Adam occupied a privileged role, one accorded to few women. Since she was neither poetic innovator nor sexual threat, she could participate actively in the "boys club" of the Spicer circle. She was much loved as a good witch or wise crone within the community, and she realized those roles powerfully in her performances. But by her particular manipulation of the romantic tradition she was able to become what she often described – a sorceress with distinct powers over and within a male community. She wielded her authority with humor and drama and, like Mrs. Mackie Rhodus, was able to keep talking in the midst of demonstrably voluble men.

JOANNE KYGER: "AN EXTENSION OF MY ARM"

Of the three women poets to be considered in this chapter, Joanne Kyger represents the closest link to the various communities discussed so far. She emerged as a writer during the heyday of the North Beach period, participating actively within the Spicer–Duncan circle as well as the Beat scene. She was a regular figure at Spicer's Sunday afternoon readings, and many of her early poems were published in magazines like *Open Space* and *J*. She was married to Gary Snyder for four years and has maintained close ties to Philip Whalen, Allen Ginsberg, and John Wieners. During the late 1960s she became associated with poets of the New York school, many of whom moved to Bolinas (as did Kyger) around this time. Kyger's work combines the Buddhist meditational concerns of Whalen, Ginsberg, and Snyder with the dailiness of Frank O'Hara and Ted Berrigan and in this respect represents an important link between the poets of the 1950s and a later generation.[30]

Like both the Beats and the New York school poets, Kyger's work stresses immediacy and spontaneity. Her poems map mundane activities like eating, cooking, gardening, and socializing with a minimum of commentary. Her work is respectful – even celebratory – of nature, but it avoids the more bardic invocations of the natural world associated with her Beat compatriots. Like Philip Whalen (whose work has exerted an important influence) Kyger's poetry often seems taken directly from the notebook page, each line registering a quick glance or momentary observation. She wants her line to be gestural, "an extension of [her] arm":[31]

> Breakfast. He assured me
> orange juice, toast & coffee.
> Just the way I like it. I flang
> the cawfee cup to de floor. After
> three times it split into a million
> pieces. She worried about the
> small supply of dope in the other room.
>   Both
> of them, Lewis and Tom, were busy
> collaborating. The record
> playing. The wind howling
> The electric heater going by
> her side, as an ache over
> increased her self. . . .[32]

Such lines resolutely refuse to editorialize, seeking instead to capture the moment, including the specific tone of voice ("I flang / the cawfee cup to de floor") and arrangement of persons around the house. At times this tendency toward the "quick take" leads to sheer nervous energy, uncontrolled and zany. Too often the poems seem to indulge distractedness for its own sake, becoming lists of unrelated observations, valued for their sheer presence rather than for any relation to a conceptual or critical frame. But at their best, Kyger's poems sustain a balance between immediacy and reflection, retaining the rush of perceptions but qualifying and refining the act of integration. As she says in another poem, "what I wanted to say / was in the broad / sweeping / form of being there."[33]

"Being there," as an autobiographical impulse, has been an important feature of San Francisco poetry in general and will be an important term in my consideration of Judy Grahn and, later, Lyn Hejinian. On the surface, Joanne Kyger's sense of autobiography, as evidenced in the lines above, seeks to erase the boundary between the life lived and any reflection upon it. But that impulse can never be realized; she must intrude upon her perceptions and test them against her desires. For all of her relaxed tone, Kyger's poems are tense with qualifications and second thoughts: "Already I wish there was something done"; "I woke up very angry because I wanted to see where they were and I couldn't see where they were"; "If something is wrong / why doesn't it change."[34] Kyger does not rearrange the events of her autobiography to form a coherent narrative; rather she sustains the oscillating motion of events and the speculative acts they engender.

Underlying Kyger's poetics of immediacy are mythopoeic and theological concerns that serve to ground the present in a larger narrative. In many of her early poems she makes use of a mythical persona (Persephone, Penelope, Circe) through whom she may examine her own life. Perhaps "persona" is the wrong word, however, since it implies a kind of rhetorical or dramatic voice that distances author from speaker. Kyger's use of persona blurs the distinction between mythical personage and herself in order to contain her own slightly scattered and distracted attentions. If, for Robert Duncan, mythopoeia implies a kind of exalted and vatic voice, for Kyger the use of myth allows her a degree of chattiness. Speaking, for instance, of Circe's transformation of Odysseus's crew, Kyger observes that

> . . . when the time came, she did right
> Let them go
> They couldn't see her when she came back
> from the ship, seating themselves and wept, the wind
> took them directly north, all day
> into the dark.
> at least they were moving again.[35]

The loose lineation, variable line lengths, casual idiom ("she did right," "at least they were moving"), and reflective tone conspire to personalize the Circe story and draw it into a more intimate frame. How different this intention is from the same story's treatment in the hands of male modernist authors like Pound and Joyce.

This synthesis of myth and personal voice is most apparent in Kyger's early book, *The Tapestry and the Web*, which concerns the Homeric account of Penelope during the period of Odysseus's wanderings. The title of the book is based partly on Penelope's name, which means "with a web over her face," and Kyger extends this etymology to include the "tapestry" that she weaves by day and unweaves by night. Thus Penelope's identity as a woman is directly related to the identity she creates through her art. Like Helen in H.D.'s *Helen in Egypt,* Penelope is both mortal woman and prophetess, wife of Odysseus and patroness of the mysteries. Her tapestry, like her life, is forever incomplete as she attempts to synthesize the "web" of stories told about her, "plucking threads / as if they were strings of a harp."[36]

The Tapestry and the Web was written outside a specific feminist discourse, although it clearly can be read, retrospectively, in such terms. The poem originated in the rhetorical alembic of the Spicer circle with its male (largely homosexual) mysteries. Robert Duncan recalls that the occasion on which the poem first appeared within that group had an almost devotional quality: "As in the scene Sunday I see Joanne Kyger kneeling. . . . As my 'rank' had been in the taking of the Chair, arguing from it."[37] Duncan's subsequent interpretation of her poem focuses on the tone of awe in the opening lines:

> Joanne Kyger's poem began "I saw"; the sound of awe lingerd as a base tone (where the word *awe* never emerges) thru the diminished o of walk, all, fall, water (for the sound of water was that sound rushing) on to the close with the word *walls*.[38]

Duncan's reading of the poem as spiritual revelation seems apt for his own concerns in poetry, but it excludes the degree to which revelation involves the gender of the speaker. The thematics of transformation, the imagery of weaving, the interplay of pronouns all pertain specifically to the woman writer in a largely male enclave. Kyger is Penelope surrounded by suitors (male writers) whom she transforms or enchants through her poem. That Kyger had to render this history in mythic terms may very well relate to certain modernist practices favored within the Spicer–Duncan circle, but it also points to an attempt to subvert the authority of that male fraternity in which she, like Helen Adam, worked.

Many of the stories in *The Tapestry and the Web* concern Penelope's relation to nature and the theme of transformation. She is identified with Persephone as well as with Venus, and through her mothering of Pan she is linked to flocks and Arcadian wildness. The story of Pan plays a particularly important role in the book since it establishes Penelope's links to the disorder and riot of nature that are figured in the Trojan War: "great turmoils that pull / through all of you." One story states that Pan's father was Hermes, who visited Penelope disguised as a ram; another states that Pan was the progeny of all the suitors. Such stories are marshaled against the Homeric version, in which Penelope patiently waits for her husband. "Just HOW / solitary was her wait?" Kyger asks;

> I notice Someone got to her that
> barrel chested he-goat prancing
> around w/his reed pipes
> is no fantasy of small talk.

> More the result of BIG talk
>> and the absence of her husband.
>>> (TW, 31)

In this absence, however, Penelope becomes a dreamer and by weaving
her dreams into her tapestry, gains her own identity beyond Odysseus:

> I believe she dreamed too much. Falling into her weaving,
>> creating herself as a fold in her tapestry.
>
> a flat dimension character of beauty
> keeping one task in mind and letting nothing *Human* touch her
> – which is pretend.
>> She knew what she was doing.
>>> (TW, 31)

Kyger, in the guise of Penelope, is also "creating herself," to the extent
that mythological sources that undergird the poem are mixed with references to her personal life: her marriage to Gary Snyder, travels to Japan
and India, a hike in the Sierras, reflections on her family, the death of her
father. But these things are merged with the Homeric stories until the
personal and mythical merge. Pan becomes the "crippled boy" in her
mother's grade school class; Odysseus's boat resembles a fishing boat
being constructed at a village in Japan; the shroud or web that Penelope
weaves for her father-in-law, Laertes, reminds the poet of her own father's death ("I had meant to write more often"); and this death resonates
with the story of Persephone:

> She finished up the web, it had to do with her
>> father she said
> using it to keep them away for many years, tricking them.
> Hermes came to get the dead suitors.
>> Persephone really died every year
>> to go down there was difficult a large dark house
> and ghost groves on either side one of white. They
>> called her terrible
>>> (TW, 61)

Just as H.D. weaves the tale of Helen out of Steisichorus, Euripides,
Homer, and others, so Kyger reinvents a Penelope who is linked to
spring rites, nature, and change. But Kyger is no modernist in her use of
The Odyssey. Myth is the mirror not of cultural survivals but of personal
choices for herself as a woman. In this sense Kyger's practice fulfills
Rich's revisionist thesis. "It has been difficult to write this," Kyger says
at the end of *Tapestry and the Web* – difficult because she must wrest a
"female presence" out of a patriarchal story. Kyger writes from within

those stories as a woman who finds herself inscribed into a myth she wishes to interrogate in her own terms. The "web" that hides Penelope becomes, through her poetic transformation, a "tapestry" in which she can gain a perspective on her life.

Like Helen Adam, Kyger draws on a range of mythological sources to tell her story, but while the former stays rigorously within the formal tradition of Scots and British narrative poetry, the latter works entirely in looser, free-verse modes. If Kyger tells her tale through mythic personae, the voice in which they speak is very much a contemporary one, full of the pauses, qualifications, and hesitations of natural speech. Thus her poems remain more reflective ("Some thing keeps escaping me") and speculative ("I guess it's good to know where you're going"), occasionally to the detriment of their critical focus. *Tapestry and the Web,* when it appeared in 1965, provided a new kind of long poem, one in which the autobiographical interests of the historical woman writer could find form in mythological materials beyond her. If Kyger drew the shape of her line from long poems like Olson's *Maximus Poems* or Gary Snyder's *Mountains and Rivers Without End,* she also understood that their historical and cultural concerns could not be hers. When she observes that "The fathers of the Sierras / once crossed here and / went beyond," she recognizes that the territory in which she is attempting to find her way has already been surveyed – by "fathers." She, like other women in the early 1960s, is waiting "for the breeze to / speed my weaving / the reverie of / memory past / what I know" (TW, 19).

JUDY GRAHN: THE UNCOMMON COMMON WOMAN

The ability to read Joanne Kyger's or Helen Adam's work in feminist terms has been aided by a more activist posture developed among women writers during the late 1960s. In the San Francisco Bay Area, this period saw the appearance of important new reading spaces, publishers, and distributors of women's literature: Alta began Shameless Hussy Press, the first women's press in the area; Susan Griffin coordinated a large conference on women poets for the University of California Extension; Joanna Griffin and Sande Fini opened a series of readings and performances at a Berkeley bar called The Bacchanall; the San Francisco State College Women's Caucus began to hold readings in the Noe Valley; and perhaps most important, the Women's Press Collective was established by Judy Grahn in 1969.[39] Although many of these events occurred after the period with which this book is concerned, they were empowered, to a certain extent, by tendencies already present in the San Francisco Renaissance.

For a lesbian poet like Judy Grahn, the historical fact of gay writing – as well as the city's relative openness to alternative social and sexual

preferences – was no small component in the development of her poetics. Although Grahn was not associated directly with the San Francisco
Renaissance, her literary voice derives, in many respects, from the populist mode of the Beats. It is hard to imagine works like "The Psychoanalysis of Edward the Dyke" or "Elephant Poem" without thinking of
Lawrence Ferlinghetti's satiric portraits of alienated fifties life or the
comic, quasi-surreal poems of Allen Ginsberg or Gregory Corso. The
strength of Grahn's early poetry depends on the odd combination of
humor and anger that gives a work like "Howl" its special power.

If the literary formation of Judy Grahn's work rests in the populist
mode of the Beats, its social formation rests in the women's movement
and, more specifically, in San Francisco's long homophile tradition,
going back to the prewar years. The city had long been a haven for
homosexuals and lesbians, and although the community was often
threatened by the homophobic public, it always had a social and even
political force in the larger demographics. Important gay political groups
like the Matachine Society, the Daughters of Bilitus, and (later) The
Alice B. Toklas Democratic Club had substantial memberships in San
Francisco from their inception, and with the emergence of a gay liberation movement in the post–Stonewall era, the city became, as John
D'Emilio says, "for gay men and for lesbians . . . what Rome is for
Catholics."[40]

To a large extent, the permission for the San Francisco gay community
to come out of the closet and become an active force in the city was
granted during the period that this book covers and by many of the same
literary events. The fact that many San Francisco poets were openly
homosexual created the illusion – if not the fact – of tolerance in the city.
Allen Ginsberg's "Howl" censorship trial, publications by Robert Duncan, Jack Spicer, James Broughton, and Robin Blaser, and even Jack
Kerouac's novels brought national attention to a city where variant sexual modes were possible. But as I have pointed out with reference to the
Spicer circle, such permission was given within a largely male, homosexual community that remained closed or even hostile to women. Denise
Levertov's "Hypocrite Women" was written in response not only to
Jack Spicer's misogyny, but to the closed, homosexual circle he supported.[41] It remained for the women's movement and its lesbian feminist
component to open a new possibility for a gay women's poetry. Judy
Grahn as much as anyone helped to create this possibility.

In order to create a gay women's poetry it was necessary to create a
woman not totally defined within male, heterosexual stereotypes. Judy
Grahn's early work involved the creation of what she called "the common woman," a figure whose power is repressed and whose beauty is
masked behind social conventions. At the same time, Grahn must re-

suscitate the common woman from the *uncommon woman,* that objectified embodiment of male desire. As she says in her poem to Marilyn Monroe, "I have come to claim / Marilyn Monroe's body / for the sake of my own."[42] Grahn must discover this woman from within a world that has not provided her with a name; hence many of the poems appear to be litanies for "she who" has no identity at all:

> the woman whose head is on fire
> the woman with a noisy voice
> the woman with too many fingers
> the woman who never smiled once in her life
> the woman with a boney body
> the woman with moles all over her
>
> (WCW, 107)

These incantatory passages suggest a communal forum in which repetition serves to unite and join, even as it differentiates.

Coinciding with the invention of a new woman is Grahn's archaeological interest in the origins of gay culture. This task is given explicit form in her book *Another Mother Tongue,* which explores archaic sources of homosexuality and lesbianism in what amounts to a popular ethnology of homoerotic culture.[43] It is "culture" that Grahn is most concerned with: that of women, and that of lesbians specifically. As one of the founders of the gay women's liberation movement on the West Coast, she has been acutely interested in what is specific to gay life: its informing myths, stereotypes, and communal signs. Her archaeological task involves exploring the words by which gays are marginalized – "butch," "fay," "queer," "dyke," – and finding their tribal or cultic origins, thus resuscitating from a despised language a new language of opposition and authority. If her historical scholarship is sometimes suspect, relying as it does on a good deal of artful speculation, it recognizes the difficulty of such ethnology: that any history of gay culture must rely on an idiom constantly under transformation, an idiom that mirrors at the same time as it satirizes the heterosexual world.

Grahn performs her archaeological work with a good deal of humor, using it to debunk certain stereotypes of gayness, both those of the straight world and those in the gay community itself. In her story "The Psychoanalysis of Edward the Dyke," she satirizes the straight psychoanalytical interpretation of lesbianism, but at the same time explores the ambivalence of the gay woman toward her own sexuality. Edward's compulsions and paranoias, as reported to her psychoanalyst Dr. Knox, are transformed into pathological symptoms of penis envy and castration compulsion. Dr. Knox sees all of Edward's problems in clinical terms, and his therapy is directed at transforming Edward (who is six feet four

inches tall) into a normal "little girl": "We will cure you of this deadly
affliction and before you know it you'll be all fluffy and wonderful with
dear babies and a bridge club of your very own." After defining Edward's "problems," Dr. Knox subjects her to shock therapy:

> Dr. Knox flipped a switch at his elbow and immediately a picture of a
> beautiful woman appeared on a screen over Edward's head. The doctor
> pressed another switch and electric shocks jolted through her spine.
> Edward screamed. He pressed another switch, stopping the flow of
> electricity. Another switch and a photo of a gigantic erect male organ
> flashed into view, coated in powdered sugar. Dr. Knox handed Edward
> a lollipop. (WCW, 30)

However humorous Grahn's story is, it deals with an interpretation of
homosexuality not uncommon during Grahn's lifetime, an interpretation
with serious consequences for the "health" of the gay community.
Grahn challenges Dr. Knox's reading of Edward's problem by refusing
to accept the language by which gays are categorized, whether in psychoanalytical or political terms. The issue of reforming the language, as
Adrienne Rich points out in her introduction to *The Work of a Common
Woman*, is central to Grahn's poetry:

> When we become acutely, disturbingly aware of the language we are
> using and that is using us, we begin to grasp a material resource that
> women have never before collectively attempted to repossess. . . . We
> might, hypothetically, possess ourselves of every recognized tech-
> nological resource on the North American continent, but as long as our
> language is inadequate, our vision remains formless, our thinking and
> feeling are still running in the old cycles, our process may be "revolu-
> tionary" but not transformative. (WCW, 7)

The transformation that Rich seeks begins with the creation of alternative models against which specific women might measure and evaluate
themselves. In her early work, Grahn created a series of portraits of
women, both lesbian and straight, which embody the diversity of the
"common woman." The result is a long series, *The Common Woman
Poems*, which has become a major document in the feminist movement.
The series mixes realistic depictions of oppressed women with a revolu-
tionary call to action:

> the common woman is as common as the best of bread
> and will rise
> and will become strong–I swear to you
> I swear it to you on my common
> woman's
> head

> (WCW, 73)

The origin of this series, as Grahn says, "was completely practical: I wanted, in 1969, to read something which described regular, everyday women without making us look either superhuman or pathetic" (WCW, 6). The women portrayed are tough and resilient, hardened by years of work in low-paying, demeaning jobs and in equally demeaning sex roles. Ella, for example, is

> . . . a copperheaded waitress,
> tired and sharp-worded, she hides
> her bad brown tooth behind a wicked
> smile, and flicks her ass
> out of habit, to fend off the pass
> that passes for affection.
> She keeps her mind the way men
> keep a knife . . .
>
> (WCW, 63)

The language in these poems is as common as the women described, straightforward and direct, with an occasional rhetorical flourish ("to fend off the pass / that passes for affection"). But the more the women are described, the less "common" they appear, each one possessing some volatile side of herself hidden beneath the surface:

> she has taken a woman lover
> whatever can we say
> She walks around all day
> quietly, but underneath it
> she's electric;
> angry energy inside a passive form.
> The common woman is as common
> as a thunderstorm.
>
> (WCW, 67)

The titles of these portraits indicate precisely where the portrait takes place: "Helen, at 9 AM, at noon, at 5:15" or "Carol, in the park, chewing on straws," as though they are photos in an album. The portraits are not idealized, and the lives the women lead are hardly heroic. Madness, abortion, failed marriages, sexual frustration, shrill invective become the unhappy legacy of the "common woman." To Grahn these features signal a potential power that must be discovered in everyday language:

> I'm not a girl
> I'm a hatchet
> I'm not a hole
> I'm a whole mountain
> I'm not a fool
> I'm a survivor

I'm not a pearl
  I'm the Atlantic Ocean
I'm not a good lay
  I'm a straight razor
look at me as if you had never seen a woman before
I have red, red hands and much bitterness

                                                        (WCW, 25)

In speaking of Joanne Kyger, I described her synthesis of autobiography and myth as an attempt to gain a perspective on her life as a woman
– that by identifying with Penelope, she could speak for herself in the
historical present. In the case of Judy Grahn, the feminist implications of
this synthesis are made explicit. "Look at me as if you had never seen a
woman before," she demands, and in much of her work she uses herself
as the focus for a larger social imperative. The common–woman portraits
may be derived from Grahn's personal life, but they attain a kind of
nobility precisely because of their bare, hard–edged presentation. They
gain mythical stature because they are so resolutely ordinary. At the
same time, Grahn's use of historical figures like Marilyn Monroe (or
Susan Griffin's use of Harriet Tubman or Adrienne Rich's use of Emily
Dickinson) represent retrievals of exceptional women to serve as simulacra for every woman. The necessity of retrieving women, common
and uncommon, from their sequestration within a patriarchal world has
been the task of a feminist poetics from the outset. Judy Grahn is no
different in this respect than other feminists in the country, but her
ability to speak as a lesbian was certainly encouraged by the large gay
community in San Francisco and the spirit of social action that had been
there from its earliest days. Grahn became the inheritor of this tradition
but also one of its most articulate disseminators.

CONCLUSION: WHOSE RENAISSANCE?

Writing about women in and of the San Francisco Renaissance is
difficult not because there were so few of them but because the standard
definition of the movement has no way of including them. The boys'
club of San Francisco bohemia, however progressive in defining new
social roles for individuals, was often blind to its own exclusionary posture. Where women are mentioned in the chronicles of the period, their
contributions are usually relegated to their "service" function. Carolyn
Cassady may be valued for her retrospective memoirs of life with Neal
and Jack, but not for her own literary attainments. The entries on Cassady and Eileen Kaufman in Arthur and Kit Knight's chronicle of the
Beat generation, *The Beat Vision,* simply memorialize their former husbands.[44] Although Joanne Kyger's major work, *The Tapestry and the
Web,* is long out of print, her journals of travel in India with her then-

husband Gary Snyder are readily available.[45] Women are conspicuously absent from major critical accounts of the period, although Kenneth Rexroth does acknowledge the pioneering work of Ruth Witt Diamant and Madeline Gleason in establishing the San Francisco State Poetry Center.[46] And although Josephine Miles *was* included in the San Francisco issue of *Evergreen,* she is almost invariably thought of as an academic fellow traveler rather than an active participant in the movement. Such omissions, subordinations, and marginalizations may reflect the roles that women played during this period, but they also suggest the endurance of a privileged narrative – what I earlier called "enabling myths" of origins – in which women are seldom the subjects.

By recognizing the contributions of women writers during the period from 1955 to 1965, we may revise that narrative somewhat, but this is only half the job. It is also necessary to discover the women who were already being invented between the lines, as it were, of male verse. These women are as much projections of that romantic ideology that I mentioned in my opening chapter as they are of the historical period with which we are concerned. They emerge from romantic conceptions of feminized nature and from a theory of creative imagination based on dualisms of form and content, action and inspiration, artist and muse. The fact that Denise Levertov and Diane DiPrima recognized those hidden women and responded to them in their own terms was crucial for the development of their individual poetics. At the same time, their "appropriations" of male discourse represent ways in which romantic narratives of natural rhythms, cyclic life, and participation are revised in terms of gender.

One of the dominant themes of feminist scholarship has been the ways that women writers have rewritten patriarchal discourse, subverting its authority while at the same time providing women with alternative discursive forms. Helen Adam's variations on stock romantic figures and Joanne Kyger's rewriting of male myth are obvious extensions of this revisionist imperative. Their work was performed within – and, I contend, against – male-centered circles in the San Francisco milieu. Judy Grahn developed her poetics in the frame of a more self-consciously feminist poetry – one that she helped to create – and, although not usually associated with the literary events described in the rest of this book, she represents a logical outgrowth of them. Like the Beats, she emphasizes plain speech and "common" subjects, but whereas Ginsberg and Kerouac often discover transcendental principles in urban landscapes, Grahn seeks the historical awareness of women's – and specifically lesbians' – condition in patriarchal America.

By concluding this chapter with figures not usually mentioned in the standard histories of the San Francisco Renaissance, I am suggesting that in order to see the contributions of women to modern literary history, we must often look outside the canonical narratives. These counternarratives challenge more than our reading of literary history; they introduce a new subject as reader. That subject, "she who" reads, must ask of the period we are studying, *Whose* Renaissance? Renaissance of *what?* If those questions are asked retrospectively, by a generation that reads through the spectacles of gender, it is thanks to figures like Denise Levertov, Diane DiPrima, Helen Adam, Joanne Kyger, and Judy Grahn. Impatient with the roles their male colleagues consigned to them, they seized upon the social and aesthetic advantages of 1950s bohemian culture and began to write "her" story in the margins of "his."

7

Approaching the Fin de Siècle

Part of the enchantment of Helen Adam's ballad opera, *San Francisco's Burning*, comes from its playful re-creation of a turn-of-the-century city, part western history, and part fantasy. Like the gaily filigreed Victorian houses for which San Francisco is famous, the literature we have been considering was built upon simple structures with considerable embellishment. "This land, where I stand," Robert Duncan announces, "was all legend / in my grandfather's time," and the task for many poets of Duncan's generation was to revive that legend so that "all the old stories / whisper once more." The rhetoric in which that legend was retold at mid-century was often, though not exclusively, that of the 1890s. The opulent diction of Pre-Raphaelite, *Yellow Book* poets from Swinburne to Dowson and Yeats can be felt in many of the poets we have considered in this book. As I pointed out in my chapter on Duncan, that rhetoric found little favor with Charles Olson and other East Coast peers who picked up a note of decadence in the Duncan circle and used it as a challenge. Whatever one may think of Olson's deprecations, the tone was there, and it became one of the characteristic features of the era's period style.

As we move ever closer to our own fin de siècle – and to the millenium that it signals – it is worth exploring how the ideals of a poetic renaissance have changed in the two decades since Jack Spicer's death. Fredric Jameson has noted that this era is characterized by an "inverse millenarianism, in which premonitions of the future, catastrophic or redemptive, have been replaced by senses of the end of this or that (the end of ideology, art, or social class; the 'crisis' of Leninism, social democracy, or the welfare state etc., etc.)."[1] Although this crisis has been expressed as such by philosophers and cultural theorists (Derrida's "The

Ends of Man" and much of Foucault's writing being two obvious examples),[2] its aesthetic version is expressed in arguments over the "literature of exhaustion," the death of the author, the crisis of the referent, the decentered subject. These discussions have concerned the status of art in an era of multinationals and computer technology and have stressed the ways that global systems of control mediate any "creative" impulse, if indeed one can speak of such a thing in the first place.

These discourses of the end are not about the failure of art so much as the inadequacy of certain metaphysical and epistemological foundations underlying aesthetic production. The "literature of exhaustion" is not about the used-upness of the novel but rather about the possibility of generating new work out of structural principles contained in previous work;[3] the death of the author is not concerned with the worthlessness of creativity but rather with the transformation of a certain artisanal ideal of writing into a more dialogical one. Far from acknowledging its own demise, recent art – and poetry in particular – has celebrated its right to exist and, more importantly, its ability to realize a certain *promesse de bonheur* of a socially critical mode.[4] Often that celebration has occurred in the opaque rhetoric of critical theory or in the hectoring tone of a populist manifesto, but the fact remains that poetry is alive and well in the 1980s, and a quick look at the local poetry calendar, *Poetry Flash*, will provide ample verification of that fact.

This continuity of activity (seldom mentioned by cultural critics) has been aided by the continuing importance of literary communities which provide a counterdiscourse to the homogenizing forces of creative writing programs and literary professionalization. As I pointed out earlier, those communities provided important continuity for writers whose lifestyles and sexual preferences were anathema to society at large, and to some degree this same communal impulse extended into the lifestyle and counterculture movements of the late 1960s and 1970s. Within subsequent generations of San Francisco writers the integrity of such communities has continued to exert an influence, although not without important modifications.

When Jack Spicer died in August 1965, the community on which he had staked so much seemed to die with him, but at the same time another was being born. As Spicer said, the Beatles, "devoid of form and color, but full of images," had invaded the North Beach jukeboxes, and what had been specific to that bohemian enclave was now diffused into the culture at large. Spicer's hostility toward this change was predictable; he had based everything on the vitality of a small insular community, and the appearance of an imported musical form from Liverpool represented a profound invasion of his private world. But one man's despair was an entire generation's hope, and for writers coming of age in the mid-1960s the new counterculture offered a synthesis of artistic freedom and social alternatives that had been lacking during the 1950s and early 1960s.

One of the changes occurring during this period was a shift in the concept of community. The North Beach scene, whether it circled around Kerouac or Spicer, continued an older bohemian tradition with roots in Europe of the early twentieth century. For this tradition, the term "community" implied shared social and artistic values that stood in opposition to middle-class culture at large. By the late 1960s, however, the term began to suggest gender, sexual, and ethnic affiliations that cut across class as well as aesthetic boundaries. Within the Latino and Asian neighborhoods of San Francisco, the growth of a new literature coincided with changes in cultural identity that went far beyond the creation of art. The sense of "difference," so essential to Spicer's Protestant poetics, was now inscribed within gender or racial terms. One did not *choose* to be different: one *was* different, by dint of race, class, or gender, and acknowledging that uniqueness became an important dimension of the new poetry. The same could be said for emerging feminist, gay, and black nationalist movements, all of which developed senses of community whose support was, to some extent, global rather than local.

This awareness of differences can be seen vividly in the emergence of bilingualism in Chicano poetry during the early 1970s. Poets like Victor Cruz, José Montoya, Roberto Vargas, and Alurista began employing a mixture of English and Spanish in an attempt to render the bicultural nature of Hispanic experience. Switching back and forth between the two languages, these "interlingual" poets pun and play with cognates (true and false) while establishing complex rhythms out of the interchange. And because the two languages are linked in a relationship of dominant to minority culture, the interchange often illustrates relations of power within the community at large. Rather than trying to reach a broad, monolingual (English-speaking) audience, the poet speaks to a specific, culturally defined audience, allowing the untranslated Spanish to stand for the Hispanic's marginal status.[5] In similar ways, gay, feminist, and black poets have incorporated idiolects particular to each subculture as a means of reinforcing group identity. Such practice is also oppositional since by employing private rhetorics and speech patterns, the poet displaces the authority of a dominant discourse that has been excluded – or left untranslated.[6]

In the late 1960s and early 1970s, this oppositional spirit among various subcultures was accompanied by a general politicization of bohemia. The nonconformist ethos of the Beats increasingly became a political stance taken by the larger Bay Area community as civil rights protests increased and the Vietnam War escalated. As I pointed out in my introduction, San Francisco has had a long history of social activism, and during the early 1960s, demonstrations, sit-ins, and strikes brought a renewed commitment to political protest. The Auto Row demonstrations, the free-speech movement at UC Berkeley, the Sheraton Palace sit-ins, the Culinary Workers strike, and other events set the tone for the next decade. San Francisco was not alone in this regard; it could no longer project itself as the single representative of some "alternate society" (as Kenneth Rexroth often said) but joined New York, Paris, Amsterdam, Tokyo, and Mexico City in a spirit of revolt and social experimentation.

The most obvious sign of change in San Francisco was demographic. The flight of the middle class to the suburbs, satirized in many a Beat poem, had left vast tracts of the inner city ready for development or exploitation. Whereas the center of artistic life had been North Beach, new centers emerged in the Mission, Noe Valley, and Fillmore districts, Berkeley, Bolinas, and, most significantly, Haight–Ashbury on the edge of Golden Gate Park. Like North Beach, Haight–Ashbury had been an ethnically mixed neighborhood, made up of Russian immigrants, blacks, and Asians with a scattering of students from the nearby medical school and San Francisco State College. With the advent of the Psychedelic Shop, the Human Be-In, and the youth movement of the mid-1960s, that ethnic mixture changed radically. The Haight–Ashbury era was more eclectic and culturally diffused than the earlier period, representing a "lifestyle" movement based less on literary interests than on a combination of new-age communalism, drug culture, antiwar activism, and alternative spiritual practices. And although many of the poets associated with the 1950s participated in the Haight–Ashbury scene, they were only part of a larger movement that had its public forum as much in rock and roll as in poetry readings.[7] Indeed, one of the central changes in poetic presentation during this period was inclusion of readings at rock concerts held in ballrooms like the Avalon or Fillmore during which Allen Ginsberg, Gary Snyder, or Michael McClure would read to large crowds on the same bill with the Jefferson Airplane or the Grateful Dead.

If one wanted to identify a single moment that dramatized a shift in literary energies and priorities it would be the Berkeley Poetry Conference in the summer of 1965, sponsored by the University of California Extension. The fact that this event occurred within the official venue of the university marks an important change from the Six Gallery reading with which I began this book and signals the important new role the university was to play in the dissemination (or absorption) of the avant garde. The event brought together members of the first-generation San Francisco scene (Robert Duncan, Allen Ginsberg, Gary Snyder, Philip Whalen) with figures associated with Black Mountain College like Charles Olson, Robert Creeley, and Edward Dorn. These poets had already been united within the pages of Donald Allen's *New American Poetry* of 1960 and at the Vancouver Poetry Conference of 1963, but this was the first time that Bay Area residents had a chance to see the "new poetry" on home ground. At this event Robert Duncan read the first twenty-five pieces in his new "Passages" series; Gary Snyder gave his important "Poetry and the Primitive" lecture; Ed Dorn discussed American Indians; Jack Spicer, in his last public appearance, lectured on poetry and politics; and during the week's most infamous event, Charles Olson gave a wild, drunken reading from the *Maximus Poems*.[8] It was a major forum for the "new American poetry," exposing the vitality of a generation that had come into its own – and exposing some of the lesions that had developed along the way. Although one might like to think that those disagreements occurred only along aesthetic lines, they also occurred around matters of power and authority within the poetry community itself.

The Berkeley Poetry Conference, however instrumental in foregrounding the accomplishments of the first generation, also announced the end of an era. Within a few years of that event, the core of the San Francisco Renaissance had moved on or passed away. Jack Spicer died of alcohol poisoning in 1965; Kenneth Rexroth moved to Santa Barbara; William Everson was living as Brother Antoninus at the Dominican Kentfield Priory in Marin County; Gary Snyder and Philip Whalen left for long stays in Japan, the former eventually moving permanently to the Sierra foothills; Allen Ginsberg, though often a visitor to San Francisco during this period, was spending most of his time on the East Coast; Jack Kerouac retired to Florida, where he died in 1969. The various members of the Spicer circle dispersed, Robin Blaser, Stan Persky, and George Stanley to British Columbia, Helen Adam to New York, and Ebbe Borregaard to Bolinas. Robert Duncan continued to live in San Francisco's Mission District but distanced himself from the more public Haight–Ashbury and North Beach milieus. The three most energetic participants in the youth culture of the day were Michael McClure, David Meltzer, and Lew Welch, although Welch gradually succumbed to alcoholism and in 1971 disappeared into the Sierra Nevadas, never to be seen again. The dispersal of the first generation was inevitable, but the generation that took its place was itself dispersed from the outset.

Describing the diversity of Bay region poetry during the past two decades would entail another book. These remaining pages will focus on two obvious extensions of the San Francisco Renaissance into the present day. Scant treatment will be given other traditions in the Bay Area – particularly those of ethnic minorities – due in part to the 1955–1965 time frame of this volume. The extraordinary growth of literature within the Asian, black, Latino, and Native American communities in the 1970s is certainly related to that earlier generation, but ethnic literature has its own internal growth and has its own literary antecedents within the minority cultures themselves. One could easily trace the influence of Ginsberg's populist voice through the work of Victor Hernandez Cruz, Lorna Dee Cervantez, Jessica Hagedorn, and Janice Mirikitani, but one would be ignoring other no less significant cultural influences (popular songs, Teatro Campesino, Latin American poetry, Native American myth, Asian-American folklore, etc.). And within these same poets one finds an equally potent reinforcement brought by Puerto Rican, Native American, Filipino, Japanese, and other international sources that do not refer so easily to the developments in San Francisco that I have described.[9]

"THE WORLD IN THE OTHER WORLD": ROBERT HASS

The most obvious change that has occurred in the past twenty years (the perennial Beat revival notwithstanding) has been a growing skepticism about the more expressive or visionary claims of neoromantics like Duncan, McClure, and Ginsberg. The elegiac rhetoric of the 1940s and the bardic chant of the late 1950s have given way to a considerably cooler tone and chastened rhetoric. At times, as in the case of "language writing," this skepticism has been embodied in formal procedures (the use of Fibonacci number series, collaboration, the "new sentence," etc.) that limit the role of personal expression. And where a process- or action-oriented aesthetics dominated much of the poetry that we have seen so far, poets of the 1980s have developed more subtle modulations of tone that return a degree of irony and self-effacement to poetry. Though these characteristics are by no means limited to Bay Area writers, they have been nurtured by and in response to many of the issues raised by the expressivist poetics that dominated the San Francisco Renaissance.

Recent writers have taken two directions in addressing the crisis of expressivity. The first, epitomized by the work of Robert Hass (and evident in other local writers like Robert Pinsky, Jack Gilbert, Denise Levertov, Diana O'Hehir, Joseph Stroud, and Gary Soto), derives from Kenneth Rexroth and Gary Snyder and emphasizes an allegorical relationship between the natural landscape and cognitive acts. The second, embodied in the work of Lyn Hejinian and others of the so-called language movement, extends from linguistically self-reflexive tendencies in Jack Spicer and Robert Duncan that stress the productive nature of language in forming the subject. Although these two tendencies have a common emancipatory goal for poetic language with respect to social practices, they differ in the specific ways that language functions in relation to those goals.

Charles Altieri has characterized the work of Hass and many of his contemporaries in terms of the "scenic mode." In such poetry (his example here is William Stafford),

> [the] work places a reticent, plain-speaking, and self-reflected speaker within a narratively presented scene evoking a sense of loss. Then the poet tries to resolve the loss in a moment of emotional poignance or wry acceptance that renders the entire lyric event an evocative metaphor for some general sense of mystery about the human condition.[10]

Altieri is not entirely happy with the scenic mode in its pure form and sees in a poet like Hass a more subtle working-out of its major presuppositions. Hass is particularly valued for refining the dramatic and emotional features of that "lyric event" so that the "mystery" is grounded in specific properties of voice.

If one of the principles of the scenic mode is its dependence on evocation of scene, one could hardly find a better example than Hass. His work often describes the natural landscape, particularly that of the coast. Hass comments on the importance of this landscape to his poetry in "Some Notes on the San Francisco Bar Area as a Culture Region." It is partly an homage to Kenneth Rexroth, who inspired the younger poet to write a poetry of place, but the debt is acknowledged in a rather roundabout way.[11] In the essay, Hass describes growing up in San Rafael, his Portuguese babysitter, life in Catholic school, playing Little League baseball, the beginnings of his literary career in an essay contest, and his discovery of poetry in an anthology bought with his prize money. In the midst of these reflections he provides a terse statement of poetics:

> Art hardly ever does seem to come to us at first as something connected to our own world; it always seems, in fact, to announce the existence of another, different one, which is what it shares with gnostic insight. That is why, I suppose, the next thing that artists have to learn is that this world is the other world. (GG, 201)

The essay complements this remark by its meandering, anecdotal quality. Just as Hass wanders among his memories of childhood that led him to Kenneth Rexroth's poetry, so we as readers are invited to discover Hass's poetics along the way. The daily world of a familiar landscape and the exotic world encountered in literature are one and the same, though the former is often invisible without the latter.

The unifying image that holds landscape and art together is the creek that flowed next to the poet's Little League field. The same creek appears in a poem by Kenneth Rexroth that Hass quotes:

> Under the second moon the
> Salmon come, up Tomales
> Bay, up Papermill Creek, up

The narrow gorges to their spawning
Beds in Devil's Gulch.[12]

Rexroth's poem, so active in rendering the specific California locale,
links Hass to his past and to the "other world" immanent in this one.
This world within the world is not a mystical quotient but something
constitutive in the "culture of the West Coast" – a synthesis of place and
propositions about the place. It is a synthesis that is fully developed in the
work of Wallace Stevens, another poet Hass quotes in the essay. The fish
that return to spawn in Papermill Creek are obeying a primitive rite of
return, which the essay, in its memorial tribute to Rexroth, imitates.
Poetry, landscape, and sexual imperative merge and follow their own
instincts, though Hass's procedure is anything but arbitrary.

The essay I have been describing appears in an anthology called *19
New American Poets of the Golden Gate*, the title including an obvious
reference to Donald Allen's earlier anthology in which the San Francisco
Renaissance was first acknowledged as a literary force. Hass follows his
essay with a poem, "Palo Alto: The Marshes," that dramatically under-
scores the influence of Rexroth on his work:

> She dreamed along the beaches of this coast.
> Here where the tide rides in to desolate
> the sluggish margins of the bay,
> sea grass sheens copper into distances.
> Walking, I recite the hard
> explosive names of birds:
> egret, killdeer, bittern, tern.
> Dull in the wind and early morning light,
> the striped shadows of the cattails
> twitch like nerves.[13]
>
> (GG, 203)

This first section of the poem establishes an identity of two sorts: a
temporal one between the speaker and the absent "She" (Mariana Richardson, whose father owned the San Rafael land grant in the late 1890s)
and a spatial one between both speakers and the tidal landscape. The
spatial bond between speaker and addressee is not only geographic –
their shared concern for a common landscape – but psychological in that
this same tidal region provides the backdrop for troubled dreams of
natural destruction and human cupidity. In establishing the literal as well
as psychic landscape, Hass acknowledges his close links to Rexroth and
Everson, who, as I have pointed out in earlier chapters, read social and
theological meanings in the text of nature. And in rehearsing "the hard /
explosive names of birds" he continues an imperative in Gary Snyder.
But whereas for Snyder naming offers a healthy antidote to human ex-

ploitation of nature, Hass recognizes a fatal complicity between the desire to name and the desire to control.

Hass views the historical transformation of the California landscape by invoking the eyes of Mariana, once glimpsed in a picture:

> Black as her hair
> the unreflecting venom of those eyes
> in an aftermath I know, like these brackish,
> russet pools a strange life feeds in
> or the old fury of land grants, maps,
> and deeds of trust. A furious dun-
> colored mallard knows my kind
> and skims across the edges of the marsh
> where the dead bass surface
> and their flaccid bellies bob.
>
> (GG, 204)

Hass's obvious pleasure in naming birds, plants, and animals is gradually qualified as he realizes his own role in the history he describes, a history that disempowered the native inhabitants of the region, and ultimately, turned the marshes into "brackish, / russet pools" where only "dead bass surface / and their flaccid bellies bob."

The poem quietly chronicles this usurpation of land from the period of land grants and settlement through the Bear Flag War and Kit Carson's raids on Indian villages. By the end, this history (Hass continues to call it a "dream") includes American adventurism in Vietnam:

> Here everything seems clear,
> firmly etched against the pale
> smoky sky: sedge, flag, owl's clover.
> rotting wharves. A tanker lugs silver
> bomb-shaped napalm tins toward
> port at Redwood City. Again,
> my eye performs
> the lobotomy of description
> Again, almost with yearning,
> I see the malice of her ancient eyes
>
> (GG, 205)

Hass recognizes that the desire to describe the landscape in such detail is part of the problem. The writer performs "the lobotomy of description" and feels the "malice" of historical judgment. When he claims that "Here everything seems clear," he refers to the time and place but also to the clarity of historical contradictions that emerge through the speaker's desultory meditation. What began as an attempt to remember the "explosive names of birds" rebounds as a mockery of that adjective when set beside "bomb-shaped napalm tins." What establishes itself, what is "etched against the pale / smoky sky" may be clear to the physical eye, but to the conscious intellect that must negotiate phenomenological claims against historical reality, the scene is quite murky.

Hass concludes by leaving many of the rhetorical tensions in place, much as he sees California as a conflicted dream of natural beauty and human despoilment:

> The otters are gone from the bay
> and I have seen five horses
> easy in the grassy marsh
> beside three snowy egrets.
>
> Bird cries and the unembittered sun,
> wings and the white bodies of birds,
> it is morning. Citizens are rising
> to murder in their moral dreams.
>   (GG, 206)

These last two quatrains are reminiscent of two other poets of place, James Wright and Robert Bly (although the ghost of Theodore Roethke hovers over the entire poem), in the way that they merge precise description with generalized statement. The final image, in its rather heavy-handed moralism, attempts to transcend the natural hieroglyph of "five horses" "beside three snowy egrets." Of course this heavy-handedness is part of Hass's method – as it is in Wright's "Lying in a Hammock at William Duffy's Farm in Pine Island, Minnesota."[14] Hass deliberately scuttles his own tendencies toward refined imagistic clarity in a moment of apotheosis and bald declaration. It is a sign of impatience, much like the famous "blackberry, blackberry, blackberry" conclusion of "Meditation at Lagunitas,"[15] a refusal of equivocation in the face of a palpable sense of loss and contradiction.

In Hass's work, craft is everywhere present yet nowhere evident, a value inherited from his former Stanford teacher Yvor Winters. Where Everson's rocking iambic cadences or Snyder's pared-down imagism foreground the materiality of language, Hass modulates his voice to attempt various dramatic responses to a crisis that is both historical and existential.[16] We "seem" to be hearing a person talking to himself ("Well, I have dreamed this coast myself"), but the discursive tone is constantly modified by lyric compression: "The star thistles: erect, surprised, / and blooming / violet caterpillar hairs." Repetition, though unenforced, is operative in producing historical ironies that undergird the poem. The "silver" salmon that Kit Carson finds upon entering an Indian Village return as the "silver" napalm tins; the "dream" of bay marshes shared by speaker and subject returns as the "moral dreams" of a civic mandate. Throughout the poem, the speaker's outrage is tempered by rhetorical balance, a balance that ultimately recognizes its own will to power.

WOMAN AND/AS SIGN: LYN HEJINIAN

In Hass's work, political agency is reflected through partial images and tentative dramatic postures. No single image is adequate; no statement is sufficient for understanding. In Heidegger's terms, the world must be unconcealed or discovered in momentary, reflective acts.[17] Implicit in this theory is the idea that there *is* a world to be discovered, preexistent and self-sufficient, for which these partial images and voices will provide a lyric and dramatic stage. To this extent, Hass continues the "immanentist" tradition that we have seen in Duncan and Snyder. For Lyn Hejinian, in contrast, value cannot be discovered but must be produced. The world exists as signs, each one invested with ideological and culturally marked interests that modify what the world "means." Although Hass and Hejinian share many of the same attitudes about the forces at work in producing that meaning, they differ sharply on the role language plays in its dissemination.

Those differences can be baldly stated as a conflict between a mimetic and what I have already defined as a performative poetics, between a poetry that represents and a poetry that acts. We can see the tension between these two theories in terms of our earlier discussion of women writers. In speaking of DiPrima, Kyger, and Grahn, I referred to feminist revisioning as a critique of the ways that women have been represented. In Kyger, this critique occurs through a rewriting of patriarchal myth; in Grahn, through a revising of role models and precedents. Adrienne Rich says that Grahn's poetry is

> among other things, a criticism of language. In setting words together in new configurations, in the mere, immense shift from male to female pronouns, in the relationships between words created through echo, repetition, rhythm, rhyme, it lets us hear and see our words in a new dimension.[18]

Of course, the idea that poetry involves a "criticism of language" is true of modernism in general, and so in order to understand the specific feminist implications of the phrase we must look more carefully at what Rich means by "language." For her, to criticize language means to place words in new arrangements for the purpose of illustrating cultural and gendered biases in conventional usage. The language itself is not changed, but its pragmatics is, insofar as a shift in pronouns will indicate a different relation between speaker and audience. Setting words in "new configurations" will not necessarily alter their basic linguistic values; Judy Grahn may challenge certain stereotypes of women without altering the mode of representation. In fact, for a work like *The Common Woman Poems*, it is essential that language retain its mimetic function so that nothing obstructs the clarity of its portraits. As radical as Rich's polemic may be, her theory of language is conservative. Revisionism, in her usage, retains the authority and integrity of the original text, while subjecting it to thematic (but not formal) transformations. In this sense, then, the patriarchal text, rather than being subverted, retains its ability to generate versions of itself.

Lyn Hejinian would certainly agree that poetry is a "criticism of language," but she would locate the critique *within* linguistic structure itself. In Hejinian's poetics, individuals (in this case, women) are not *represented* by language so much as they are constituted *within* it and are thus subject to those empowered to wield it. To use language in a traditional representational or narrative manner is to retain the structure of differences (male–female, master–slave, word–referent) by which individuals are oppressed. For Hejinian, language is a social construction that serves certain class, ethnic, and gendered interests. To change language at the level of its material plane is not simply to "see differently," as Rich implies, but to change social relations themselves. It is a utopian project whose origins lie in the European avant garde as well as in the theoretical writings of the Russian formalists and French feminists, but it has become a major concern of a number of writers in the Bay Area, loosely gathered under the rubric "language writing."[19]

The poetics of language writing offers the greatest challenge to the largely expressivist bias that I have been discussing in this book. In important ways, the group emerges out of the spirit of linguistic play and opposition characterized by Jack Spicer and Robert Duncan, but its epistemological basis is very different. It has been the subject of much contention within the Bay Area community, provoking "poetry wars" in the pages of local journals.[20] The argument concerns the nature of poetry itself, whether it is regarded as a vehicle of communication for some prior meaning or a material component in the production of meaning. To its detractors, language writing threatens the expressive potential of poetry and the authority of the autonomous subject that is its basis. For feminist poets anxious to reach a wider audience and serve specifically social ends, language poetry may seem an irrelevant, formalist exercise. But for feminist poets like Lyn Hejinian, Carla Harryman, Leslie Scalapino, Johanna Drucker, Kathleen Fraser, Beverly Dahlen, and others (not all of whom would be considered "language" poets, by any means) the term "woman" is a concept enmeshed in social discourses that can be deciphered only by a radical defamiliarization of the language itself.[21]

The best introduction to Lyn Hejinian's views on the subject can be found in her essay "The Rejection of Closure," in which she calls for an "open text," one that "emphasizes or foregrounds process, either the process of the original composition or of subsequent compositions by readers."[22] The reader of the "open text" is not regarded as a consumer of a closed, formally bounded work but as a co-creator along with the author. Because she is not given certain rhetorical or linguistic clues (chronological narrative, complete sentences, consistent point of view, etc.) to direct her reading, this ideal reader must work with a plurality of possible texts. Hejinian invokes the work of French feminists like Luce Irigaray and Helene Cixous who have seen in modernist and postmodern "open texts" the possibility of a "woman's language" not dependent on the Freudian (oedipal) structure of desire and the teleological imperative that undergirds it. A "woman's language" must create "variousness and multiplicity" both syntactically and semantically; it must acknowledge its own intertextuality, whether those texts derive from patriarchal language or from the writings of other women.

In attacking the expressivist paradigm of writing, language writers have paid particular critical attention to the poetic line and its presumed relation to an ideal of voice and presence. Charles Olson's idea of the line as a score for the voice and Allen Ginsberg's idea of the line as a dimension of mantric chant represent only two versions of what many language writers would regard as an idealist position. In an essay entitled "The New Sentence," Ron Silliman focuses on the sentence as the basic poetic unit since it is defined not by psychological or acoustic determinants (the line as score for the voice) but by linguistic means.[23] But Silliman's "new sentence" not so much connotes a different use of syntax as involves a different patterning of sentences such that each is generated by the previous in a nondiscursive, nonsyllogistic fashion.

Lyn Hejinian's use of such sentencing can be seen in *My Life*, in which the decontextualizing features of the new sentence serve to qualify the chronological narrative of autobiography:

> Learning to listen, that is taught not to talk. Can one take captive the roar of the city. Simon says sounds from the schoolyard. If I'm standing here then I must be positive. We are taking from the neighbor's rain, which goes damp and tight around my waist. Obey the best. We were like plump birds, then, walking stiffly in a sandy wind along the shore. Foxtails, the juice of a peach, have fallen on the flesh of the book. The secret of the song was that one couldn't hum it; the melody was elusive or not apparent at all. Women, I heard, should speak softly without mumbling. The obvious analogy is with music.[24]

Each sentence here is logical enough in its internal structure, but no element seems to lead logically to the next. We read a text whose individual sentences have been rearranged or in which certain essential connectives have been erased. Reference to a childhood maxim ("better seen than heard") leads to a question about being able to capture the "roar of the city" which leads to a reference to the schoolyard game "Simon

Says," and on to a statement about being "positive." The logic of connection is to some extent associational – references to sound, music, and listening predominate – but point of view and perspective are blurred.

Despite the constantly shifting address, this passage has a unifying "theme" dealing with the nature of games and their rules. The clearest statement of this theme is found in the proposition "If I'm standing here then I must be positive" or in the reference to Simon Says, a game that depends on one's ability to obey commands quickly. These remarks deal with the binary logic of children's games in which players assume "positive" and "negative" positions in a ludic parody of adult behavior. Such games have a special resonance for women, who are often the silenced listeners to *what* Simon says. The idea that girls should speak softly without mumbling or that one should learn to listen is a bit of adult wisdom whose social consequences have only recently been challenged.

References to speaking and silence are extended to music, which is another kind of discourse based on rule-governed conventions. When Hejinian asserts that "the analogy is with music," she refers both to the organization of her sentences and to the way that women's silence is analogous to the "elusive" properties of music. Each of these sentences is about "learning to listen," developing the ability to differentiate subjectivity from the rules by which subjectivity is inherited. In short, the passage is both *from* Hejinian's autobiography ("We were like plump birds, then, walking stiffly in a sandy wind along the shore") and *about* the process of its construction.

At a structural level, *My Life* argues with its title by refusing to conceptualize personal history into a unified narrative frame. Incidents, memories, and observations are free to resonate among themselves. Marjorie Perloff observes that this liberation of words and phrases from a narrative logic diminishes the possessive dimension of autobiography (*my* life) and make it about the "archetypal life of a young American girl."[25] At the same time, Hejinian has controlled the arrangement of memories, incidents, and associations by limiting the number of sentences per chapter and the number of chapters overall to thirty-seven, the age at which she wrote *My Life*. In republishing the book at age forty-five, she remained true to her procedure by adding eight new chapters and eight sentences to each. This imposition of formal controls organizes semantic interplay between individual sentences, even as it liberates sentences to interact with each other.

The principles by which sentences proceed within each chapter are controlled by a variety of factors, some phonic, some imagistic, and some syntactic. Consider the following:

> I was shy of my aunt's deafness who was [my uncle's] sister-in-law and who had years earlier fallen into the habit of nodding agreeably. Wool station. See lightning, wait for thunder. Quite mistakenly, as it happened. The afternoon happens, crowded and therefore endless. Thicker, she agreed. It was a tick, she had the habit, and now she bobbed like my toy plastic bird on the edge of its glass, dipping into and recoiling from the water. But a word is a bottomless pit. (ML, 7)

The remark about the aunt's nervous tick that begins the passage is interrupted by other things but is revisited several sentences later, this time linked to a memory of a toy bird, "dipping into and recoiling from the water." The conjunction that begins the next sentence would seem to extend the previous, but it leads to a general remark about language being "a bottomless pit." We retain the images of bobbing aunt and bird in our minds, and so the image of a word as a "bottomless pit" seems an appropriate, if unexpected, complement; what would otherwise be an abstraction (the endlessness of language) is suddenly materialized in the whimsical image of a toy dipping into a physical word. It is this kind of associative logic that makes *My Life* anything but "arbitrary" in its growth.

This attempt to materialize language by exposing its arbitrary, systemic nature has obvious precedents in modernists like Williams and Stein. For Hejinian, the task has an additional critical function in exploring the interdependencies of that material word and the "self" that is produced therefrom. Far from being nonreferential or "anticontent," as some have argued, language writing takes the issue of representation as a problematic issue – not as a self-evident fact but as an ideology in need of deconstruction. The word *is* a "bottomless pit," and only by recontextualizing it can one test its depth.

Robert Hass would no doubt agree that language, to be seen as ideology, must be re-seen as material artifact. But his work differs from Hejinian's in the form that this recontextualizing must take. For him, rhetoric retains its expressive potential to highlight and suggest affective states; for Hejinian, rhetoric is not in service to but is a dimension of those states and thus must be foregrounded as figuration. For Hass, poetry refers to the interaction between a speculative, skeptical intellect and a natural world of fundamental value. He tests his perceptions by trying out new dramatic postures, some self-effacing and some boldly polemical, not to "fix" the landscape but to discover how he is written into it. Hejinian also wants to understand how she is "written" into the landscape, but her method is to invite participation between her composition and the one the reader creates in its interstices. These may seem minor distinctions in the larger history of poetry, but they have increasingly divided poets into opposed and opposing camps, one holding

out for the continuity of a lyric tradition from the first-generation romantics and the other holding out for a fundamental "postmodern"
aporia. This argument has surfaced with considerable urgency (although
not between Hass and Hejinian, by any means) in San Francisco, whose
literary reputation has, to some extent, been based upon extreme forms
of confession and personalism. Hass and Hejinian represent two important qualifications of this tendency, even as they exemplify the difficulties
of escaping it.

CONCLUSION: A CITY ON A HILL

The work of Lyn Hejinian represents the most extreme version
of a personalist or autobiographical impulse that we have seen in earlier
chapters of this book. *My Life* rejects the idea of a single, unified subject
and the narrative logic by which it may be constituted. As a feminist,
Hejinian does not depend on mythic or archetypal principles underlying
identity (the cult of the goddess, atavistic survivals), nor does she project
a unified vision of women's biological or economic oppression. And
because it is difficult to find some thematic representation of women in
her work, one might see it as a regression to a kind of impersonal
formalism. This accusation is usually made by critics who have not read
language writing very carefully – who look at any concern with formal
structure as a denial of imagination, content, or expression. By treating
these qualities as self-evident poetic values, such critics signal the ideology they inhabit, one built upon that narrow reading of romanticism
with which I began this book.[26]

By concluding *The San Francisco Renaissance* with language writing, I
would like to suggest the unexpected variations that an "ideology of
romanticism" must accommodate. Rather than see the work of this
group as a total break with the poetics we have been addressing, I would
see it as representing a new stage in a romantic theory of language, one
based less on the artist's imaginative and expressive powers than on a
skepticism about language's ability to represent. The definitive remark
on the subject was made not by a "language poet" but by Jack Spicer in
1960: "Where we are is in a sentence." The ramifications of this remark
are still unfolding.

The origins of this linguistic skepticism predate our era by at least two
hundred years. They can be found in Kant's and Schopenhauer's theories
of the sublime and in the "dejection" poems of Coleridge, Shelley, and
Blake. They can be found, as Paul de Man has shown, in the structure of
romantic imagery itself, which is able to constitute presence "but, by the
same token [is] unable to give a foundation to what it posits except as an
intent of consciousness."[27] And in a larger, philosophical sense, such a
bifurcation between intention and language can be found in Nietzsche's

genealogical critique of morality or Heidegger's etymological analysis of the structure of *Dasein*. Jack Spicer's poetics of dictation may attempt to "transcend" the rational ego, but at the same time it acknowledges the essential otherness of language and, by extension, the degree to which the self is constituted *by* language. These are all variations of that central romantic problematic of the sign: In order to represent thoughts "too deep for tears," the poet must use words, and words are ultimately inadequate to fulfill the intentional purposes to which they are put. "It is very difficult," Jack Spicer says: "We want to transfer the immediate object, the immediate emotion to the poem – and yet the immediate always has hundreds of its own words clinging to it, short-lived and tenacious as barnacles. And it is wrong to scrape them off and substitute others. A poet is a time mechanic not an embalmer."[28]

This linguistic skepticism led to a highly rhetorical or elegiac poetry during the 1940s and, later, to the jazz-inspired or visionary poetry of the Beats. In my introduction I characterized such a poetics as "performative" in that poetry was expected to enact rather than represent, to touch rather than educate, to perform rather than describe. As William Everson points out, the rhetorical poetry of his generation was not much in favor within the academic establishment – and therein lay its power.[29] By its sheer bravura and grandiloquence it could cut across rational discourse to a realm of feeling and intuition that lay beyond words. Although I have emphasized this performative tendency as a response to the New Critical metaphysical lyric, I would also suggest that these strategies were developed in response to the alienation and malaise of the postwar era. The creation of a new poetry was directly linked to the need for alternative social forms during a period of consensus and conformity.

In my introduction I argued that the San Francisco Renaissance was based on a series of enabling myths invented for the purpose of shoring up a sense of community. These myths circled around ideals of energy, primitivism, and participation that would link the individual to a subterranean realm of vitality lacking in the social world. Theodor Adorno has described the role that such myths play as the immanence of society in art, the presence of social tensions in an art that attempts to distance itself from that society: "Works of art are after-images or replicas of empirical life, inasmuch as they proffer to the latter what in the outside world is being denied them."[30] Granted Adorno is discussing what he thinks of as autonomous modern art, whereas we are describing a poetry that was often committed to specific social and political agendas. Still, the point can be made that it was not so much the "content" of these enabling myths that created an alternative poetics as their function in signaling a desire for community acutely felt at this time. If there was a disparity between poetic claim and social practice, it was largely the result of attempting to justify aesthetic acts by transcendental principles. Poets sought a "ground" outside language obtainable only through language, and in the breach they found themselves enmeshed in a series of contradictions.

Whatever contradictions there may have been between theory and practice, the enabling myths generated were responsible for things larger than literature. In the inflated claims for "authenticity of lifestyle" can be found the origins of later counterculture and New Left thinking that would have a decisive effect on community during the late 1960s. In the various formulations of "open" versus "closed" texts can be found new approaches toward noncoercive theories of reading and pedagogy that have had an impact on current education. And as I said earlier, the gains of feminism, ethnic identity, and gay rights owe something to the spirit of "disaffiliation" celebrated by Rexroth in his earlier essays on San Francisco. However "mythic" these enabling myths, they were formulated within communities that stood in self-conscious opposition to the dominant culture. In these myths we may read something of the Protestant impulse that characterizes our literature in general.

The second, and even third, generations of San Francisco writers have built upon the spirit, if not the letter, of the first generation, enlarging the populist thrust on one hand and curbing the rhetorical excesses on the other. There is still a degree of internecine warfare going on between various literary factions (Beat versus academic, language writing versus populist), but rather than disparage such conflicts as signaling the decline of some original, unified movement I would see them as carrying on a tradition of opposition that was there from the beginning. And rather than attempt to unify all of the communities of the San Francisco literary community under one heading, I would see them as reflecting a necessary diversity and pluralism in a time of globalized ideologies. When poets become so satisfied with the status quo that they forget to respond, democratic consensus will truly have done its job.

San Francisco as a literary frontier (in the sense of outer limit as well as province) has been a contentious and cranky place, overdetermined, grandiose, and at times pompous. It has also believed in literature enough to argue about it, sometimes in excess. We may see in the disparity between its desire for cohesion and the reality of its sectarianism some of the tensions of American life in general: democratic institutions versus self-centered individuals, expansion versus exploitation, individualism versus the ensemble. On a national scale, these tensions are worked out within the myth of a "city on a hill" that claims belatedness as a sign of divine largesse. Because that community was founded late in the history

of a corrupt world, it might serve as a fulfillment of an ancient covenant.[31] The modern writers of the West imported this Puritan myth to a
city built on several hills, rewriting that covenant in secular and no less
social terms. We may continue to read their narratives as a measure of the
community we have – and the community we have yet to realize.

Notes

PREFACE

1 Raymond Williams, *The Sociology of Culture* (New York: Schocken, 1982), pp. 10–11. See also idem, *Keywords: A Vocabulary of Culture and Society* (New York: Oxford University Press, 1976), pp. 76–82.
2 Robert Duncan, *Bending the Bow* (New York: New Directions, 1968), p. 6.
3 Robert von Hallberg, *American Poetry and Culture, 1945–1980* (Cambridge, Mass.: Harvard University Press, 1985), p. 4.
4 Ibid., p. 8.
5 On John Crowe Ransom's response to Duncan, see Ekbert Fass, *Young Robert Duncan: Portrait of the Poet as Homosexual in Society* (Santa Barbara, Calif.: Black Sparrow Press, 1983), p. 151.

INTRODUCTION

1 The most comprehensive history of the San Francisco Renaissance can be found in Lawrence Ferlinghetti and Nancy Peters's *Literary San Francisco* (San Francisco: City Lights Books; Harper & Row, 1980). Like most other anecdotal accounts, it focuses on the North Beach scene, although it offers an interesting perspective on the activist political tradition of San Francisco writing in general. Other accounts can be found in Barry Gifford and Lawrence Lee, *Jack's Book* (New York: St. Martin's, 1978); Ann Charters, *Kerouac* (New York: Warner Paperback Library, 1974); Tom Clark, *Jack Kerouac* (San Diego, Calif.: Harcourt Brace Jovanovich, 1984); Aram Saroyan, *Genesis Angels* (New York: Morrow, 1979); David Kherdian, *Six Poets of the San Francisco Renaissance: Portraits and Checklists* (Fresno, Calif.: Giligia Press, 1967); Michael McClure, *Scratching the Beat Surface* (San Francisco: North Point Press, 1982); Gerald Nicosia, *Memory Babe: A Critical Biography of Jack Kerouac* (New York: Grove Press, 1985); *The Beat Vision*, ed. Arthur Knight and Kit Knight (New York: Paragon House, 1987). The appendixes to Allen Ginsberg's *Howl: Original Draft Facsimile, Transcript and Variant Versions . . .*, ed. Barry Miles (New

York: Harper & Row, 1986), offer useful discussions of the Six Gallery reading, the *Howl* trial and the early 1950s period in general. Also see the individual entries in *The Beats: Literary Bohemians in Postwar America,* ed. Ann Charters, Dictionary of Literary Biography, vol. 16 (Detroit, Mich.: Gale Research Co.).

2 Jerome J. McGann, *The Romantic Ideology: A Critical Investigation* (Chicago: University of Chicago Press, 1983), p. 1.

3 Accounts of the Six Gallery reading can be found in most of the entries listed in note 1. See particularly McClure's *Scratching the Beat Surface.* See also Robert Duncan, unpublished interview with Eloyde Tovey concerning Bay Area poetry, Bancroft Library, University of California, Berkeley, pp. 6–7; Thomas Albright, *Art in the San Francisco Bay Area, 1945–1980: An Illustrated History* (Berkeley and Los Angeles: University of California Press, 1985), pp. 85–6.

4 Jack Kerouac, *The Dharma Bums* (New York: NAL, 1958), p. 13.

5 McClure, *Scratching the Beat Surface,* p. 24.

6 Ibid., pp. 24–6; "Point Lobos Animism" is reprinted in *Hymns to St. Geryon and Dark Brown* (San Francisco: Grey Fox, 1980).

7 Harold Bloom and David Bromwich, "American Poetic Schools and Techniques (Contemporary)," in *Princeton Encyclopedia of Poetry and Poetics,* ed. Alex Preminger, Frank J. Warnke, and O. B. Hardison, Jr. (Princeton, N.J.: Princeton University Press, 1974), p. 918.

8 Daniel Hoffman, *The Harvard Guide to Contemporary American Writing* (Cambridge, Mass.: Harvard University Press, 1979), p. 518.

9 Stephen Schwartz, "Escapees in paradise: Literary life in San Francisco," *New Criterion* 4, no. 4 (1985), p. 2.

10 It is odd that Schwartz should focus much of his invective on the North Beach Beat scene, since he himself has been strongly identified with that very community. He was the editor of *Anti-Narcissus,* a San Francisco–based surrealist magazine. His work is represented in the surrealism supplement of *City Lights Anthology,* ed. Lawrence Ferlinghetti (San Francisco: City Lights, 1974), and his poetry has been published in numerous local magazines like *Bastard Angel* and *Beatitude* as well as the Chicago-based surrealist magazine *Arsenal,* which has featured numerous San Francisco writers.

11 On America's distrust of popular literature, see Jane Tompkins, *Sensational Designs: The Cultural Work of American Fiction, 1790–1860* (New York: Oxford University Press, 1985).

12 Jack Spicer, "The Poet and Poetry: A Symposium," *Occident* (Fall 1949), p. 45. Reprinted in *One Night Stand and Other Poems* (San Francisco: Grey Fox, 1980), p. 92.

13 William Blake, *Jerusalem* (14:29), in *The Poems of William Blake,* ed. W. H. Stevenson and David Erdman (London: Longman Group, 1971), p. 654.

14 Robert Duncan, "Ode for Dick Brown," in Robert Duncan and Jack Spicer, *An Ode and Arcadia* (Berkeley, Calif.: Ark Press, 1974), p. 25.

15 Frank Norris, "An Opening for Novelists: Great Opportunities for Fiction Writers in San Francisco," *San Francisco Wave* 16 (May 22, 1897); p. 7, reprinted in the Norton Critical Edition of *McTeague* (New York: Norton, 1977), p. 254.

16 According to early Spanish accounts, the state of California was thought to be an island and was represented as such in early navigational maps. See, for instance, the map in Ferlinghetti and Peters, *Literary San Francisco,* p. 4.

17 Kevin Starr, *Americans and the California Dream, 1850–1915* (Santa Barbara, Calif.: Peregrine Press, 1981), p. 42.

18 David Wyatt, *The Fall into Eden: Landscape and Imagination in California* (Cambridge University Press, 1986), p. 5.

19 On the origins of California literature see Wyatt, *The Fall into Eden;* James D. Hart, *A Companion to California* (New York: Oxford University Press, 1978); Starr, *Americans and the California Dream;* Ferlinghetti and Peters, *Literary San Francisco,* pp. 1–120; Lawrence Clark Powell, *California Classics: The Creative Literature of the Golden State* (Los Angeles: Ward Ritchie Press, 1971); Franklin Walker, *San Francisco's Literary Frontier* (Seattle: University of Washington Press, 1969); William Everson, *Archetype West: The Pacific Coast as a Literary Region* (Berkeley, Calif.: Oyez, 1976).

20 Joaquin Miller, "In San Francisco," in *The Poetical Works of Joaquin Miller,* ed. Stuart Sherman (New York: Putnam, 1923), p. 158.

21 Quoted in Everson, *Archetype West,* p. 28.

22 Ibid., p. 27.

23 William Everson, in "The San Francisco Renaissance: A Reappraisal," conference held at the University of California, San Diego, February 10, 1982. Audio tape held in the Mandeville Department of Special Collections, University Library, University of California, San Diego.

24 Kenneth Rexroth, *American Poetry in the Twentieth Century* (New York: Herder & Herder, 1971), p. 137.

25 Kenneth Rexroth, interview in David Meltzer, ed., *The San Francisco Poets* (New York: Ballantine, 1971), p. 30.

26 Kenneth Rexroth, "San Francisco's Mature Bohemians," *The Nation* 184, no. 8, (1957), p. 159.

27 Kenneth Rexroth, "Noretorp-Noretysh," *Evergreen Review* 1, no. 2 (1957), p. 15.

28 Gary Snyder, in "The San Francisco Renaissance: A Reappraisal."

29 Ibid.

30 Lew Welch, "The Song Mount Tamalpais Sings," in *Ring of Bone: Collected Poems, 1950–1971* (Bolinas, Calif.: Grey Fox, 1973), pp. 121–2; Gary Snyder, "A Walk," in *The Back Country* (New York: New Directions, 1968), p. 11. See also Robert Kern, "Recipes, Catalogues, Open Form Poetics: Gary Snyder's Archetypal Voice," *Contemporary Literature* 18, no. 2 (1977), pp. 173–97.

31 Jack Spicer, *The Collected Books of Jack Spicer,* ed. Robin Blaser (Los Angeles: Black Sparrow Press, 1975), p. 176.

32 Frank O'Hara, "Meditations in an Emergency," in *The Collected Poems of Frank O'Hara,* ed. Donald Allen (New York: Knopf, 1971), p. 197.

33 Jack Kerouac, "The Railroad Earth Part I," in *The New American Story,* ed. Donald Allen (New York: Grove, 1965), p. 132.

34 Ibid., p. 136.

35 Lawrence Ferlinghetti, "Autobiography," in *A Coney Island of the Mind* (New York: New Directions, 1958), p. 60.

36 John Hollander, "Poetry Chronicle," *Partisan Review* 24, no. 2 (1957) p. 297.

37 Lawrence Ferlinghetti, "Note on Poetry in San Francisco," in *Casebook on the Beat,* ed. Thomas Parkinson (New York: Crowell, 1961) p. 124.

38 Helen Adam, "I Love My Love," in *The New American Poetry,* ed. Donald M. Allen (New York: Grove, 1960), p. 114.

39 Dylan Thomas made two reading tours to the West Coast, the first in 1950 and then in 1952.

40 On jazz in San Francisco see Ralph J. Gleason, "San Francisco Jazz Scene," *Evergreen Review* 1, no. 2 (1957), pp. 59–64.

41 Charles Altieri, "From Symbolist Thought to Immanence: The Ground of Postmodern American Poetics," *boundary 2* 1, no. 3 (1973), pp. 605–41. A rewritten version of this essay appears as the introduction to Altieri's *Enlarging the Temple: New Directions in American Poetry during the 1960's* (Lewisburg, Pa.: Bucknell University Press, 1979).

42 John Keats, letter to George and Thomas Keats, December 21, 27, (?), 1817 in *The Selected Poems and Letters by John Keats,* ed. Douglas Bush (Boston: Houghton Mifflin, 1959). The distinction about "negative capability" is important to make here since Keats's letters have been marshaled by the New Critics to verify ideas of impersonality and aesthetic autonomy. In another well-known passage from his letters, Keats, writing to Richard Woodhouse on October 27, 1818, says the following: "A poet is the most unpoetical of any thing in existence; because he has no Identity . . . he is certainly the most unpoetical of all God's Creatures. If then he has no self, and if I am a Poet, where is the Wonder that I should say I would write no more?"

43 Altieri, "From Symbolist Thought to Immanence," p. 607.

44 William Spanos, "Breaking the Circle: Hermeneutics as Disclosure," *boundary 2* 5, no. 2 (1977), p. 423. See also Paul Bové, *Destructive Poetics: Heidegger and Modern American Poetry* (New York: Columbia University Press, 1980).

45 Altieri, "From Symbolist Thought to Immanence," p. 611.

46 Robert Duncan, *Bending the Bow* (New York: New Directions, 1968), p. v; Michael McClure, Foreword to *Rare Angel* (Los Angeles: Black Sparrow Press, 1974); Jack Spicer, *The Collected Books of Jack Spicer,* p. 33; Jack Kerouac, "Essentials of Spontaneous Prose," in *The New American Story,* p. 271.

47 See *The Poetry Reading: A Contemporary Compendium on Language and Performance,* ed. Stephen Vincent and Ellen Zweig (San Francisco: Momo's Press, 1981).

48 Jack Kerouac, "146th Chorus," in *Mexico City Blues* (New York: Grove, 1959), p. 146.

49 J. L. Austin, *How to Do Things with Words* (Cambridge, Mass.: Harvard Univ. Press, 1975), pp. 4–11. For a critique of Austin's theory of the performative utterance, see Emile Benveniste, "Analytical Philosophy and Language," in *Problems in General Linguistics,* trans. Mary Elizabeth Meek (Coral Gables, Fla.: University of Miami Press, 1971), pp. 231–8.

50 Ibid., p. 236. For a fuller treatment of the possibilities of applying speech act theory to literature see Mary Louise Pratt, *Toward a Speech Act Theory of Literary Discourse* (Bloomington: Indiana University Press, 1977). I have dis-

cussed the role of the performative utterance in relation to Wallace Stevens in "Notes Beyond the *Notes: Wallace Stevens and Contemporary Poetics,*" in *Wallace Stevens and Modernism,* ed. Albert Gelpi (Cambridge University Press, 1985), pp. 141–60.

51 Altieri, *Enlarging the Temple;* Robert Pinsky, *The Situation of Poetry: Contemporary Poetry and Its Traditions* (Princeton, N.J.: Princeton University Press, 1976); Ralph Mills, *The Cry of the Human: Essays on Contemporary American Poetry* (Urbana: University of Illinois Press, 1975); Cary Nelson, *Our Last First Poets: Vision and History in Contemporary American Poetry* (Urbana: University of Illinois Press, 1981).

52 Jack Kerouac, "The Philosophy of the Beat Generation," *Esquire* 49, no. 3 (1958), pp. 24–5.

53 Daniel Bell, *The End of Ideology* (New York: Free Press, 1960), p. 288.

54 Christopher Lasch, *The Agony of the American Left* (New York: Random House, 1968).

55 David Riesman, *The Lonely Crowd: A Study of the Changing American Character* (New Haven, Conn.: Yale University Press, 1950).

56 Irving Howe, "Mass Society and Post-Modern Fiction," *Partisan Review* 26, no. 3 (1959), p. 435.

57 Burroughs, quoted in *The Beats,* part 1, p. xiii.

58 Gary Snyder, "North Beach," in *The Old Ways* (San Francisco: City Lights, 1977), p. 45. Although I am emphasizing community in the San Francisco Bay Region, the same need for community that Snyder expresses existed in other parts of the country. Such was the case among poets at Black Mountain College during the early 1950s and within the New York school of poets and painters, where contact among members occurred on a daily basis. I am less concerned with forms of community that develop around a magazine or a concept in which the major contact occurs through the mails, although one could say that a certain kind of community formed around *Poetry* magazine under Harriet Monroe's editorship when poets from Europe and the United States regularly "met" within its pages. And one could also say that the seeds of Black Mountain as a community were being planted in Cid Corman's magazine *Origin* some years before Black Mountain College came under Charles Olson's rectorship.

59 Allen Ginsberg to Louis Ginsberg, February 2, 1958, Allen Ginsberg Papers, Butler Library, Columbia University, New York.

60 Allen Ginsberg, "America," in *Collected Poems, 1947–1980* (New York: Harper & Row, 1984), p. 148.

61 Jean-François Lyotard, *The Postmodern Condition: A Report on Knowledge,* trans. Geoff Bennington and Brian Massumi (Minneapolis: University of Minnesota Press, 1984), p. xxiv.

62 See Fredric Jameson, "Postmodernism, or the Cultural Logic of Late Capitalism," *New Left Review* 146 (July–August 1984), pp. 53–92. See also Jean Baudrillard, "The Precession of Simulacra," in *Simulations,* trans. Paul Foss, Paul Patton, and Philip Beitchman (New York: Semiotext(e), 1983), pp. 1–79.

63 On the "culture industry," see Max Horkheimer and Theodor W. Adorno,

The Dialectic of Enlightenment, trans. John Cumming (New York: Seabury, 1969), pp. 120–67.

64 Ferlinghetti, "Autobiography," p. 63.

65 Robert Duncan, "Poem Beginning with a Line by Pindar," in *The Opening of the Field* (New York: New Directions, 1960), p. 64.

1 THE ELEGIAC MODE

1 Robert Duncan and Jack Spicer, *An Ode and Arcadia* (Berkeley, Calif.: Ark Press, 1974), p. 21. Duncan has always credited Rexroth with recognizing the elegiac impulse in Bay Area poetry following the war, but in an interview on July 12, 1982, Duncan said that an even more important model was the British poet George Barker. Indeed, many of Barker's "secular" and "sacred elegies" are reminiscent of Duncan's work of the mid-1940s.

2 William Carlos Williams, "Asphodel, That Greeny Flower," in *Pictures from Brueghel and Other Poems* (New York: New Directions, 1962), p. 168.

3 Delmore Schwartz, "The Present State of Poetry," in *Selected Essays of Delmore Schwartz,* ed. Donald A. Dike and David H. Zucker (Chicago: University of Chicago Press, 1970), p. 44. The conservative nature of forties poetry is discussed in James E. B. Breslin, *From Modern to Contemporary: American Poetry, 1945–1965* (Chicago: University of Chicago Press, 1984), pp. 23–52.

4 David Antin, "Modernism and postmodernism: Approaching the present in American poetry," *boundary 2* 1, no. 1 (1972), p. 118.

5 The "Modern Masters" series was held at Throckmorton Manor on Telegraph Avenue, south of the University of California campus. For a thorough history of this period, see Ekbert Faas, *Young Robert Duncan: Portrait of the Poet as Homosexual in Society* (Santa Barbara, Calif.: Black Sparrow Press, 1983), pp. 205–64.

6 T. S. Eliot, "Ulysses, order and myth," *Dial* 75 (1923), p. 483. Reprinted in *The Modern Tradition: Backgrounds of Modern Literature,* ed. Richard Ellmann and Charles Feidelson, Jr. (New York: Oxford University Press, 1965), p. 679.

7 Samuel Hynes, *The Auden Generation: Literature and Politics in England in the 1930's* (New York: Viking, 1976).

8 Robert Duncan, *The Years as Catches* (Berkeley, Calif.: Oyez, 1966), p. vi. In a notebook entry from this period discussing "An Apollonian Elegy," Duncan speaks of "a suffering without language seeking to take body in words, now finds body in 'Apollo's' imagined suffering." Robert Duncan papers, Notebook B, Bancroft Library, University of California, Berkeley.

9 William Everson, *Earth Poetry: Selected Essays and Interviews,* ed. Lee Bartlett (Berkeley, Calif.: Oyez, 1980), p. 35.

10 Kenneth Rexroth, "The Phoenix and the Tortoise," in *The Collected Longer Poems of Kenneth Rexroth* (New York: New Directions, 1968), p. 64; hereafter cited in the text as CLP.

11 Thomas Parkinson, "September Elegy," *The Ark* 1 (n.d.), p. 71.

12 Thomas Parkinson, "Phenomenon or Generation," in *A Casebook on the Beat* (New York: Crowell, 1961), p. 283.

13 Ibid., p. 282.
14 See the interview with Rexroth in *The San Francisco Poets*, ed. David Meltzer (New York: Ballantine, 1971), p. 9.
15 Among Winters's best-known students are J. V. Cunningham, Ann Stanford, Thom Gunn, Edgar Bowers, and Robert Hass.
16 Lawrence Hart, "Some Elements of Active Poetry," *Circle* 6 (1945), p. 7.
17 See the special "Activist" issue of *Circle* no. 6, (1945) from which these examples are taken.
18 Spicer's debt to Miles can best be seen by the fact that he dedicated his *Collected Poems: 1945–1946* to her. A facsimile version of this hand-printed, hand-bound pamphlet was republished in 1981 by Oyez Press, Berkeley, Calif.
19 Duncan, "Ode to Dick Brown," in *Ode and Arcadia*, p. 24.
20 Kenneth Rexroth, *The Alternative Society: Essays from the Other World* (New York: Herder & Herder, 1970). See also his *Communalism: From Its Origins to the Twentieth Century* (New York: Seabury, 1974).
21 Kenneth Rexroth, *Collected Shorter Poems* (New York: New Directions, 1966), p. 89; hereafter cited in the text as CSP.
22 Kenneth Rexroth, *An Autobiographical Novel* (Santa Barbara, Calif.: Ross-Erickson, 1978), p. 338.
23 Kenneth Rexroth, Introduction to William Everson, *The Residual Years* (New York: New Directions, 1968), p. xv; hereafter cited in the text as RY.
24 On Everson's relation to Roethke, see the interview in *The San Francisco Poets*, pp. 82–3.
25 Ibid., p. 92.
26 Albert Gelpi, Afterword to *The Veritable Years: 1949–1966* (Santa Barbara, Calif.: Black Sparrow Press, 1978), n.p.
27 Unpublished interview with William Everson, conducted by Steven Henry Madoff, September 1980.
28 M. H. Abrams, *Natural Supernaturalism: Tradition and Revolution in Romantic Literature* (New York: Norton, 1971), pp. 95–6.
29 For a discussion of Everson's first marriage and its dissolution, see the interview with him in Meltzer, ed., *The San Francisco Poets*, p. 83.
30 Brother Antoninus [William Everson], *Robinson Jeffers: Fragments of an Older Fury* (Berkeley, Calif.: Oyez, 1968), p. 14.
31 Everson, *Earth Poetry*, p. 35.
32 Robert Duncan papers, notebook, Bancroft Library, University of California, Berkeley.
33 Ibid.
34 On the circumstances surrounding the composition of "Medieval Scenes," see the preface to *Medieval Scenes: 1950 and 1959* (Kent, Ohio: Kent State University Libraries, 1978). Also see Robert Bertholf's afterword to this volume.
35 Faas, *Young Robert Duncan*, pp. 225–41. The dominant theme of Duncan's discussion of the Berkeley period, both in his published interviews and in personal conversations with the author, is that the term "renaissance" for his circle had specific historical and philosophical connotations. It was not a term that described a group of writers who happened to be living in Berkeley;

rather, it referred to their particular concerns with medieval and Renaissance studies. Most important was the idea of a brotherhood steeped in the study of art, history, and philosophy and that had, behind it, a sense of occult or mystical theology.

36 Robert Duncan, "The Years as Catches," in *The First Decade: Selected Poems, 1940–1950* (London: Fulcrum Press, 1968), p. 15; hereafter cited in the text as FD.

37 Robert Duncan, Introduction to *The Years as Catches: First Poems (1939–1946) by Robert Duncan* (Berkeley, Calif.: Oyez, 1966), pp. vi–vii.

38 Robert Duncan, "Returning to the Rhetoric of an Early Mode," in *Roots and Branches* (New York: New Directions, 1964), p. 89.

39 Robert Duncan, *Caesar's Gate: Poems, 1949–50* (Berkeley, Calif.: Sand Dollar Press, 1972), p. ix.

40 Robert Duncan, jacket blurb for *The First Decade*.

41 See Robert Duncan, "The Poetics of Music: Stravinsky," *Occident* (Spring 1948), pp. 53–4. Reprinted in Fass, *Young Robert Duncan*, p. 335.

42 Robert Duncan, "Sonnet 3," in *Roots and Branches* (New York: New Directions, 1964), p. 124.

2 "THE DARKNESS SURROUNDS US"

1 Paul O'Neil, "The Only Rebellion Around," in *A Casebook on the Beat*, ed. Thomas Parkinson (New York: Crowell, 1961), p. 236.

2 Ibid., p. 235.

3 Norman Podhoretz, "The Know-Nothing Bohemians," in *A Casebook on the Beat*, pp. 203–4.

4 Ibid., p. 204.

5 Jack Kerouac, *On the Road* (New York: NAL, 1957), p. 111; hereafter cited in the text as OR.

6 Lucien Levy-Bruhl, *Primitive Mentality*, trans. Lilian A. Clare (Boston: Beacon, 1966), chap. 1.

7 Robert Creeley, "I Know a Man," in *The Collected Poems of Robert Creeley* (Berkeley and Los Angeles: University of California Press, 1982), p. 132.

8 In an interview with Michael André, Creeley argued against the impulse to read the "he" of the tenth line as the one who says "drive":

> The poem protects itself. . . . I like the impulse of "drive," then "he said." I could have said, period, you know
>
>> drive. He sd, for
>> christ's sake
>
> But "he" doesn't say "drive."

Robert Creeley, *Contexts of Poetry: Interviews, 1961–1971* (Bolinas, Calif.: Four Seasons Foundation, 1973), p. 209.

9 Jack Kerouac, "Essentials of Spontaneous Prose," in *A Casebook on the Beat*, p. 66.

10 Jack Kerouac, "Origins of the Beat Generation," *Playboy* 6 (June 1959), p. 32. Reprinted in *A Casebook on the Beat*, pp. 68–76.

11 See Tim Hunt, *Kerouac's Crooked Road: Development of a Fiction* (Hamden, Conn.: Archon Books, 1981), for the most thorough discussion of Kerouac's "road" book.

12 On the limitations of the expressive ideal see Charles Altieri, "From Experience to Discourse: American Poetry and Poetics in the Seventies," *Contemporary Literature* 21, no. 2 (1980), pp. 191–224.

13 Allen Ginsberg, "Notes for *Howl and Other Poems*," in *The New American Poetry*, ed. Donald M. Allen (New York: Grove, 1960), p. 415.

14 James E. B. Breslin, *From Modern to Contemporary: American Poetry, 1945–1965* (Chicago: University of Chicago Press, 1984), p. 65.

15 Allen Ginsberg, *Howl: Original Draft Facsimile Transcript and Variant Versions . . .* , ed. Barry Miles (New York: Harper & Row, 1986).

16 Richard Eberhart, *To Eberhart from Ginsberg: A Letter About "Howl"* (Lincoln, Mass.: Penmaen Press, 1976), p. 16.

17 Allen Ginsberg, "The Art of Poetry VIII," *Paris Review* 37 (1966), pp. 14–55; hereafter cited as *Paris Review* interview.

18 *A Casebook on the Beat*, p. 70.

19 Catherine Stimpson, "The Beat Generation and the Trials of Homosexual Liberation," *Salmagundi* 58–9 (Fall 1982), p. 376.

20 Ibid., p. 375.

21 Quoted by Seymour Krim in his introduction to Jack Kerouac, *Desolation Angels* (London: Panther, 1966), p. 19.

22 Ibid., p. 65.

23 Kenneth Rexroth, "Disengagement: The Art of the Beat Generation," in *A Casebook on the Beat*, pp. 179–93.

24 D. H. Lawrence, "Whitman," in *Studies in Classic American Literature* (New York: Viking, 1964), pp. 163–77.

25 Jack Kerouac, *Excerpts from Visions of Cody* (New York: New Directions, 1960), p. 5. Quoted in Hunt, *Kerouac's Crooked Road*, p. 121. I will be referring to the complete *Visions of Cody* (New York: McGraw-Hill, 1972), hereafter cited as VC in the notes and text.

26 Quoted in Hunt, *Kerouac's Crooked Road*, p. 121.

27 Gerald Nicosia, *Memory Babe: A Critical Biography of Jack Kerouac* (New York: Grove, 1983), p. 371.

28 VC, 99–100. As this passage makes clear, Proust is an important source for Kerouac, but like so much else in the novel, the use of the French writer is filtered through Cody. At one point in the tapes, Cody says " 'cause we're both concerned about, ah, memory, and just relax like Proust and everything. So I talk on about that as the mind and remembers and thinks and that's why it's difficult for, to keep, ah, a balance, you know" (VC, 146). For Cody, Proust "represents" a certain kind of writer (one concerned with memory and relaxation), but Duluoz is the one who is able to translate Proustian problems of memory and sensation into narrative terms and thus gain the "balance" that Cody cannot achieve.

29 Cody spends most of his time in the tapes talking about talking. Kerouac's use of tape transcriptions does not, as some commentators have claimed, give a clear sense of Cody's conversational brilliance but rather of his extreme self-consciousness.

30 Letter from Allen Ginsberg to Jack Kerouac, June 12, 1952, Allen Ginsberg Papers, Butler Library, Columbia University, New York.

31 Ibid.

32 Letter from Jack Kerouac to Allen Ginsberg, May 18, 1952, Allen Ginsberg Papers, Butler Library, Columbia University, New York.

33 Ginsberg claims that "Howl" was an attempt to create "long saxophone-like chorus lines I knew Kerouac would hear *sound* of–taking off from his own inspired prose line really a new poetry." Allen Ginsberg, "Notes for *Howl and Other Poems*," in *The New American Poetry*, ed. Donald M. Allen (New York: Grove, 1960), p. 415.

34 Ibid., p. 415.

35 Letter from Allen Ginsberg to Louis Ginsberg, January 1957, Allen Ginsberg Papers, Butler Library, Columbia University, New York.

36 Allen Ginsberg, *Allen Verbatim: Lectures on Poetry, Politics, Consciousness*, ed. Gordon Ball (New York: McGraw-Hill, 1974), p. 20.

37 See Ginsberg's lengthy discussion of Cezanne's influence in his *Paris Review* interview, pp. 24–31.

38 Allen Ginsberg, "Howl," in *Collected Poems, 1947–1980* (New York: Harper & Row, 1984), pp. 130–1; hereafter cited as CP in the text.

39 Marjorie Perloff, "A Lion in Our Living Room," *American Poetry Review* 14, no. 2 (1985), p. 38.

40 *Paris Review* interview, p. 16.

41 Letter from Allen Ginsberg to John Hollander, quoted in Jane Kramer, *Allen Ginsberg in America* (New York: Random House, 1969), p. 176.

42 Michael McClure, *Ghost Tantras* (San Francisco: n.p., 1964), p. 58.

43 "An Interview with Michael McClure," *San Francisco Review of Books* 3, no. 8 (1977), p. 15.

44 Michael McClure, "Interview," in *The San Francisco Poets*, ed. David Meltzer (New York: Ballantine, 1971), p. 261.

45 Michael McClure, "Phi Upsilon Kappa," in *Meat Science Essays* (San Francisco: City Lights, 1966), pp. 7–23. Reprinted in *The Poetics of the New American Poetry*, ed. Donald Allen (New York: Grove, 1973), pp. 416–29.

46 "Phi Upsilon Kappa," p. 13.

47 Michael McClure, *Star* (New York: Grove, 1970), p. 61.

48 Michael McClure, "Mozart and the Apple," in *Scratching the Beat Surface* (San Francisco: North Point, 1982), p. 115.

49 Michael McClure, "Hail Thee Who Play!" in ibid., p. 164.

50 *The San Francisco Poets*, p. 259.

51 Michael McClure, *!The Feast!* in *The Mammals* (San Francisco: Cranium Press, 1972), p. 60.

52 Quoted from jacket blurb of *The Mammals*.

53 Michael McClure, *The Meatball*, in *Gargoyle Cartoons* (New York: Delacorte, 1971), p. 45.

54 Michael McClure, *Gorf* (New York: New Directions, 1976), p. 59.

55 Michael McClure, "Poetics," in *Antechamber & Other Poems* (New York: New Directions, 1978), p. 17.

56 Without mentioning the Beats by name, Robert Lowell acknowledges the

influence of a trip to the West Coast in creating his confessional style in *Life Studies*. See his interview with Frederick Seidel in *Robert Lowell: A Collection of Critical Essays*, ed. Thomas Parkinson (Englewood Cliffs, N.J.: Prentice-Hall, 1968), p. 18.

57 Transcripts from the trial have been published as *The Howl of the Censor*, ed. J. W. Ehrlich (San Carlos, Calif.: Nourse, 1961).

58 Gregory Corso, "Power," in *A Casebook on the Beat*, p. 84.

3 "SPOTTING THAT DESIGN"

1 John Ciardi, "Epitaph for the Dead Beats," *Saturday Review* (February 6, 1960), p. 11. Reprinted in *A Casebook on the Beat*, ed. Thomas Parkinson (New York: Crowell, 1961), pp. 257–65.

2 Herbert Gold, "The Beat Mystique," *Playboy* (February 1958), p. 85. Reprinted in *A Casebook on the Beat*.

3 Rexroth discusses his religious awakening in *An Autobiographical Novel* (Garden City, N.Y.: Doubleday, 1966), pp. 247–52, 332–9.

4 Kenneth Rexroth, *Communalism: From Its Origins to the Twentieth Century* (New York: Seabury, 1973).

5 John Crowe Ransom, "Poetry: A Note in Ontology," in *Critical Theory Since Plato*, ed. Hazard Adams (New York: Harcourt, Brace & World, 1971), p. 880.

6 Charles Altieri, *Enlarging the Temple: New Directions in American Poetry During the 1960's* (Lewisburg, Pa.: Bucknell University Press, 1979), p. 55.

7 D. H. Lawrence, "Preface to the American Edition of *New Poems*," in *The Poetics of the New American Poetry*, ed. Donald Allen and Warren Tallman (New York: Grove, 1973), p. 71.

8 On catalogues and lists in Snyder see Robert Kern, "Recipes, Catalogues, Open-Form Poetics: Gary Snyder's Archetypal Voice," *Contemporary Literature* 18, no. 2 (1977), pp. 173–97.

9 It could be suggested that Wordsworth's imperative to "look steadily at the subject" might suggest a pictorialist aesthetic based on an entirely mimetic theory of language, but as Paul DeMan says, "This urge to keep the eye on the subject is only Wordsworth's starting point and . . . perhaps more than any poet, he appreciates the complexity of what happens when eye and object meet. The delicate interplay between perception and imagination could nowhere be more intricate than in the representation of a natural scene, transmuted and recollected in the ordering form of Wordsworth's poetic language." Paul DeMan, "Landscape in Wordsworth and Yeats," in *The Rhetoric of Romanticism* (New York: Columbia University Press, 1984), p. 126.

10 Gary Snyder, "The *East–West* Interview," in *The Real Work: Interviews and Talks, 1964–1979* (New York: New Directions, 1980), p. 98; hereafter cited in text as TRW. Subsequent references to Snyder's poetry in the text and the notes will appear as follows: *The Back Country* (New York: New Directions, 1968), BC; *Earth House Hold* (New York: New Directions, 1969), EHH; *Myths and Texts* (New York: New Directions, 1978), MT; *Regarding Wave*

(New York: New Directions, 1970), RW; *Riprap and Cold Mountain Poems* (San Francisco: Four Seasons Foundation, 1966), R; *Turtle Island* (New York: New Directions, 1974), TI.

11 Snyder discusses the role of koan study in an interview with Dom Aelred Graham collected in *Conversations: Christian and Buddhist,* ed. Dom Aelred Graham (New York: Harcourt, Brace, & World, 1968), p. 65.

12 On the "wisdom-oriented line" of Mahayana Buddhism, see TRW, p. 94.

13 Altieri, *Enlarging the Temple,* pp. 128–50.

14 Philip Whalen, *Heavy Breathing: Poems, 1967–1980* (San Francisco: Four Seasons Foundation, 1983), p. 28; hereafter cited in text as HB. Other references to Whalen's work will be the following: *Off the Wall: Interviews with Philip Whalen* (San Francisco: Four Seasons Foundation, 1978), OW; *On Bear's Head* (New York: Harcourt, Brace, & World, 1969), OBH.

15 On "communities of practice," TRW, pp. 136–37.

16 Gary Snyder, "The Poet and the Primitive," lecture given at the Berkeley Poetry Conference, University of California, Berkeley, Friday, July 16, 1965. Audiotape in the Mandeville Department of Special Collections, Central Library, University of California, San Diego. A revised and abbreviated version of this lecture is printed in *The Poetics of the New American Poetry.*

17 Gary Snyder, "Statement on Poetics," in *The New American Poetry,* ed. Donald M. Allen (New York: Grove, 1960), p. 420.

18 Robert Kern relates this effacement of the subject in Snyder to Roman Jakobson's characterization of metonymy:

> We are given a naming of things without a name, a deliberately elliptical utterance that suggests the purest kind of attention to the world beyond the self. As Roman Jakobson points out in his pioneering article on metonymy and metaphor, one characteristic of the kind of aphasia ("similarity disorder") that tends toward the exclusively metonymic pole of discourse is the omission of the subject of the sentence, an omission that results in the type of utterance which takes a purely predicative form and whose subjects are thus not defined so much as rendered through their consequences and effects.

Robert Kern, "Gary Snyder and the Modernist Imperative," *Criticism* 19, no. 2 (1977), p. 163.

19 "The Poet and the Primitive" (lecture version).

20 "The Poet and the Primitive" (printed version in *The Poetics of the New American Poetry,* p. 395).

21 Michael Davidson, "Exiled in the Word: Orality, Writing and Deconstruction," *New Wilderness Letter* 2, no. 8 (1980), pp. 43–7.

22 On Snyder and landscape see Wai Lim Yip, "Aesthetic Consciousness of Landscape in Chinese and Anglo-American Poetry," *Comparative Literature Studies* 15, no. 2 (1978), pp. 211–41. I have also benefited from Professor Yip's unpublished essay on the same subject, "Against Domination: Gary Snyder as an Apologist for Nature."

23 See Kern, "Recipes, Catalogues, Open Form Poetics," p. 177. See also Altieri, *Enlarging the Temple,* pp. 131–50, for what is perhaps the best critique of Snyder's later work.

24 On the influence of Lloyd Reynolds, see Philip Whalen, OW, pp. 12–13, 42.

25 Allen, *The New American Poetry*, p. 420.
26 Several of Whalen's notebooks have been published in facsimile, among them *Highgrade* (San Francisco: Coyote's Journal, 1966); *Intransit: The Philip Whalen Issue* (Eugene, Ore.: Toad Press, 1967); *The Invention of the Letter: A Beastly Morality* (copyright Philip Whalen, 1966).
27 The poet visits the sites described in the poem in a documentary made by National Educational Television in its "Poetry USA" series.
28 Geoffrey Hartman, "Romanticism and Anti-Self-Consciousness," in *Beyond Formalism: Literary Essays, 1958–1970* (New Haven, Conn.: Yale University Press, 1970), pp. 298–310.
29 Frank O'Hara, "Meditations in an Emergency," *The Collected Poems of Frank O'Hara*, ed. Donald Allen (New York: Knopf, 1971), p. 197.

4 "CAVE OF RESEMBLANCES, CAVE OF RIMES"

1 On Duncan's version of the San Francisco Renaissance, see the following: "A conversation with Robert Duncan" (with Eloyde Tovey), Bancroft Library, University of California, Berkeley; "The San Francisco Renaissance: A Reappraisal," conference held at the University of California, San Diego, February 10, 1982 (audiotape at the Mandeville Department of Special Collections, University Library, University of California, San Diego); Michael Davidson, "Robert Duncan," in *The Beats: Literary Bohemians in Postwar America*, part I, ed. Ann Charters, Dictionary of Literary Biography, vol. 16 (Detroit, Mich.: Gale Research Co.), pp. 169–80; Robert Duncan, Letters to Robin Blaser and Jack Spicer, *Ironwood* 22 (Fall 1983), pp. 96–133.
2 Duncan, Letters to Robin Blaser and Jack Spicer, p. 106.
3 Charles Olson, "Against Wisdom as Such," in *The Human Universe and Other Essays*, ed. Donald Allen (New York: Grove, 1967), p. 67.
4 Robert Duncan, *The Opening of the Field* (New York: Grove, 1960), p. 7; hereafter cited in the text as OF. Subsequent references to Duncan's work will be abbreviated as follows: *Bending the Bow* (New York: New Directions, 1968), BB; *Fictive Certainties: Essays by Robert Duncan* (New York: New Directions, 1985), FC; *Roots and Branches* (New York: Scribner, 1964), RB.
5 In Duncan's letters to Blaser during the late 1950s, the issue of literary movements becomes a central point. Duncan was initially unwilling to contribute to Donald Allen's *New American Poetry* anthology since the editor wanted to place him in the "San Francisco Renaissance" section (which included Blaser, Jack Spicer, Brother Antoninus (William Everson), James Broughton, Madeline Gleason, Lawrence Ferlinghetti, Lew Welch, Richard Duerden, Philip Lamantia, Bruce Boyd, Kirby Doyle, and Ebbe Borregaard). Duncan felt that his appropriate context was that of Black Mountain poets like Charles Olson and Robert Creeley. See Duncan's letters to Blaser in *Ironwood* 22, pp. 126–31.
6 On Duncan's relationship to Hellenistic and Christian traditions, see "Two Chapters from *H. D.*," *Tri-Quarterly* 12 (Spring 1968), pp. 67–98.
7 Robert Duncan, Unpublished preface to *Opening of the Field*, Notebook A, Robert Duncan papers, Bancroft Library, University of California, Berkeley, p. 97.

8 Robert Duncan, "The *H. D. Book,* Part I: Chapter 2," *Coyote's Journal* 8 (1967), p. 27.

9 "Interview with Robert Duncan," in *Towards a New American Poetics: Essays and Interviews,* ed. Ekbert Faas (Santa Barbara, Calif.: Black Sparrow Press, 1978), p. 82.

10 Robert Duncan, "Pages from a Notebook," in *The New American Poetry,* ed. Donald M. Allen (New York: Grove, 1960), p. 407.

11 Charles Olson, "Against Wisdom as Such," in *Human Universe and Other Essays,* ed. Donald Allen (New York: Grove, 1967), p. 68.

12 Charles Olson, "Maximus to Gloucester, Letter 17 [withheld]," in *The Maximus Poems,* ed. George Butterick (Berkeley and Los Angeles: University of California Press, 1983), p. 185.

13 Don Byrd, "The Question of Wisdom as Such," in *Robert Duncan: Scales of the Marvelous,* ed. Robert J. Bertholf and Ian W. Reid (New York: New Directions, 1979), pp. 38–55.

14 See Charles Olson, "Equal, That Is, to the Real Itself," in *Human Universe and Other Essays,* pp. 117–22.

15 This quotation, from which my title is derived, appears in Duncan's poem "Apprehensions," in RB, p. 39.

16 Michael A. Bernstein, "Bringing It All Back Home: Derivations and Quotations in Robert Duncan and the Poundian Tradition," *Sagetrieb* 1, no. 2 (1982), p. 184.

17 Robert Duncan, "Beginnings: Chapter 1 of the *H. D. Book,* Part I," in *Coyote's Journal* 5–6 (July 1966), pp. 3–31.

18 Duncan, "The *H. D. Book,* Part I: Chapter 2," p. 27.

19 On Jacob and the Angel, see "The Truth and Life of Myth," in FC, p. 8.

20 Duncan, "Two Chapters from *H. D.,*" p. 67.

21 Duncan discusses the occult tradition in his family background in "Occult Matters" [Part I, Chapter 5 of *The H. D. Book*] in *Stony Brook* 1–2 (Fall 1968), pp. 4–19.

22 Ibid., p. 18.

23 William Carlos Williams, "The Descent," in *Pictures from Brueghel* (New York: New Directions, 1962), p. 73.

24 Sören Kierkegaard, *Repetition,* ed. and trans. Howard V. Hong and Edna Hong (Princeton, N.J.: Princeton University Press, 1983), p. 149.

25 Robert Duncan, "Man's Fulfillment in Order and Strife," FC, 125. See also "Notes on the Structure of Rime," in *Maps* 6 (1974), pp. 42–52.

26 Duncan discusses the role of "persons of the poem" in an interview with Kevin Power, "A Conversation with Robert Duncan," *Revista Canaria de Estudios Ingleses* 4 (April 1982), pp. 100–3.

27 On the "First Beloved" see "An Interview with Robert Duncan" (by Jack R. Cohn and Thomas J. O'Donnell), *Contemporary Literature* 21, no. 4 (1980), pp. 513–48.

28 Letter from Jack Spicer to Robert Duncan (1962), *Acts* 6 (1987), p. 30.

29 Such intertextuality can be seen throughout Duncan's work, but it is particularly in evidence in *The Opening of the Field,* where almost every poem incorporates remarks taken from conversations, letters, and essays. "Poetry, a

Natural Thing" draws upon statements made in a letter to Duncan by John Crowe Ransom (" a little heavy, a little contrived"); "Keeping the Rhyme" quotes from a letter from Pound to Duncan ("We must understand what is happening"); "A Storm of White" draws from a poem by Robert Creeley that was sent in a letter; "A Storm of White," "Atlantis," "The Natural Doctrine," and others incorporate epistolary remarks.

30 Duncan's relation to Dante is best articulated in his essay "The Sweetness and Greatness of Dante's *Divine Comedy*," in FC. But see also "Changing Perspectives in Reading Whitman," in the same volume, as well as his long series based on Dante's prose, "Dante Etudes," in *Groundwork: Before the War* (New York: New Directions, 1984), pp. 94–134.

31 The full passage from *Inferno* XV reads as follows:

> We were already so far removed from the wood that I should not have seen where it was had I turned to look back, when we met a troop of souls that were coming alongside the bank, and each looked at us as men look at one another under a new moon at dusk; and they knit their brows at us as the old tailor does at the eye of the needle.

Dante Alighieri, *The Divine Comedy,* trans. Charles S. Singleton (Princeton, N.J.: Princeton University Press, 1970), vol. 1, *Inferno* text, pp. 154–5.

32 In Patrick S. Diehl's English version, this sonnet is listed as "Rime" 15, the first strophe of which is translated as follows:

> Guido, I wish that Lapo, you, and I
> Were taken up by strong ensorcelment
> And set in ship, whatever winds were sent,
> Who'd go the way we chose (no matter why),

Dante's Rime, trans. Patrick S. Diehl (Princeton, N.J.: Princeton University Press, 1979), p. 49.

33 Harold Bloom, *The Anxiety of Influence: A Theory of Poetry* (New York: Oxford University Press, 1973).

34 On Duncan and hieroglyphs see Charles Altieri, "The Book of the World: Robert Duncan's Poetics of Presence," *Sun and Moon* 1 (Winter 1976), pp. 66–94. A version of this essay appears in Altieri's *Enlarging the Temple: New Directions in American Poetry during the 1960's* (Lewisburg, Pa.: Bucknell University Press, 1979), pp. 150–63.

35 Robert Duncan, "The Beginning of Writing," in *Writing Writing: A Composition Book* (Portland, Ore.: Trask House, 1971) n.p. Originally printed by Sumbooks in the spring of 1964.

36 Robert Duncan, "Writing at Home in History," in *Writing Writing,* n.p.

37 On Psyche and the Pindar poem see Wendy MacIntyre, "Psyche, Christ and the Poem," *Ironwood* 22 (Fall 1983), pp. 9–22.

38 Duncan, "Two Chapters from *H. D.,*" p. 68.

39 Ezra Pound, "The Phantom Dawn," in *The Spirit of Romance* (New York: New Directions, 1968), p. 16.

40 William Carlos Williams, "Asphodel, That Greeny Flower," in *Pictures from Brueghel,* p. 168.

41 Ralph Waldo Emerson, "Hamatraya," in *Selections from Ralph Waldo Emerson,* ed. Stephen E. Whicher (Boston: Houghton Mifflin, 1960), p. 437.

42 Roy Harvey Pearce, "Whitman and Our Hope for Poetry," in *Historicism Once More: Problems and Occasions for the American Scholar* (Princeton, N.J.: Princeton University Press, 1969), p. 327.

43 Robert Duncan, "Occult Matters," in *Stony Brook* 1–2 (1968), p. 19.

44 On Duncan's homosexuality see Ekbert Faas, *Young Robert Duncan: Portrait of the Poet as Homosexual in Society* (Santa Barbara, Calif.: Black Sparrow Press, 1983), and "Interview with Robert Duncan," *Gay Sunshine* 40–1 (Summer–Fall, 1979), n.p.

45 Bernstein, "Bringing It All Back Home," p. 178.

5 "THE CITY REDEFINED"

1 On Blabbermouth Night and the Spicer circle in general, the best sources are a series of interviews conducted by Lew Ellingham and published in the following magazines: *Jimmy and Lucy's House of 'K,'* 4 (June 1985), pp. 61–8; *Acts* 3 (1984), n.p.; *No Apologies* 3 (Fall, 1984), pp. 74–88; *No Apologies* 4 (n.d.), pp. 6–20; *Soup* 4 (1985), pp. 101–7; *Ironwood* 28 (Fall 1986), pp. 152–64; *Line* 9 (Spring 1987), pp. 59–69. See also *Manroot* 10 (Fall 1974–Winter 1975): Robert Duncan, Introduction to Jack Spicer, *One Night Stand,* ed. Donald Allen (San Francisco: Grey Fox Press, 1980); James Herndon, *Everything as Expected* (San Franscisco: n.p., 1973). Robert Duncan conducted an extensive interview with Eloyde Tovey on the San Francisco writing scene with particular emphasis on the Spicer circle, which is available at the Bancroft Library, University of California, Berkeley. Jack Spicer discusses Blabbermouth Night in "The Vancouver Lectures [no. 1]," *Caterpillar* 12 (July 1970), pp. 181–2.

2 Jack Spicer, *The Collected Books of Jack Spicer,* ed. Robin Blaser (Los Angeles: Black Sparrow Press, 1975), p. 133; hereafter cited as CB. Abbreviations of other Spicer publications will be as follows: *Caterpillar* magazine, 12 (July 1970), CAT; *One Night Stand and Other Poems,* ed. Donald Allen (San Francisco: Grey Fox Press, 1980), ONS.

3 CAT, 184. A lengthy excerpt from the "Vancouver Lectures" appears in *The Poetics of the New American Poetry,* ed. Donald Allen (New York: Grove, 1973), pp. 227–34.

4 James Herndon, "Thus Jack Spicer Refuted Child Psychology," *Manroot* 10 (Fall 1974–Winter 1975), p. 56.

5 CB, 125. The "explanatory note" to this poem indicates that the laws of physics as well as of love are determined by the language in which they are expressed: "What Beatrice did did not become her own business. Dante saw to that. Sawed away the last plank anyone he loved could stand on."

6 Robert Duncan, "The Underside," unpublished manuscript in the Poetry/Rare Books Collections, University Libraries, State University of New York, Buffalo, p. 5.

7 Duncan regards this side of Spicer as a cultivation of a permanent boyhood ethos whose origins can be found in Tom Sawyer or the stories of Penrod and Sam. Duncan relates this spirit of boyhood to Spicer's early poetry community in Berkeley: "We were – Robin Blaser and I – in 1946–1950, for him,

members of his secret boys' club, hero-friends and teammates in this new game of poetry. Playing poetry. He wanted to keep us true to the game. That was always what the public meant to him – the public a game has, the public of poetry like the public of baseball or football." Ibid., p. 3.

8 *University of California Occident* (Fall 1949), p. 43. Republished in ONS, pp. 90–2.

9 *Occident,* p. 44; ONS, 91.

10 Ibid., p. 45; ONS, 92.

11 Frank O'Hara, "Personism," in *Poetics of the New American Poetry,* p. 355.

12 This is the general thrust of Robin Blaser's afterword to *The Collected Books of Jack Spicer,* entitled "The Practice of Outside," as it is in the essays included in the special issue of *boundary 2* devoted to Jack Spicer's work (*boundary 2* 6, no. 1 [1977]), including my own essay in that volume. Although the present chapter makes use of portions of that earlier essay I have revised its treatment of Spicer's theological terms to account for the issue of community.

13 On Spicer's anarchist politics, James Herndon remembers "the appearance of Jack at pompous, highly-organized politics meetings in VFW hall at Berkeley; only students representing organizations could speak and vote – Jack's appearance causing an uproar among both Wallacites and Socialists etc. big argument about his credentials and Jack announced he represented the 'Committee for Anarchist Unity' – an organization which he then admitted consisted only of himself, since there could 'By definition be no unity among more than one anarchist' " (CB, 376).

14 I am adapting terms developed by Mikhail Bakhtin, who uses "dialogic" in terms of the novel but whose remarks could as easily refer to much postmodern poetry. See "Discourse in the Novel," in *The Dialogic Imagination,* ed. Michael Holquist (Austin: University of Texas Press, 1981), p. 276. I have developed the possibilities of Bakhtin's work for poetics in "Discourse in Poetry: Bakhtin and Extensions of the Dialogical," *Code of Signals: Recent Writings in Poetics* (*Io* 30), ed. Michael Palmer (1983), pp. 141–50.

15 Spicer's remarks on the City of God and its relation to community are spelled out in his first Vancouver lecture, published in CAT, p. 202.

16 Jack Spicer, *Language* (San Francisco: White Rabbit Press, 1965). The essay was Spicer's only "professional" publication as a linguist. Spicer did publish a review of the Johnson edition of Emily Dickinson's *Complete Poems:* John L. Spicer, "The Poems of Emily Dickinson," *Boston Public Library Quarterly* (July 1956), pp. 135–43; partially reprinted in *Ironwood* 28 (Fall 1986), p. 207.

17 Colin Christopher Stuart and John Scoggan, "The Orientation of the Parasols: Saussure, Derrida, and Spicer," *boundary 2* 6, no. 1 (1977), p. 228. See also Robin Blaser in CB, p. 318.

18 See Bruce Boone, "For Jack Spicer – and a Truth Element," *Social Text* (Spring–Summer, 1983) pp. 120–6.

19 The letters to Graham Mackintosh and Jim Alexander are published in CAT, pp. 83–114.

20 See Lori Chamberlain, "Ghostwriting in Test: Translation and the Poetics of Jack Spicer," *Contemporary Literature* 26, no. 4 (1985), pp. 432–3.

21 See Blaser in CB, p. 322.

22 Jean Doresse, *The Secret Books of the Egyptian Gnostics* (New York: Viking, 1960), p. 50. See also Norman M. Finkelstein, "Jack Spicer's Ghosts and the Gnosis of History," *boundary 2* 9, no. 2 (1981), pp. 89–90.

23 As described in CB, 322.

24 I have discussed this theme in "Incarnations of Jack Spicer: *Heads of the Town up to the Aether*," *boundary 2* 6, no. 1 (1977), pp. 103–34.

25 I am grateful to Ron Loewinsohn, who reminded me of Creeley's pervasive influence on poets in San Francisco – including Spicer. Although Spicer's lyrics in "Homage to Creeley" are a good deal more fragmentary and broken than Creeley's, they do manifest something of the same compression and emotional energy.

26 Spicer's attitude toward his own biography is graphically presented in the biographical note in Donald Allen's *The New American Poetry* (New York: Grove, 1960), p. 445: "Jack Spicer: does not like his life written down. He was born in Hollywood in 1925. Anyone interested in further information should contact him at The Place, 1546 Grant Avenue, San Francisco."

27 Spicer's misspellings ("wonderfly," "Glouchester") are consistent with his practice elsewhere in his work. At the White Rabbit Symposium and Jack Spicer Conference in San Francisco, June 1986, Spicer's spelling was discussed, and it was pointed out by Robin Blaser that although Spicer was a terrible speller, he did not want his misspellings changed since they, like the poems themselves, were dictated and thus should remain as they were.

28 Of course, in *The Holy Grail* of 1962, Spicer does create at least a partial utopia in the form of King Arthur's knights of the round table. Elsewhere in that book, Spicer refers to Oz as another heavenly kingdom. Both the grail legends and the Oz stories are tales adapted by Spicer to his own uses; his later "diamond" image is very much his own creation.

29 Selected comments from "Jack Spicer at the Berkeley Poetry Conference, July 14, 1965." Phonotape at the Archive for New Poetry, Mandeville Department of Special Collections, University Library, University of California, San Diego.

30 Allen Ginsberg, "Kral Majales," in *Collected Poems 1947–1980* (New York: Harper & Row, 1984), p. 353. On Spicer's response to Ginsberg, see Blaser in CB, p. 300.

31 Roy Harvey Pearce, *The Continuity of American Poetry* (Princeton, N.J.: Princeton University Press, 1961), p. 5.

6 APPROPRIATIONS

1 This event is described in Lew Ellingham, *"Poet, Be Like God": Jack Spicer's Circle in San Francisco, 1956–1965* (unpublished), chap. 6, p. 16.

2 Jack Spicer, "For Joe," in *The Collected Books of Jack Spicer*, ed. Robin Blaser (Los Angeles: Black Sparrow Press, 1975), p. 62. Hereafter referred to in the text as CB.

3 Denise Levertov, "Hypocrite Women" in *O Taste and See* (New York: New Directions, 1964), p. 70.

4 Shari Benstock, *Women of the Left Bank: Paris, 1900–1940* (Austin: University of Texas Press, 1986).

5 Gertrude Stein, "Patriarchal Poetry" in *The Yale Gertrude Stein*, ed. Richard Kostelanetz (New Haven, Conn.: Yale University Press, 1980), pp. 106–46.

6 Diane DiPrima, *This Kind of Bird Flies Backward* (New York: Totem Press, 1958); *Dinners and Nightmares* (New York: Corinth Books, 1961; enlarged edition, 1963).

7 Robert Duncan, "The Underside," unpublished manuscript, Robert Duncan papers, Poetry/Rare Books Collection, University Libraries, State University of New York, Buffalo.

8 Quoted in Joyce Johnson, *Minor Characters* (Boston, Mass.: Houghton Mifflin, 1983), p. 79.

9 Barbara Ehrenreich, *The Hearts of Men: American Dreams and the Flight from Commitment* (Garden City, N.Y.: Doubleday, 1983), p. 52. On women in bohemia, see Ellen Kay Trimberger, "Feminism, Men, and Modern Love: Greenwich Village, 1900–1925," in *Powers of Desire: The Politics of Sexuality*, ed. Ann Snitow, Christine Stansell, and Sharon Thompson (New York: Monthly Review Press, 1983), pp. 131–52; Virginia M. Kouidis, *Mina Loy: American Modernist Poet* (Baton Rouge: University of Louisiana Press, 1980); Catherine Stimpson, "The Beat Generation and the Trials of Homosexual Liberation," *Salmagundi* 58–59 (Fall 1982), pp. 373–92.

10 Ehrenreich, *Hearts of Men*, p. 54.

11 See Paul O'Neil, "The Only Rebellion Around," in *A Casebook on the Beat*, ed. Thomas Parkinson (New York: Crowell, 1961), pp. 232–46.

12 Margaret Homans, *Women Writers and Poetic Identity: Dorothy Wordsworth, Emily Bronte, and Emily Dickinson* (Princeton, N.J.: Princeton University Press, 1980), p. 13.

13 Gary Snyder, "Praise for Sick Women," in *Riprap and Cold Mountain Poems* (San Francisco: Four Seasons Foundation, 1965), p. 10.

14 Diane DiPrima, *Selected Poems 1956–1975* (Plainfield, Vt.: North Atlantic Books, 1975), p. 39. In this later reprinting of the poem, DiPrima has added an epigraph from Snyder's poem ("The female is fertile, and discipline / (contra naturam) only / confuses her"). In the poems's initial publication in *Yugen* in 1958, the epigraph does not appear.

15 Adrienne Rich, "When We Dead Awaken: Writing as Re-Vision," in *Adrienne Rich's Poetry*, ed. Barbara Charlesworth Gelpi and Albert Gelpi (New York: Norton, 1975), p. 90.

16 Christina Rossetti, "Goblin Market," in *The Complete Poems of Christina Rossetti* Vol. I, ed. R. W. Crump (Baton Rouge: Louisiana State University Press, 1979), p. 23.

17 Helen Adam and Pat Adam, *San Francisco's Burning: A Ballad Opera* (Brooklyn, N.Y.: Hanging Loose Press, 1985), p. 56. Hereafter referred to in the text as SFB.

18 Quoted in Lew Ellingham, *"Poet, Be Like God"*, chap. 6, p. 17.

19 Helen Douglas Adam, *Charms and Dreams from the Elfin Pedlar's Pack* (London: Hodder & Stoughton, 1924); *The Elfin Pedlar and Tales Told by Pixy Pool* (London: Hodder & Stoughton, 1923).

20 Sandra M. Gilbert and Susan Gubar, *The Madwoman in the Attic: The Woman Writer and the Nineteenth-Century Literary Imagination* (New Haven, Conn.: Yale University Press, 1979), pp. 3–44.

21 Nina Auerbach makes a similar point about Victorian projections of woman as monster or demon. See *Woman and the Demon: The Life of a Victorian Myth* (Cambridge, Mass.: Harvard University Press, 1982), p. 17.

22 Helen Adam, "The Fair Young Wife," in *Turn Again to Me and Other Poems* (New York: Kulchur Foundation, 1977), pp. 13–15.

23 All of these poems appear in *Turn Again to Me*, pp. 49–50, 99–101, 102–3, 104–6.

24 Ibid., p. 106.

25 Ibid., p. 15.

26 *San Francisco's Burning* was first published in 1963 by Oannes Press, for which edition Jess Collins created drawings that testify not only to the Victorian setting of the play but to the painter's debt to Art Nouveau design. These drawings have been reproduced in the 1985 Hanging Loose version.

27 This debate occurred between Robert Duncan and James Broughton and forms the basis for the former's poem, "What Happened: Prelude," which appears in *Roots and Branches* (New York: Scribners, 1964), pp. 97–106. In the prose "prelude" to the poem, Duncan recalls that *San Francisco's Burning*, was presented twice in San Francisco, the first at Ebbe Borregaard's Museum in a reading version with Helen and Pat Adam only, and again at James Broughton's Playhouse near Aquatic Park. Duncan characterizes the first as the "authentic form" in which it was performed with Helen Adam "evoking by candlelight, by the manipulation of a fan, and by her marvelous voice, a Theater immediate to the imagination, true to the inner vision of the Underworld." But in Broughton's production, Duncan claims that Adam "denies the inspiration of her tunes and . . . seeks to improve the play to suit the dictates of the Stage." Duncan's feeling that James Broughton and Kermit Sheets, the play's directors, had distorted Adam's original intent led him and others to boycott its production, creating, as Lew Ellingham says, "open wounds in the poetic community of Helen Adam's friends" (*"Poet, Be Like God,"* chap. 17, p. 2).

28 The image of the worm as a figure of death is, of course, an ancient one, but Adam's derivation may owe something to Bram Stoker's *The Lair of the White Worm*. According to Nina Auerbach, the Dracula figure at the center of the book is "in her true self a giant white worm older than mankind, living at the bottom of a deep and fetid well that crawls with the repulsive vitality of vermin, insects, and worms" (*Woman and the Demon*, p. 25).

29 I am grateful to Jess Collins and Ron Loewinsohn for reminding me of the existence of these "mechanical marvels" in San Francisco during this period.

30 See *On the Mesa: An Anthology of Bolinas Writing*, ed. Joel Weishaus (San Francisco: City Lights, 1971). On Joanne Kyger and the Bolinas milieu, see Bill Berkson, "Joanne Kyger," in *The Beats: Literary Bohemians in Postwar America*, part 1, ed. Ann Charters, Dictionary of Literary Biography, vol. 16 (Detroit, Mich.: Gale Research Co.), pp. 324–8.

31 Joanne Kyger, "Three Versions of the Poetic Line," *Credences* 2, no. 1 (1977), p. 63.

32 Joanne Kyger, *Joanne* (Bolinas, Calif.: Angel Hair, n.d.), n.p.

33 Ibid.

34 Joanne Kyger, *Places to Go* (Los Angeles: Black Sparrow Press, 1970), pp. 9, 47, 82.

35 Ibid., p. 9.

36 Joanne Kyger, *The Tapestry and the Web* (San Francisco: Four Seasons Foundation, 1965), p. 33; hereafter referred to as TW in the text.

37 Robert Duncan, *As Testimony* (San Francisco: White Rabbit Press, 1966), p. 13.

38 Ibid., p. 18.

39 On women's poetry readings see Frances Jaffer, "For Women Poets, For Poetry: A Journal Entry," in *The Poetry Reading: A Contemporary Compendium on Language and Performance,* ed. Stephen Vincent and Ellen Zweig (San Francisco: Momo's Press, 1981), pp. 58–63.

40 John D'Emilio, "Gay Politics, Gay Community," *Socialist Review* 11, no. 1 (1981), p. 77.

41 Levertov comments on the poem and its occasion in an interview:

> So for my poem, what I meant was that women (at that pre-Feminist, or at least pre-late-20th-century Feminist period) might also think that genitalia were not pretty, visually – but their *function* was not visual anyway, so why should they be. I said "hypocrite" because the thought was one not commonly admitted. I later came to see how much of women's self-deprecation came from macho male attitudes. That occasion was also my first exposure to homosexual males as a group – I had, and continue to have, individual homosexual friends but I find homosexual males and lesbians uncongenial in groups, when they reinforce each other's sexism toward heterosexuals.

Ellingham, *"Poet, Be Like God"*, chap. 6, p. 18.

42 Judy Grahn, (untitled), in *The Work of a Common Woman: The Collected Poetry of Judy Grahn, 1964–1977* (Trumansburg, N.Y.: Crossing Press, 1978); hereafter referred to as WCW in the text.

43 Judy Grahn, *Another Mother Tongue: Gay Words, Gay Worlds* (Boston: Beacon, 1984).

44 Carolyn Cassady, "Life with Jack and Neal," and Eileen Kaufman, "Laughter Sounds Orange at Night," in *The Beat Vision: A Primary Sourcebook,* ed. Arthur Knight and Kit Knight (New York: Paragon House, 1987), pp. 29–51, 259–67.

45 Joanne Kyger, *The Japan and India Journals, 1960–1964* (Bolinas, Calif.: Tombouctou, 1981).

46 Kenneth Rexroth, *American Poetry in the Twentieth Century* (New York: Herder & Herder, 1971), p. 140.

7 APPROACHING THE FIN DE SIÈCLE

1 Fredric Jameson, "Postmodernism, or the Cultural Logic of Late Capitalism," *New Left Review* 146 (July–August 1984), p. 73.

2 Jacques Derrida, "The Ends of Man," in *Margins of Philosophy,* trans. Alan Bass (Chicago: University of Chicago Press, 1972) pp. 109–36.

3 John Barth, "The Literature of Exhaustion," *Atlantic Monthly* 180 (August 1967), pp. 29–34.

4 I use Stendhal's phrase, *promesse de bonheur,* in the sense in which it was used within the Frankfurt school, namely, as a definition of art's utopian project. As Martin Jay summarizes, "Kant's notion of the disinterestedness of beauty was therefore wrong: true art was an expression of man's legitimate interest in his future happiness." Martin Jay, *The Dialectical Imagination: A History of the Frankfurt School and the Institute of Social Research, 1923–1950* (Boston: Little, Brown, 1973), p. 179.

5 The best introduction to interlingualism in Chicano poetry can be seen in magazines like *Maize* and *Revista Chicano-Riquena* and through the publications of Arte Publico Press. Also see Susan Bassnett, "Bilingual Poetry: A Chicano Phenomenon," *Revista Chicano-Riquena* 13, nos. 3–4 (1985), pp. 137–47.

6 For an excellent discussion of gay language as oppositional, see Bruce Boone, "Gay Language as Political Praxis: The Poetry of Frank O'Hara," *Social Text* 1, no. 1 (1979), pp. 59–92.

7 On rock music and poetry readings, see William Everson, *Archetype West: The Pacific Coast as a Literary Region* (Berkeley, Calif.: Oyez, 1976), chap. 19. The best survey of Bay Area poetry readings is by Stephen Vincent, "Poetry Readings/Reading Poetry: San Francisco Bay Area 1958–1980," in *The Poetry Reading: A Contemporary Compendium on Language and Performance,* ed. Stephen Vincent and Ellen Zweig (San Francisco: Momo's Press, 1981), pp. 19–54.

8 Many of the Berkeley Poetry Conference lectures have been published. See, e.g., Gary Snyder, "Poetry and the Primitive," in *Earth House Hold* (New York: New Directions, 1969), pp. 117–30; Edward Dorn, *The Poet, the People, the Spirit* (Vancouver, B.C.: Talonbooks, 1976); Charles Olson, "Reading at Berkeley," in *Muthologos: The Collected Lectures and Interviews,* vol. 1, ed. George Butterick (Bolinas, Calif.: Four Seasons Foundation, 1978) pp. 97–156; Jack Spicer, "Lecture and Reading at the Berkeley Poetry Conference, July 1965," phonotape at the Mandeville Department of Special Collections, University of California, San Diego.

9 The best survey of writing among the Bay Area's ethnic communities can be found in the pages of *Yardbird* and *Y-bird,* edited by Ishmael Reed.

10 Charles Altieri, *Self and Sensibility in Contemporary American Poetry* (Cambridge University Press, 1984), p. 10.

11 Robert Haas, "Some Notes on the San Francisco Bay Area as a Culture Region: A Memoir," in *19 New American Poets of the Golden Gate,* ed. Philip Dow (San Diego, Calif.: Harcourt Brace Jovanovich 1984); hereafter referred to in the text as GG.

12 Kenneth Rexroth, "Time Spirals," in *The Collected Shorter Poems of Kenneth Rexroth* (New York: New Directions, 1966), p. 220.

13 "Palo Alto: The Marshes" first appeared in *Field Guide* (New Haven, Conn.: Yale University Press, 1973), pp. 24–7.

14 James Wright, "Lying in a Hammock at William Duffy's Farm in Pine Island, Minnesota," in *Collected Poems* (Middletown, Conn.: Wesleyan University Press, 1971), p. 114.

15 Robert Hass, "Meditation at Lagunitas," in *Praise* (New York: Ecco Press, 1978), pp. 4–5.

16 Stanley Kunitz describes this quality of unobtrusive voice in his introduction to *Field Guide:* "It [is] as if the voice were the continuation of a long soliloquy that had only just now become audible, without straining to be heard, without breathing harder – a clear musical voice that modulates itself as it flows and that enjoys caressing the long vowel sounds" (p. xi).

17 Heidegger's concept of truth as "unconcealment" (*aletheia*) is developed in his essay "The Origin of the Work of Art," in *Poetry, Language and Thought*, trans. Albert Hofstadter (New York: Harper & Row, 1971), pp. 39–7.

18 Adrienne Rich, "Power and Danger: The Work of a Common Woman by Judy Grahn," in Judy Grahn, *The Work of a Common Woman: The Collected Poetry of Judy Grahn, 1964–1977* (Trumansburg, N.Y.: The Crossing Press, 1978), p. 8.

19 A good overview of the language movement is presented by Marjorie Perloff, "The Word as Such: L=A=N=G=U=A=G=E Poetry in the Eighties," APR 13, no. 3 (1984). Reprinted in *The Dance of the Intellect: Studies in the Poetry of the Pound Tradition* (Cambridge University Press, 1985), pp. 215–38. See also the following: Lee Bartlett, "What Is 'Language Poetry'?" *Critical Inquiry* 12, no. 4 (1986), pp. 741–52; Charles Bernstein, *Content's Dream* (Los Angeles: Sun and Moon Press, 1986); Barrett Watten, *Total Syntax* (Carbondale: Southern Illinois University Press, 1985); *The L=A=N=G=U=A=G=E Book*, ed. Bruce Andrews and Charles Bernstein (Carbondale: Southern Illinois University Press, 1984); *Writing/Talks*, ed. Bob Perelman (Carbondale: Southern Illinois Press, 1985). Two recent anthologies of language writing offer a capacious overview: *In the American Tree*, ed. Ron Silliman (Orono, Maine: The National Poetry Foundation, 1986); *Language Poetries*, ed. Douglas Messerli (New York: New Directions, 1987).

20 Most of this warfare has been carried out in the pages of San Francisco's poetry newsletter, *Poetry Flash*, although salvos were fired from *Rolling Stock*, *The New Criterion, Exquisite Corpse, Contact II*, as well as the *San Francisco Chronicle*. The conflict began with an article on Robert Duncan (David Levi Strauss, "On Duncan and Zukofsky on Film: Traces Now and Then," *Poetry Flash* 135 [June 1984]), which brought letters from Ron Silliman, Jacqueline Cantwell, and Stephen Rodefer in the next issue. A longer and more heated exchange occurred with a review essay by the linguist George Lakoff ("On Whose Authority?" *Poetry Flash* 147 [June 1985]), to which Tom Clark wrote a response at the request of the editors ("Stalin as Linguist," *Poetry Flash* 148 [July 1985]). This article occasioned vehement letters from writers on both sides of the fence in the next several issues: Bob Perelman, Gloria Frym, David Bromige, Frederick Pollack, Frances Butler, Jerry Estrin, John J. Richards, Mike Tuggle, Edward Dorn, Jill Duerr, Darrell Gray, Debbie Linton, Michael Anderson, Roberto Bedoya, and Joe Sadfie. A version of Clark's

essay was published under the same title in *Partisan Review* 54, no. 2 (1987), pp. 299–304.

21 These and other women writers have been featured in *HowEver,* a journal of experimental writing and feminist discourse, edited by Kathleen Fraser, Frances Jaffer, and Rachel Blau DuPlessis and published by San Francisco State University.

22 Lyn Hejinian, "The Rejection of Closure," *Poetics Journal* 4 (May 1984), p. 135.

23 Ron Silliman, "The New Sentence," *Hills* 6–7 (1980), pp. 190–217. I have discussed Silliman's prose and that of other language writers in "Writing at the Boundaries," *New York Times Book Review* (February 24, 1985), pp. 3, 28–9, and in "Sentence, Discourse and the New Prose," *Fiction International* 15, no. 2 (1984), pp. 125–32.

24 Lyn Hejinian, *My Life* (Los Angeles: Sun & Moon Press, 1980), p. 39; hereafter referred to in the text as ML.

25 Marjorie Perloff, "The Word as Such," in *The Dance of the Intellect,* p. 225.

26 This ideology can be viewed in the essay by Tom Clark in *Poetry Flash* mentioned in note 20, but see also Jack Gilbert, "The Craft of the Invisible," *Ironwood* 24, 12, no. 2 (1984), pp. 156–61, and my response to Gilbert in the subsequent issue.

27 Paul de Man, "The Intentional Structure of the Romantic Image," in *Romanticism and Consciousness,* ed. Harold Bloom (New York: Norton, 1970), p. 69. See also Tilottama Rajan, *Dark Interpreter: The Discourse of Romanticism* (Ithaca, N.Y.: Cornell University Press, 1980), pp. 13–26.

28 Jack Spicer, from "After Lorca" in *The Collected Books of Jack Spicer,* ed. Robin Blaser (Los Angeles: Black Sparrow Press, 1975), p. 25.

29 See the last chapter of Everson's *Archetype West.* See also, in the same context, Robert Duncan's introduction to *The Years as Catches* (Berkeley, Calif.: Oyez, 1966), in which he describes his own interest in and application of the rhetorical mode during the 1940s.

30 Theodor Adorno, *Aesthetic Theory,* trans. C. Lenhardt (London: Routledge & Kegan Paul, 1984), p. 6.

31 Frances FitzGerald has employed John Winthrop's famous phrase in discussing four American communities, among them the gay community of San Francisco's Castro District. See her *Cities on a Hill: A Journey Through Contemporary American Culture* (New York: Simon & Schuster, 1986).

Index